Praise for *A School*

This inspirational book is much more than a report of building ethos in a publicly funded selective sixth-form school. Don't dismiss it as a quirk that creates a newly privileged class. Instead it is a model of how school leadership enriched by a deeply human hinterland can transform students, teachers and a community. Poetry, art, music, people, hope, trust: all play a part in founding a fresh culture that turns lives and expectations around. Visionary education can make social change possible – here's one way.

Anne Watson, Professor Emeritus,
Department of Education, University of Oxford

A School Built on Ethos cleverly combines poetry, philosophy and knowledge into a comedic jaunt through the author's mind as he delivers a wondrous series of captivating assemblies to his student body. The reader cannot help but be swept along with the flow as they meander through each chapter, which conclude with real words of hard-won wisdom. These narrate an insight into how James Handscombe has established success in his school and instilled life-long values into his students, and these same values will provide acuity for any school leader.

Clive Hill, Lead Practitioner for Science, Archway Learning Trust,
and a member of the Chartered College of Teaching Council

Handscombe is the Montaigne of education writers. His book is a beautifully written smorgasbord; a feast of thought spread out before you. Or maybe it would be better thought of as a carefully curated exhibition, the exhibits chosen for the light they shed on each other and, obliquely, on the process of leading a school. Handscombe never tells you what to do. Instead, he provides fleeting glimpses by means of an extraordinary range of assembly topics in which the breadth of his interests and erudition sparkle and glister as he cajoles, exhorts and guides the students who have been privileged – whether they knew it or not – to be present at these addresses in which the very human core of a school is refracted.

David Didau, Senior Lead Practitioner for English,
Ormiston Academies Trust, and author of *Making Kids Cleverer*

This is a book about how an incredibly successful school built its ethos – but it's not just about this school, as the principles elucidated here can be applied to any school. Through a series of assemblies and commentaries by the founding principal of Harris Westminster Sixth Form, the book outlines the key principles involved in creating excellence through building ethos in a school. These principles – Harris Westminster's driving ideas of ambition, perseverance and legacy – can be adapted for any context.

A School Built on Ethos is by turns entertaining, thoughtful, stretching and deeply interesting. James Handscombe demonstrates very clearly that while every school leaves a legacy of some kind, a legacy of excellence can indeed be planned for and created with ambition and perseverance.

Sir Dan Moynihan, Chief Executive, Harris Federation

A School Built on Ethos offers a personal take on the world of education via an ingenious idea, whereby head teacher James Handscombe has written each chapter around assemblies delivered at his school over the past few years. That his school is Harris Westminster – a sixth-form school that serves a wide range of students yet is situated right in the centre of Britain's power and privilege, pomp and circumstance – gives this book a unique edge, too. Handscombe teaches us all a number of lessons from (sometimes literally) his pulpit, yet manages to make the style more conversational than preachy. This is to his credit.

A book that is a joy to dip in and out of, *A School Built on Ethos* conjures up an array of fascinating situations and characters, but it is the advice drawn from experience that will resonate long after the book has been read that will bring readers to it, safe in the knowledge that they are in the good hands of a thoughtful and empathetic head teacher.

Martin Robinson, education consultant
and author of Trivium 21c and Curriculum

An honest, touching and inspirational tale with pearls of wisdom and useful practical ideas.

Katharine Birbalsingh, Head Teacher, Michaela Community School

Many books about education are purely utilitarian; you open them up in the hope of learning how to do something better. Whilst *A School Built on Ethos* offers plenty in this regard, it does much more besides too. Furthermore, there are sadly too few education books that work as a piece of literature; however, this book shares a narrative to savour and get lost within as James Handscombe takes you on a fascinating journey of how a school comes into being, in both a physical sense but also as something that transcends its bricks and mortar. It is also a delightfully funny read as James meanders from one digression to another in weaving his captivating story. The scripts of assemblies that pepper the book are particular high points and I turned the page on each one feeling enriched. They also beautifully illustrate the points made in each section of the book and enable you to see the author who walks his talk on a daily basis.

I adore *A School Built on Ethos* for many reasons. It is wonderful to read about school leadership from someone who clearly loves their job, their school and their students. And as well as giving many practical points on school leadership, James also sets out a clear case that a school is more than a building, a timetable and a budget; it is a community and one that needs an ethos to bring people together and give them a common purpose.

I cannot recommend this book highly enough.

Mark Enser, Head of Geography and Research Lead,
Heathfield Community College, and author of
Teach Like Nobody's Watching and *Powerful Geography*

Harris Westminster is a gem and it has been a privilege to work with and get to know many of their students. James' book provides a peek behind the door of why this school and the students themselves are such a success. James is an inspiring, passionate and dedicated school leader and educator, and in this book his passion and enthusiasm is infectious and jumps right off the page.

A School Built on Ethos offers an insight into the framework that differentiates this school and enables it to achieve all it does.

Janine Glasenberg, Head of EMEA Graduate Recruiting,
Goldman Sachs

This book charts brilliantly the establishment of a school's ethos through the use of assemblies, as James Handscombe shares assembly content, purpose and reflections with the reader as thoughtful learning orientations. Harris Westminster's assemblies provide collective space for the orator to draw upon their intellectual interests to inspire, provoke, encourage and pique the curiosities of the audience that are situated at the threshold of adulthood. This collection of assemblies are bold, at times brave, and are grounded in a collective humanity which seeks to encourage and unite in a common scholarly purpose – that of human flourishing. If Ofsted's notion of 'cultural capital' is to equip children and young people with 'the essential knowledge that pupils need to be educated citizens, introducing them to the best that has been thought and said and helping to engender an appreciation of human creativity and achievement' then I am certain this assemblage of content achieves this benchmark. I think the French sociologist Pierre Bourdieu, often associated with the concept of 'cultural capital', would approve too. Having said that, this is not a book whose purpose is to satisfy Ofsted nor, as James opines, one that offers some sort of educational elixir for those that seek to transpose its content word for word in the hope they too can replicate the outcomes of Westminster Harris. If anything, this book gives permission for educators to share not only their knowledge and love of learning but to connect enquiring intellects to the brilliance of humanity. Finally, the ancient Greek philosopher Plato held the view that children should not be exposed to "chance stories" fashioned by "chance teachers", fearing that such offerings would leave a questionable and indelible imprint on a young mind. However, Harris Westminster's success is because they did, and do, take a chance. For this is their ethos. And it is one we can all learn from.

Claire Birkenshaw, Lecturer in Childhood and Education,
Leeds Beckett University, and former head teacher

A School Built on Ethos

Ideas, assemblies and hard-won wisdom

James Handscombe

Crown House Publishing Limited
www.crownhouse.co.uk

First published by
Crown House Publishing Limited
Crown Buildings, Bancyfelin, Carmarthen, Wales, SA33 5ND, UK
www.crownhouse.co.uk

and

Crown House Publishing Company LLC
PO Box 2223, Williston, VT 05495, USA
www.crownhousepublishing.com

First published 2021.

Cover image © sveta – stock.adobe.com.

British Library Cataloguing-in-Publication Data
A catalogue entry for this book is available from the British Library.

Print ISBN 978-178583533-9
Mobi ISBN 978-178583551-3
ePub ISBN 978-178583552-0
ePDF ISBN 978-178583553-7

LCCN 2021932050

Printed and bound in the UK by
Charlesworth Press, Huddersfield, West Yorkshire

For my Grandparents.

Contents

Preface

Oswald Bastable says that he never reads prefaces and that there is not much point in writing things just for people to skip.[1] But there are some things that, whilst not crucial to the story, may be useful to know before you embark on the book. So, trusting that the sort of people who don't read prefaces are also the sort of people who are more interested in the action than in the author's philosophy, I shall attempt to set out here, in this semi-secret chapter, what kind of book this is.

[Pause whilst the author thinks.]

This is more difficult than I had thought, but here goes.

It is a history of a school told through the experiences of its principal using the lens of weekly assemblies to cast light on the ethos and idiom of the community, with the hope that the reader will be encouraged to think about the central role that ethos has in any organisation and, perhaps, absorb some of the author's ideas on the idioms that work well in an educational setting.

If that sounds rather vague then perhaps you will find this a rather vague book – although I hope not, because I feel quite passionate about the school whose story I am telling, and I absolutely believe that our ethos is both amazing in itself and impressive in how it has carried us from small beginnings to significant success.

What I can't do is tell you how to set up and run a successful school, because my thesis is that it is in the idiosyncrasy that a school triumphs, it is in being unusual that a community is created, and it is by thinking strategically about the way in which an organisation differs from the norm that a leader shapes its success. The chapters of this book are therefore to be thought of as stories or parables whose characters are not heroes to be copied, but totems to illustrate an idea and from whose mistakes and triumphs lessons can be learned. I thought about

1 E. Nesbit, *The Story of the Treasure Seekers* (London: T. Fisher Unwin, 1899), ch. 2. Available at: http://www.gutenberg.org/ebooks/770.

trying to distil each chapter into a few bullet points and give you some 'brass tacks' to go away with, but even here I found myself pulling away from being too prescriptive. Trying to make the ideas precise and universal was like pinning mist to the wall, and so the 'Final Thoughts' sections are more impressionist – brass tacks painted by Monet (in my next book I will channel Dali and have surreal commentaries to terminate each chapter).

I hope, then, that you find the book interesting and inspiring. I hope that there are places where you think, 'What a great idea!' but also that you sometimes think, 'What on earth is he worrying about here?' or 'I'd never have fallen into making that mistake.' I hope that you will find it amusing (and I should warn you that the playful and possibly heavy-handedly literate tone of this preface is one that continues – I enjoy a good literary reference) and thought-provoking. I hope that you will learn something. I hope also that it will make you think about the power of assemblies: that they have a central role in a school, that they are the principal's set piece – the one moment in the ebb and flow of a school when everything is neatly ordered and everyone is, for a few minutes, listening, and that how they are conducted and what is said sets the tone for everything else.

Oswald says that chapters in which nothing happens are boring, so I should move swiftly on to Chapter 1 in which something does, but before I do, I should make an apology to all those who have worked to make Harris Westminster the place it is but I have failed to give enough credit in this book (particularly those from the Harris Federation and Westminster School who were involved before me and handed over a project that had received a great deal of thought and work and whose marks are etched deeply into the school psyche). Thank you.

Acknowledgements

Particular thanks go to the leadership team who have supported, developed and enriched the Harris Westminster ethos. From an authorial perspective, I am particularly grateful to those whose assemblies decorate this tome: Fiona, Al, Claire and especially Nic; but in truth the school owes just as much to the ideas, integrity and wisdom of Paul, Tristan, Mark and Kiylee. Assemblies are not just those published here and leadership is far more than assemblies.

In putting this book together I have reflected on how much the development of an ethos is a two-way process; that we put ideas out to the school in what we say, what we do and how we do it, but for it to be absorbed and embedded there needs to be a sympathetic reciprocation from the school community. So thank you to those students and staff who, credited or not, have responded to the assemblies and our other decisions and innovations, who have criticised or applauded or, best of all, who have asked questions and sought clarification and understanding.

As I mentioned in the preface I, and the school, owe a huge debt of gratitude to the Harris Federation and Westminster School for their support. Far too many people have been involved for me to name them all, but special mention should go to Stephen, Gary and particularly Patrick, the headmasters who have supported the project; to Dan for giving me the job; to Carolyn who has repeatedly helped me to believe it was possible when all evidence was against; and to Rodney whose patient liaison work between the two schools was completely vital.

Thank you also to Westminster Abbey, who provided the locations for our assemblies (without which this book would have been much shorter), and to John who provided cups of Earl Grey tea and a sympathetic ear when I needed it.

Thanks go to my wife, Louisa, who has put up with first the school and more recently this book taking up a large proportion of my time, energy and emotional equilibrium. Supportive when I have doubted my direction and challenging when I have got too full of myself, I am (as is routinely pointed out by my loving family) lucky to be married to her.

My daughters, Frankie and Zoë, are inspirations. Frankie has provided me with those elements of popular culture that post-date 1990 and a window onto the home life of a sixth-form student that I would otherwise have been trying to recall from my own dim and distant experience. Zoë has refreshed my zest for life with her enthusiasm for all things, her fearless approach to challenges and her surprising (and not justified by the evidence) confidence that whatever the problem, I will be able to fix it just right.

Thank you to my parents, Rob and Meg, for encouraging my approach to assemblies, for reading through and enjoying the jokes – even the ones that the students missed first time round. Thank you for teaching me the lesson that if you practise something enough you get better at it.

Thank you to all those who read through the text in its formative stages and to those who gave advice on how to write it or get it published. Mark, Paul, Anne, Martin, Michelle – your advice has been invaluable.

Rabindranath Tagore says 'depth of friendship does not depend on length of acquaintance'.[1] Thank you to Yaz, Oran, Sean, Fargrim, Corinthia and D.M. for demonstrating this to me through 2020.

Finally, I owe a huge debt of gratitude to Crown House for agreeing to publish this manuscript and to the team for turning it from a messy Word file into a veritable book. They have all been magnificent, particularly Emma Tuck, whose editing has been faithful, kind and good-natured.

1   R. Tagore, *My Reminiscences* (Zhingoora Books, 2012), p. 230.

Chapter 1

Beginning

One of the things that people want to know when they hear about Harris Westminster is how it got started – how do you go from a world in which there is no such thing to one in which 600 students are tucked away behind a bland Westminster façade every day? The idea sprang from an alignment of the interests of the Harris Federation and Westminster School, but the first steps out of discussion and into reality (or, at the very least, into a reality that included me) were taken when a principal was advertised for in the summer of 2013. The process of recruitment was what I would later recognise as very Harris Westminster – one day of pedagogy, processes and ruthless questioning in Crystal Palace followed by a grand interview in a fourteenth century chamber once used by royals to die in (Henry IV) or to become king (Henry V, not coincidentally). That evening was (coincidentally) the Speech Day at my school and so, having been offered the job and finding myself needing to invent an answer to that question of beginning, I sat on the stage in front of a large crowd of parents and students half listening to the guest speaker and half wondering how one could go about creating from scratch the school spirit that had built up over fifty years and now permeated the community that surrounded me.

As I sat there, I found myself reaching for words – words that would encapsulate and communicate, words on which I could build, words that would create direction and allow others (hopefully, eventually) to travel with me, words that could lie at the heart of a school ethos, words that would last. Inspired by the speaker, by the prize-winning students (whose names it was my job to read out) and by a very real sense of the enormity of the task, I settled on three words: ambition, perseverance and legacy. This tricolon summed up how I felt that evening and also (starting a tradition of investing words with multiple meanings) encapsulated the qualities I thought would be most valuable in potential students. For me sitting there that evening, ambition was an excuse to dream big, to think about creating the best school in the country, to stoke the fires of self-confidence that had nudged me towards applying for the role in the first place. Legacy was the sense both that I should build for the future, create structures and traditions that could long outlive me, and that the success of the school would be seen in the mark its students made on the world and not just in their grades. And perseverance was the understanding that I had made some big promises and that keeping them would involve keeping on – I couldn't expect every day to be a celebration of brilliance such as the one I was part of that evening. And then I wanted students who would dream big, set themselves high targets and then, upon meeting them, set higher ones; I wanted students who would go out into the world and make a difference, make it better for others and not just more comfortable for themselves; and I wanted students who would keep going, who would get over setbacks, who would help with the building of the school (metaphorically rather than physically, I hoped – the interview panel had been rather cagey about the location we would be using).

Two things came out of that evening of reflection. The first is the tricolon that still lies at the heart of the school ethos and is proudly displayed on the wall of the entrance corridor: Ambition, Perseverance, Legacy; the second is the idea that Harris Westminster Sixth Form would be a school in which words had power, resounded, were invested with meaning and shared. This is a book about those words, and particularly about the words that were shared with the whole school in assemblies, standing at the front of St Margaret's Church or in the pulpit of Westminster Abbey, before hundreds of expectant faces – words that built and shared and communicated an ethos. In a chapter on beginnings, it is appropriate to begin with an assembly on the Harris Westminster approach to beginning. Not the very first Harris Westminster Assembly – I am afraid that has been lost in the sands of time. Two very early assemblies follow later in this chapter, but right now we begin *in medias res*. One of the things about which I hope to interest my readers is the development of the ethos from those three words to something that has the strength and depth to underpin an entire school. This assembly from three years in is a kind of foreshadowing for that development, a glimpse into the future that I would have loved to have had back in 2013.

You must imagine me stepping up to the pulpit of Westminster Abbey as the bongs of Big Ben fail to fade into the background (the bell having been silenced for repair), without notes (as will become apparent) and with a worried look on my face.

Beginning – 19 April 2017

I have left my notes in my office but it is nine o'clock, too late to go back. I will just begin. The beginning of summer, the beginning of a new term and a wonderful time to speak about beginnings, so I will speak to you about beginnings – or I would, but I don't know where to begin. The sages say to start at the very beginning – it is, apparently, a very good place to start. They go on to explain that when you read you begin with ABC, but they do not, unfortunately, specify how you begin when you deliver an assembly, and so I find myself in the right place, at the right time, needing to start but not knowing where or how.

Maybe I should begin by telling you of the time I explained mechanics and purpose to the principal of Harris Battersea. He listened attentively and then said, 'Yes – excellent. Of course, purpose is just another kind of mechanics.' That is an interesting comment and one that is worth developing, but I know how I plan to end this assembly and I am not sure how to get there from that beginning.

I plan to end by quoting four lines from the poem on the whiteboard in my office and so maybe I should begin with some poetry. Maybe I should update you on my progress towards memorising six poems this year, but I have received criticism from one of your number that my assemblies tend to emphasise literature at the expense of maths and science; of course, I have also received criticism that my Twitter feed fetishises mathematics, so perhaps I can't win. I value all of these areas of learning, but an assembly is fundamentally a wordy creation and it is, therefore, understandable, I hope, that I reach for the geniuses of language in order to felicitate my delivery.

Perhaps, however, and in light of the two poetry-heavy assemblies I have given recently, I should spare you too much this morning and instead begin with the information that on 13 March 1781, William Herschel discovered the planet Uranus – the first planet to be discovered by telescope. But Herschel is buried in Slough of all places and maybe I should reach for one of those memorialised in this building – Admiral Sir Cloudesley Shovel, for example. I suspect I could develop an excellent naval analogy, but too many of you will not have admired his tomb and it is hidden on the south aisle.

So, maybe I should begin with you. I could start by congratulating you on your house drama, by expressing my delight at being able to be part of that celebration of your thespian talents and by linking that celebration to this term and explaining that the exams are to your studies as the opening night is to weeks of rehearsals, and that therefore, if you have studied correctly, exams, as much as the end of exams, are a celebration. That would make this week's Year 13 mocks a dress rehearsal and I don't want to give the impression that I think of exams as a bit of fun. I know exams are not fun – they are deadly serious – but that doesn't stop them from being a celebration of how clever you are.

I don't know how to begin and now I have wittered away 500 words, so maybe I should take a deep breath, clear my decks and get started.

I love the idea of clearing my decks – a nautical term for the beginning of a combat that resonates pleasingly with the scholarly act of clearing my desk – and so, with a clear desk and cleared decks, I shall leap into a pre-prepared paragraph on the discovery of Neptune: something I know well and feel confident about and which will illuminate my main point once I get to it. After the discovery of Uranus, the new planet was watched carefully by astronomers who discovered that it wobbled in its orbit from what would be expected based on the laws of gravity. From this, two astronomers – John Couch Adams and Urbain Le Verrier – deduced that there must be another planet out there and were able to use mathematics to calculate its location. Simultaneously, or almost so, they pointed at an area of sky and said, 'Look there.' Unfortunately, there the similarities end because as students differ so do scientists, and John Couch Adams was careless in his mechanics, sloppy in his workings and messy in his laying out, whilst Urbain Le Verrier was slightly slower but careful and accurate. Adams pointed first but Le Verrier pointed to where Neptune actually was. The British establishment claimed for many years therefore that they should share the glory, but unfortunately this is not how an exam board would see it and nor, now, does the international community. The glory belongs to Le Verrier alone. They both had excellent purpose in understanding that there was a planet out there, but Le Verrier's mechanics were better.

Le Verrier was excited by this and went on to calculate that Mercury's orbit was also wobbly. He therefore predicted another planet, Vulcan, between the sun and Mercury. Sadly, no matter how carefully they looked (and after his success with Neptune they looked very carefully), nobody could find a planet where he was pointing. This was due to the disappointing fact that there was no planet there. Le Verrier's mechanics were fine again – the orbit was wobbly – but his purpose let him down because he didn't know about general relativity (living, as he did, considerably before Einstein). General relativity explains many things, one of which is the wobbliness of Mercury's orbit.

And so we hook into the question of whether purpose and mechanics are the same thing: can you learn to do all of your studies by rote? Could a computer be programmed to pass A levels? Well, I suspect it could: I suspect that at a basic C-grade level the questions are routine, the explanations required are straightforward and most of the essays needed could be memorised, but I think that to get full marks, to get an A*, you need to properly understand, you need to be able to think around the question, you need to be able to bring something interesting and original to the analysis. There is no excuse, however, for missing out on those C-grade marks in the manner of John Couch Adams: if the examiners are willing to give you marks for memorising quotes or formulae or dates or essay structures or graphs or techniques, then you should just memorise them. If I can memorise the poems that go on my wall, then you can memorise the things you need to know for your exams. And so we return to the poem currently on my whiteboard.

It is called 'Invictus' and was written by William Ernest Henley. The last stanza goes like this:

> *It matters not how strait the gate,*
>
> *How charged with punishments the scroll,*
>
> *I am the master of my fate,*
>
> *I am the captain of my soul.*

Right now you are masters of your fate as well as captains of your souls, but time is sweeping you on and exams are a celebration of how clever you are, whether you like it or not. Every mark you gain is a testament to the hours of work you have put in, and every one you should have gained but don't is a sad reflection on your study habits: first nights tend to show up those who haven't learned their lines. And so we get back to the question of how should one begin on a task that seems unmanageably large, where the stakes are scarily high and where there is no obvious starting point. I have a neatly enumerated list of tips on how to begin, garnered from my experience, in this assembly on beginnings. Listen up – you all have exams this term.

- Clear your decks and your desk. You can't work in the middle of a mess and you can't begin with something hanging over you. Do the jobs you have been putting off – throw out the rubbish that you neither know to be useful nor believe to be beautiful – and that is a quote from the third William of the day – William Morris.[1]

- Get rid of distractions. Cancel social engagements, put the Xbox in the attic, change your Snapchat password and forget the new one, tell your friends you will see them in a couple of months. You are the captain of your soul, and the admiral will remind you that a distracted captain crashes the ship.

- Balance mechanics and purpose but know that the quick wins are all mechanics – memorise important things, make as much as you can into a routine you can follow, learn the patterns. This is why, by the way, Year 12s need to be digging as deeply into the purpose of their subjects as they can now: by this time next year it will be too late to get your head round the really hard ideas. Treating purpose like mechanics will get you a C but no further.

- Learn drop-ins. Like the piece on the discovery of Neptune, you can memorise a paragraph or a proof that you can then drop into an answer and gain some marks for a perfectly constructed section because you haven't had to work it out on the day. In fact, you will have guessed that this whole assembly was constructed off site and dropped into place this morning.

- And, finally, just begin. It is easy to put off getting started, to dither, to vacillate, to squander time and to end up being a hostage to fortune, but your ambition is wedged into one of the stones of the abbey. You

---

1   W. Morris, 'The Beauty of Life' (lecture delivered at the Birmingham Society of Arts and School of Design, 19 February 1880). In *Hopes & Fears for Art: Five Lectures* (London: Longmans, Green, and Co., 1919). Available at: http://www.gutenberg.org/ebooks/3773.

know where you want to end up and you can get there if you start from here – you are the master of your fate.

By 2017, the ethos was up and running, the students had joined the school and so it was possible to have an assembly that played a little with the format (I usually read from a prepared script but, sometimes, as on this occasion, I indulge the urge to show off and commit it to memory). It was also possible to play with the jargon of the school: mechanics, purpose and celebration are all words that we have adopted and developed. At its heart, though, this assembly is a development of the thread that started at the Speech Day in 2013: words being used to educate, amuse and intrigue; words being used to model, support learning and enable the students to get better, to develop the skills that would bring them closer to their ambition.

Back to the beginning, though, and what happened next: what do you do when the euphoria of being appointed to your dream job dies down and you find yourself with a three-word ethos and little else to build a school upon? Obviously, my 2017 self would have cleared my desk, but in 2013 I hadn't yet come across this excellent piece of advice, and, anyway, I was still employed in my previous school until 1 January 2014 and in the meantime there were plans to be made and students to recruit on top of my existing job.

I spent the summer pondering the kind of school I wanted to create – a place of learning, a sanctuary from ignorance but also a place that would send its graduates out ready to face and change the world. The idea of changing the world, of developing a generation of young people whose diversity, intelligence and passion would create a shift in the social structures of the nation (which, to this day, sounds overblown as an ambition), was in my thinking throughout those months, and it nearly became the tagline: 'Ambition, perseverance, legacy: changing the world'.

A little reflection showed that this sounded more like voluntary service and less like the academic sixth form I was hoping to create. Our actual unofficial motto came about through an interview I gave for the

Evening Standard in the autumn.[2] This was the first time I had spoken to a newspaper journalist since, I think, I was 16 and in the local press for having a notable collection of GCSEs. Once again, the Harris and Westminster teams had come together to create the opportunity: the Harris communication experts from the mysteriously named 8hwe had set up the interview and it took place in the headmaster's study at Westminster School. By this point I had gone past the point of no return; there was no mileage in being daunted – the entire experience was beyond anything I had done before. My comfort zone was a dot on the distant horizon, and so I smiled broadly and talked enthusiastically about the wonderful institution we were building.

That interview helped me to understand the 'we' in that last phrase: this wasn't just my school, my idea, my impossible commitment, my inevitable crashing downfall when the impossibility was realised; it was a team with contributions and commitments from the Harris Federation and Westminster School (neither of which are in the business of inevitable crashing downfalls). I also saw that I was bringing something to that partnership, that my experience of being an academic high-flyer in a state school, of being a comprehensive kid at Oxford, of being an Oxford graduate teaching in state schools would be important if we were to pull this off.

For a few days after the publication of the article, friends and relatives would tell me that they had seen it. Generally, they were positive about how I had come across but the recurring theme in their comments was, 'You do say "learning is amazing" a lot.' This was news to me – I had certainly never caught myself doing so (although it was, and remains, a thesis with which I agree). I reread the article and, in a short piece with even less quoted text, it did, indeed, turn out that I had repeated that phrase. Either embrace your idiosyncrasies or be forever ashamed of them goes the ancient proverb (or it would if I were in charge of creating ancient proverbs), and so I decided that I would say 'learning is amazing' a lot and let whoever wanted laugh. 'Ambition, perseverance, legacy: learning is amazing' would be the

---

2   A. Davis, 'State Sixth Forms Aren't Inspiring Pupils, Says New Academy Head', *Evening Standard* (16 October 2013). Available at: https://www.standard.co.uk/news/education/state-sixth-forms-aren-t-inspiring-pupils-says-new-academy-head-8883485.html.

ethos and tagline with which I would try to win the hearts (and, more importantly, minds) of London's teenagers.

Shortly after the *Evening Standard* interview we held our launch event for some of those teenagers, and again the partnership had pulled out the stops to impress (looking back, this may have been to impress me as much as the prospective students). The event was at the House of Lords in one of their reception rooms. Students from 11–16 schools and Harris academies had been invited, and lined up to speak were the headmaster of Westminster, Boris Johnson (then mayor of London) and the principal designate of Harris Westminster Sixth Form (me). We were all herded into this amazing venue, stunned by the architecture, charmed by the history and symbolism, intimidated by the airport-style security and then stood about nervously making conversation. I did my best to give the impression of a nerveless and consummate party-goer for whom this kind of affair was second nature – and, to put the students at ease, to find out something about them, to commit their names to memory (Thomas, Chloe, Laura and Daniella are still lodged there years later). My success (or otherwise) in this goal is unrecorded.

Then the time for speeches could be delayed no longer – we had been waiting for Boris to kick us off but he had been caught up in something more pressing than our launch. Stephen Spurr, the head of Westminster, started with the importance of academic qualifications and his commitment to the partnership, and then it was me (I was meant to be the last of the three speakers; it turned out that I was to be last of two). I talked about the environment Harris Westminster would provide, the culture, the opportunities, and then I said, 'But the best thing about this school is not the amazing subject specialists who will teach you, not the library of books you can get lost in, not the lectures, guest speakers, visitors and trips …' *Bang!* The door behind me was flung open and slammed into the oak-panelled wall. 'Oh, oh, I'm sorry, am I late?' bellowed the tousle-haired celebrity. I cleared my throat, '… not the support of the mayor of London. No, the best thing about this school is you: amazing young people coming together from all over the city to learn together, here at the centre of things.'

The amazing location of the school, in central Westminster, is an important component of the provision. We are hugely fortunate to be located where we are (in a building that was kept top secret for many months: when our first cohort of students came to take their entrance exams and we walked them over to Methodist Central Hall so I could talk to them – the first opportunity I had to do so with the whole group together – all I could say was that it was within a stone's throw of where they sat, and then ask them not to throw stones at it). This is a privilege that we take advantage of – and I think that any school which doesn't take advantage of all their advantages is missing a trick – and one for which I am grateful to the team who worked on the project (and to the Department for Education for finally signing off on the cost of the central London building – the £45 million price tag appears to be the going rate for real estate on Tothill Street, but it made the front pages of the newspapers).

The amazing location and the opportunities that it offered was also an idea that was picked up by Nic Amy in one of our earliest assemblies.

Stop and Wonder – 17 September 2014

An assembly by Nic Amy

It is nine o'clock on a Wednesday morning. In this Remembrance term, I want you to think back over the last few weeks and to remember. It is nine o'clock on *this* Wednesday morning. Exactly one week ago today we were sitting on coaches, just outside the abbey, ready to embark on a remarkable journey to Cambridge. Exactly two weeks ago today we were all arriving at Steel House for the very first day of your brand new school. Exactly four weeks ago was the eve of GCSE results. The day before you opened that envelope or travelled into your old school for one final time to unfold the results of your hard work over the last two years.

What do you remember of those last four weeks? You have moved from uncertainty about your futures to the normality and routine of sixth-form life in four short weeks. It has passed so incredibly quickly. So will the next four and then it will be half-term and you will be almost a quarter of your way through Year 12. *Tempus fugit.* Time flies. What will you remember of that first half-term? How do you make sure that this Remembrance term is a term to remember? How do you capture the key moments? How will this fleeting period of your life be part of your legacy? Because very soon memory will morph into legacy.

Well, today I am going to encourage you to remember two things. Two things that, on the surface at least, might appear contradictory. I am going to encourage you to remember to stop … and to go. To be still and to be bustlingly busy.

Firstly, to stop. To stop still. To pay attention. To look closer and to see more. To find moments of calm in busy days. Moments to read, to listen, to look, to care. But I am also going to encourage you to go. To go with all your energy and ambition. To go to things. To go out of your comfort zone. To take risks. To embrace opportunities. To be amazing.

So, let us stop for a moment. Take stock. Stop and think. When we look closer we see the beauty in everything around us; we recognise the amazing buildings, people and possibilities which surround us. We see the unexpected: the things that everyone else misses, as the wonderful talk in Monday's assembly reminded us. Don't miss out: the cultural perspectives course that wasn't your first choice will be the one that lights up your imagination, if you let it.

So, we stop and reflect and are still. But we also go on: manically and restlessly and ambitiously. You are the pioneers. Let us chart new ground. Learning is amazing, yes, but you are amazing too. Do I really mean that? Well, yes. What is my evidence? What does Harris Westminster Sixth Form look like through my eyes? What do I see? I have met many of you to talk about your timetable and your choices, and I have been impressed, without exception, by your ambition and by your focused, intelligent commitment to choosing a programme of subjects which will give you the very best shot to study your first-choice course at your first-choice university.

Getting into the top universities is hugely competitive; you know that and know how hard you will need to work to give yourself the best chance. Some of you need to continue to improve your note-taking and organisational skills in lessons (but more of that in your tutorial on Friday), those of you who want to take girls' football as an option need to remember to sign up in reception today, and the debating teams aren't ready to win a big competition yet. But they will be.

They have the ambition and the potential. Indeed – and to quote the line from Wordsworth which came into my mind as I was cycling over Westminster Bridge this morning – you all have the ambition and potential to be, like this incredibly city, 'All bright and glittering in the smokeless air.' You are amazing, but then so are the opportunities available to you. Don't let them pass you by. Stick at it. Persevere. Take the difficult route.

Last week I taught the U. A. Fanthorpe poem 'Not My Best Side' to my English class. It is based on a Uccello painting which hangs in the free National Gallery in Trafalgar Square. It is only a ten-minute walk away. I encouraged all my set to go and look at this remarkable work. I wonder if they did? Go do. You have astonishing opportunities if you choose to take them. Go and follow up your cultural perspectives courses in political thought, in the media, in current affairs. Find out more. Pay attention. Tomorrow is a historic day: people in Scotland (including voters your age) will decide whether or not Scotland will become independent. That is a decision that will resonate through history – and particularly with those of you studying the reign of James I in history lessons. I hope also that you noticed the Scottish theme of the poem of the week.

It is now just after nine o'clock on Wednesday morning. We have collectively stopped. We have looked closer and we have seen more. Now it is time to go. Stop and go. Go forward with your ambition and your perseverance – don't wait for tomorrow; use the opportunities that today will offer to shape your legacy now. You are amazing. Make sure, therefore, that today you stop … and then go: go, now, and do something remarkable.

Some of the students I had met at the House of Lords were sitting in St Margaret's Church on Parliament Square listening to that assembly, and both they and the school had been through a lot and come a long way during the intervening ten months. They had all completed the application form, spent a cold Saturday in January being examined and a very wet one in February being interviewed. They had also studied for, sat and passed their GCSE exams. Meanwhile, I and others had been busy getting the school ready for them.

My first action following Boris Johnson's appearance at that meeting was to break my leg – a rugby injury that necessitated an operation, a metal plate, time off work and a period of hopping around on crutches.

Thus it was that at the other open events that autumn, instead of seeing a school full of students, teachers, books and resources (as is traditional on such occasions), those young people considering Harris Westminster were treated to me, standing at a lectern with one leg wrapped in a purple cast.

At one of those events, amongst the questions I was asked was, 'Why would you have school on Saturday?' To be fair to the student who asked this, it was a question I had asked myself several times. It was a structure that we were inheriting from Westminster School and one that was necessary to keep our curricula parallel (something that would be important to provide support for teachers and to make sure that our pitch and trajectory were right). It was also something that was going to require quite a radical change in my own lifestyle and a great deal of accommodation from my family (the details of which I was yet to work out). Rather than admit this concern, I kept on message: 'Because learning is amazing and because Saturday is an amazing day on which to learn – we want to fill your two years with as much learning as we possibly can and Saturday school is an excellent way to do this.' Judging from their faces, I think several students changed their mind about coming to Harris Westminster at that point.

Enough, however, were charmed by my unbridled enthusiasm – or believed the promises of an amazing and enriching experience, or were simply short of good alternatives – and we had 374 applicants signed up for the entrance exams which took place in January at the Royal Horticultural Halls (another amazing venue), by which time I had shed both plaster cast and crutches.

The exams and interview make up the selection process by which we pick out students who have the ability and desire to learn that they will need to keep on top of the Harris Westminster curriculum, and they are also clear statements of intent. The exams are based on the Westminster School entrance exams and are targeted away from rote learning and towards application of knowledge. The interviews are modelled on Oxbridge admissions interviews and measure subject affinity and enthusiasm and speed and ownership of learning. By putting prospective students through this process, we are emphasising the importance of knowledge rather than cramming for an exam; we are focusing on a direction of travel rather than current location; and we are saying to students that we don't believe they should rule out any university destination on the grounds that it is too grand or difficult.

This is a model for how ethos has permeated all the structures of the school – how Harris Westminster may be physically built on Tothill Street but its operation is grounded on every level in that ethos. Whenever we can, we make everything we do not merely functional but also something that reflects, operates within or communicates the ethos of ambition, perseverance and legacy; something that says 'learning is amazing'.

One good example of this is the school's term names. State schools tend to follow a fairly sensible structure of naming terms after seasons: autumn term is followed by spring term (we elide winter term because nobody can face it) and then we have summer term. Westminster School, however, for reasons that are lost in history, have Play term, Lent term and Election term, and so the door was open for us to do something interesting with the term names. Following Westminster exactly would lack meaning – both Play and Election refer to occasions in their school calendar that wouldn't appear in ours – and so I looked further afield. Copying Oxbridge would be tempting if it weren't for the fact that they don't align: Oxford has Michaelmas, Hilary and Trinity; Cambridge has Michaelmas, Lent and Easter. I decided that we should therefore have term names that were different to anywhere else (it seems that all the cool kids are doing it), but that they would be names we could invest with meaning, term names that would help to develop the ideas at the heart of the school. The names I came up with were Remembrance, Resilience and Celebration. Each of these had a surface meaning: Remembrance is the term containing 11 November, Remembrance Day; Resilience is the term of January and February, when it is cold and dark and hard; and Celebration leads into the end of term, final exams for the Year 13s and the summer holidays. They also each have a nuance – Resilience and Celebration will come up in later chapters; conveniently, the other meaning of Remembrance was the subject of an assembly in the first weeks of the school's opening.

The Other Meaning of Remembrance –
8 September 2014

We call this Remembrance term and, on the face of it, there is good reason for doing so: this is the term in which Remembrance Day lies and Harris Westminster will have a service at the abbey – this year on Remembrance Day itself. This meaning of remembrance – remembering those who came before, especially those who fought and died for our freedoms – is one we will explore later in the term, but there is more to the name than that.

This weekend I was up in Cambridge, checking that it is still there in advance of our visit tomorrow, and attending the golden wedding anniversary celebrations of my parents-in-law. They have been married for fifty years, and if that doesn't deserve a jolly good knees-up I don't know what does. Their particular version of a knees-up involved a quite delicious dinner, after which my father-in-law gave a little speech and a pianist came on to play some music. The first piece played by the pianist was 'Moonlight in Vermont', which, not coincidentally, was the music to which they had got engaged in the summer of 1963, and it seemed appropriate after fifty years of marriage to remember where it had all started. I don't think this was the first time that Paul, my father-in-law, had thought back to that evening: he talked to us about having made the decision that he wanted to spend the rest of his life with this woman (presumably shortly before that night – it takes a little while to procure a suitable ring). He then smiled, rather shyly for someone who is usually over-brimming with confidence, and said, 'And I've jolly nearly done that.'

The engagement took place at an Oxford college and the dinner was held at one in Cambridge, and during the music I pondered for a while on those strange places of learning, on universities in general and on how they can be made sense of by a visitor or, more precisely, by a group of potential students looking around maybe for the first time. Why is there, in the middle of the Fens, a group of ornate grey stone buildings and over in the Cotswolds another – this group of yellowish brown? The answer lies in the people who live and work there because they were there first and the buildings followed them – or were at least built up to house them. The people were those who wanted to know more, to think more deeply, and they formed small communities because if you want to ask hard questions, it is good to have others around to help you answer them. Their answers were valuable and brought wealth and the wealth paid for the buildings, but it is the people and their questions that are the key to the place.

We are visiting this week, and I hope there will be opportunities to ask them questions and I hope that you will have questions to ask. One question that I commend to you, both this week and in your future, is, 'How do we know that?' It is easier and quicker to believe someone when they tell you something but often you only get at the truth when you ask, 'How do we know?' For years, people knew that heavy objects fell faster than light ones until Galileo questioned this: 'How do we know?' he asked, dropping different sized cannonballs off the Tower of Pisa. That the Battle of Hastings was won by the Normans, partly as a result of a feigned retreat by William's knights, is interesting enough, but by asking, 'How do we know?' we find ourselves in Mr Murphy's cultural perspectives class examining the weight of different kinds of evidence. Fermat's Last Theorem is easy to state ($a^n + b^n = c^n$ has no integer solutions if n is greater than 2) and easy to believe: try as you might you won't find two cubes that add together to make a third one. But the question, 'How do we know?' led to three centuries of mathematics, creating and exploring new ideas. The theorem is conclusively proved but the exploration of that mathematics continues.

For the tourist, the buildings are the amazing thing about Oxford and Cambridge – these great old colleges more like cathedrals than anything else but without an altar. For the students and academics who live there, the central point is not an altar but a question, or series of questions, and the buildings are a place to live, to eat, to sleep, to play and to fall in love, which brings me back to my parents-in-law.

Fifty years is a long time to be married and it is not all spent in the dream world of a college ball with music playing and a beautiful girl in your arms; inevitably bits of it are tough, and it is only by getting through those tough bits that you get to your golden wedding anniversary. Listening to Paul, it was clear that part of what had got him through the tough bits was remembering back to where it had begun and the decision he had made, and so it seems sensible that we should take a moment here to remember why we are setting out on the next two years (a sixth-form course is shorter than a lifetime's marriage but equally likely to have some tough bits) and to make a commitment to ourselves that we will see it through. Getting to the best university you can; having qualifications that you know represent a real achievement; knowing that you have spent two years learning as hard, efficiently and effectively as you are able; and setting yourself up to be in the best position to face the rest of your lives – something like that is why you are here, I think. Take a moment. Make the commitment. Make this moment something that you can remember when the homework piles up and you are not sure it is worth it. It really is: you can say to yourselves, 'It's leading somewhere, it's taking me somewhere I want to go – I remember making that decision.' That is the other meaning of remembrance.

From the very beginning of the school these assemblies have played a key role in the development of ethos. We use them to explain how we want students to behave or how we want them to think; we use them to broaden cultural understanding and to throw out nuggets of learning to be picked up and investigated later; we use them to deliver edicts and to set challenges; and we use them for fun, to enjoy being clever and to give students the opportunity to enjoy being clever by picking up on allusions or call-backs. I sometimes think we place too much emphasis on them – that we expect too much if we hope that students will listen to and retain fifteen minutes of fast-paced, densely packed speech rich in allusion and wordplay. There is good reason for this concern: it is certainly not the case that every word of every assembly is memorised by every person in the church, but it is not our way to step back from a challenge – and so we keep them pitched high, keep them asking more from the students than they can easily give, keep enjoying every joke that gets a ripple of laughter (not all of them do), keep delighting in every student who approaches us during the week to compliment or criticise something that struck them.

The assembly is a wonderful vehicle for sharing learning, for sharing ideas, for sharing ethos; you get to unpack an idea, develop it, twist it and send it out into the world changed – hopefully for the better. The assembly is also a rather wonderful art form: it is a piece of writing of around 1,500 words to be enjoyed by a very specific audience whose tastes you know, whose purpose in being there is agreed and whose attention, by and large, you can rely on. During the first year we had two whole school assemblies every week in St Margaret's Church; I would take Monday and the vice principal, Nic Amy, would take either Wednesday or Friday (days being juggled to work around the diary of a church that still serves the House of Commons). Having been proud of my assemblies in my previous job and rather conceitedly believing myself to be the best in the business, I was alarmed to discover that we had employed someone who was cleverer, more practised and vastly more literate than I was. In the good-natured game of academic one-upmanship that became assembly ping-pong (with ideas and developments being passed from one to (or at) the other), I had to do better, be better, to improve on my beginnings.

Let us, therefore, move on from beginnings to Nic and the rest of the team.

Final Thoughts

- Words come with meaning but they can also be given meaning. Words that are unambiguous, that have only one meaning, are not working hard enough.

- Assemblies are a vehicle for teaching and learning – about the school, about life, about the world. They should never be boring.

- The most amazing thing about any school is the students.

- Building a school on ethos means taking every opportunity to communicate the ethos, and also every opportunity to live the ethos, to show by doing as well as saying.

Chapter 2

Teamwork

I had formally started work on 4 January 2014 and the entrance exams were two bewildering weeks later. As soon as they were done, we started the hunt for a vice principal and shortly thereafter for the rest of the team. Picking the right person as vice principal was more important even than I realised at the time (although I took the process very seriously, telephoning anyone who showed an interest in the advert and making notes in my little green book of all knowledge – an A5 notebook I had been given for Christmas and the first in an annual progression of books of all knowledge).

I knew I needed someone who was different enough to have complementary skills in some areas, someone with strong enough views that my madder ones would be challenged and yet someone who was sufficiently similar for us to get on, for there to be understanding.

We had an excellent field and invited half a dozen candidates to come to Harris Crystal Palace to teach a lesson and then to be interviewed. The second day's ordeal (for a reduced field) moved to Westminster School to observe a lesson, to feed back to me (in role as the teacher) and then for another interview. We found we had two candidates we wanted to employ: Nic Amy, who was an experienced senior teacher, and Paul Murphy, who had a lot of potential and experience outside education (he had been a lawyer in a previous life) but would be new to senior leadership. After much agonising (on the basis that I really wanted to employ them both) we offered the vice principal job to Nic and, once he had agreed to the deal, did some creative accountancy and invented a catch-all middle leader post of head of faculty (the faculty of learning) to Paul. I think it was the job title that swung it. Now there were three of us: one maths teacher (me), one English teacher (Nic) and one historian (Paul).

We could now get on with advertising for the other teaching jobs. Back of the envelope calculations based on the choices of our applicants suggested that we needed two more maths teachers (counting me as a quarter), an English teacher (counting Nic as a half), one and a quarter biologists, one and a quarter chemists, a physicist, a geographer, an economist, a philosopher, half an art teacher and a linguist, if we could find one who could speak French and Spanish. Three quarters of Paul would be our history teacher. You may be able to spot some flaws in our reasoning or, at least, some challenges that would emerge from the calculations, but now was not the time to worry about those details; now was the time to cast our net upon the waters and see what teachers we could catch.

Meanwhile, a location had been procured and work was beginning on the architectural task of turning a rather tired office block into a modern school. To start with, this was a paper exercise, taking the Tube into North London to meet with architects, builders, project managers and some mysterious people who were none of those things but would make sure that anything which required a pipe or wire had the appropriate pipe and/or wire. For everyone else around the table, transforming a building from one thing into another was a process they had been through several times; for me, however, this was a new and bewildering experience. I stared at the plans, listened hard to what was being said and did my best to imagine what it would mean for the school. Where would the hall go? What about the canteen? Was the library large enough? Were there enough toilets? At this point the school was very much a figment of our collective imaginations, and so we should see what the Harris Westminster annals have to say about imagination (this assembly is one of Nic's and you will recognise his style from 'Stop and Wonder': his contribution to the assemblies and to the school ethos was such that I couldn't get through the first chapter without giving him a voice).

On Imagination – 18 May 2015

An assembly by Nic Amy

I want to take as my theme this morning: imagination.

Imagination: 'The power or capacity to form internal images or ideas of objects and situations not actually present to the senses, including remembered objects and situations, and those constructed by mentally combining or projecting images of previously experienced qualities, objects, and situations.'[1]

Just imagine.

Last week I was preparing for Poetry Society. That runs at 4pm on Tuesday, by the way, and you are all welcome. Keep going to those clubs and societies. That is what scholars do. And there is time: time to continue with your sport and exercise (which, in any case, is beneficial to your study); time to continue interests beyond the curriculum; and time to work astonishingly hard in preparation for examinations.

So, in Poetry Society last week we were looking at a poem by the great Edward Thomas (who died on the Western Front, at Arras, in April 1917). The poem is called 'Old Man'; it is a powerfully compelling meditation on memory. In preparation for the session I was reading other poets and critics writing about Thomas; that process of reading deeply in preparation for a lesson is something that I would strongly commend to you.

Browsing through JSTOR, I happened upon an excellent essay by the former Poet Laureate, Andrew Motion.[2] JSTOR, by the way, is a superb resource: a gateway to hundreds of thousands of articles, books and journals, and available to all of you through the library tiles on the student portal. I commend it to you without hesitation (although you may need help and support in searching it successfully – please ask if you do – the librarian would be the best person to start with). And, if you claim, 'But JSTOR has an arts and literature bias,' I will put my hands up and say, 'Fair enough,' so it is rather wonderful that we now have access to the *New Scientist*, *Student BMJ* and *The Economist*. A little bit of imagination in searching out the resources that are available to you goes a long way. I commend them all to you.

But, I digress. Imagination.

I was reading Andrew Motion on Edward Thomas on JSTOR. He was talking about paths and places, and I learned (and I didn't know this before) that Robert Frost wrote his wonderful 'The Road Not Taken' ('Two paths diverged in a yellow wood, / … and I — / I took the one less traveled by, / And that has made all the difference') for Edward Thomas.

---

1   See https://www.oed.com/view/Entry/91643.
2   A. Motion, 'The Poem and the Path', *The Hudson Review* 63(1) (2010): 19–54. Available at: http://www.jstor.org/stable/25703712.

But, I digress again.

Reading Motion, I enjoyed his turn of phrase to describe Thomas' sense of place in the poem. He calls it a 'local habitation'. But then I thought: hey, hang on, I recognise that. There were no quotation marks but it wasn't his phrase – it is Shakespeare's.

It made me think of T. S. Eliot, writing in *The Sacred Wood* in 1920, who said: 'One of the surest of tests is the way in which a poet borrows. Immature poets imitate; mature poets steal; bad poets deface what they take, and good poets make it into something better, or at least into something different.'[3] Just like one of Eliot's 'mature' poets, Motion had stolen that phrase. Plagiarism, surely? Well, no, not at all, I would argue, but the literary critical justification for that claim runs to longer than another digression in this assembly; come along to Poetry Society instead.

For one thing, because I can't resist one very brief aside, Motion *wants* his reader to recognise the borrowing. 'Local habitation' is from *A Midsummer Night's Dream*. At the beginning of Act 5, Duke Theseus is talking to Hippolyta in anticipation of their nuptials and the resolution of the play: the matches for the lovers and the performance by the mechanicals (including the incredible Bottom) of their terrible play. Anyway, here is what Theseus says. And I got so excited by rediscovering these remarkable lines that I immediately sent them to your English teachers in a fit of: isn't-our-subject-rather-amazing.

> *The lunatic, the lover and the poet,*
> *Are of imagination all compact:*
> *One sees more devils than vast hell can hold,*
> *That is, the madman; the lover, all as frantic,*
> *Sees Helen's beauty in a brow of Egypt:*
> *The poet's eye, in fine frenzy rolling,*
> *Doth glance from heaven to earth, from earth to heaven;*
> *And, as imagination bodies forth*
> *The forms of things unknown, the poet's pen*
> *Turns them to shapes, and gives to airy nothing*

3   T. S. Eliot, 'Philip Massinger'. In *The Sacred Wood: Essays on Poetry and Criticism* (London: Faber & Faber, 1997 [1920]), pp. 104–121 at pp. 105–106.

A local habitation and a name.

Such tricks hath strong imagination,

That, if it would but apprehend some joy,

It comprehends some bringer of that joy;

Or in the night, imagining some fear,

How easy is a bush supposed a bear![4]

We can all empathise with this, no? With the power of the imagination: 'in the night, imagining some fear, / How easy is a bush supposed a bear!'? It might not have been a bush that you mistook and your imagination might have conjured up something even more terrifying than a bear, but we have all, surely, under the cover of night, imagined some terrible forms lurking in the shadows.

It was the subject (the power of our imaginations to scare the life out of ourselves) of the wonderful poem by the Renaissance poet Fulke Greville ('In night, when colours all to black are cast') that we looked at the week before in Poetry Society. Tuesday, 4pm. I commend it to you.

In these lines, as he talks about the poet's pen, Theseus also gives us an amazing insight into the power of creative writing. What does he say? Firstly, he identifies the power of looking. I quote my favourite book about education, Jonathan Smith's *The Learning Game* where he encourages us to 'look closer' that we might 'see more'.[5] Looking closer, seeing more. That is the stuff of learning. The poet's gaze is special, though. His looking is supercharged. His eye, in a wonderfully coined metaphor, glances from heaven to earth and back again 'in fine frenzy rolling'. We might roll our eyes sarcastically, sardonically. The poet does so in celebration, in a precisely, beautifully calibrated alliterative 'fine frenzy'. It is a 'frenzy' – almost out of control with the excitement of the looking and the seeing – but qualified 'fine' (extensive, exact, scrupulous, critical); the fine qualification of the frenzy applies the critical control of scholarship to the passion and excitement of learning.

Imagine that eye greedily taking in the world around us: gradually moving from earth to heaven and back again. Imagine glancing up at St Margaret's as you came in this morning: 'Grass, weedy pavement, brambles, buttress, sky'. But it was with imagination and with Motion's turn of local habitation that we

---

4   W. Shakespeare, *A Midsummer Night's Dream*, Act V, sc. I, ll. 7–22.

5   J. Smith, *The Learning Game: A Teacher's Inspirational Story* (London: Abacus, 2002).

started. So, before we finish, let us take a couple of minutes to think about those most famous lines from Theseus' speech:

And, as imagination bodies forth

The forms of things unknown, the poet's pen

Turns them to shapes, and gives to airy nothing

A local habitation and a name.

Imagination is the agent, the actor, the craftsman. And the craft it enacts is wonderfully represented as 'bodying forth'. Turning the inanimate (literally, without a soul) into animation (literally soulful): the tangible, the whole, the that-with-the-substance-of-a-body.

It is 'the poet's pen' that performs these tiny miracles of imagination, taking 'airy nothing' and turning it to 'shapes', giving it, to quote Motion on Thomas, stealing from Shakespeare's Theseus: a 'local habitation' and, of course 'a name' (which is the subject of Thomas' 'Old Man', by the way).

The poet's pen is taking the insubstantial, the unordered, the incorporeal and bodying it forth: giving it an exact and critical 'special shell' of a body. Giving 'to airy nothing / A local habitation and a name.'

And here is what my Year 13 literature class would call 'the reach' – where we take a critical reading just a little too far. So, excuse me please, but let us think of these wonderful lines in the context of what is at the front of all of our minds this week: your upcoming examinations. I hope you are practising. Past papers, past questions, practising the stuff that you are finding hard (not the things you have already mastered). Over and over again until you get it right and can get it right time after time: time and time again, until you can get it right *habitually*.

That is the attitude you need in terms of preparing for examinations. Preparation, practice is the key. But back to imagination: with each examination you sit you are confronted with the blank page, the carte blanche, the tabula rasa. It is your blank slate which only your imagination can fill up through the action of your pen.

You are charged with filing the examination paper with the fruits of your practised imagination, giving 'to airy nothing / A local habitation and a name.' And I wish you all the very best in those examinations. Celebrate your powers of imagination: look closer to see more and body forth something truly amazing.

To Harris Westminster, Nic brought a huge enthusiasm for some things about which I knew very little: poetry, Shakespeare and (although I am embarrassed to say it) educational literature. Poetry Society was a very real and wonderful thing: an example of something that was entirely on message, in ethos and yet which I would never have been able to run myself. The success of the sixth form is built on such activities where someone (occasionally me, but most often someone else) has been inspired, had an idea and run with it, relying on the enthusiastic engagement of the students and the uncensoring approach I took to leadership to make it work. I am sure there is a nice way to tie in Shakespeare here, with the eyes of Harris Westminster rolling in fine frenzy and the teachers acting as pens to give to these wild ideas a local habitation and a name, but maybe I need to ask Nic to shape it for me.

JSTOR was also an enthusiasm of Nic's – it is, he admitted, less useful for the mathematically inclined than for the arts and humanities students – and he worked with the librarian and other teachers to train students in its use. A superb resource full of articles, ideas, opportunities for imagination and digression. To digress myself, briefly, some of the language in the assembly above may seem unusually selected unless you have at your fingertips the works of Philip Larkin. One of the poems that had been covered in Poetry Society (but not credited in this assembly) was Larkin's 'Church Going'. I happened to pop into Nic's office shortly before this meeting of the society and he handed me a copy of the poem, saying that it was the best poem of the twentieth century. The phrases dropped into the assembly were a challenge to Poetry Society (and to me) to recognise and relish.

Back in 2014, the interviews took place on a very rainy Saturday in February – storm warnings abounded and public transport was disrupted to the point where, getting up extremely early, I tweeted that I would be riding in on a dolphin. Interviewers were begged and borrowed from across the Harris Federation – consultants, principals, vice principals – and to their number were added kind friends, a Westminster teacher or two, Nic and I. Students came into the great hall of Westminster School (an amazing location and a wonderful resource to be offered for the day) and we peppered them with hard questions, looking for students who perked up when they didn't know something rather than being intimidated; young people who wanted to learn, not ones who thought they knew everything already. Once all the data had been collected in, I applied a series of fiendish formulae in a large Excel spreadsheet to identify the highest scoring and sent out offer letters.

One of the complications in giving offers was that some subjects – art history, German, drama, Latin, and music – were offered through our partnership with Westminster School, and the students for those subjects would be attending Westminster lessons. This meant that they had to meet not only the overall standards to get a place at Harris Westminster, but also needed to demonstrate high levels of aptitude for those particular subjects. Additional interviews (and music auditions) were organised, some difficult conversations were had about available options (some of which worked out very fortuitously: one student who had originally chosen music switched to art history after such a conversation, did amazingly well and went on to study at the Courtauld Institute), and then we were sorted.

Our music provision was something that niggled at the back of my mind: how can you have a school without music? And if the music students had their lessons at Westminster, how would Harris Westminster manage to have an orchestra, choir, band or any kind of extracurricular music? I took this question to the architects, and we found a way to build a music room into the school – not for year one (for which it was quickly clear that we would only have three floors, no school hall or canteen and very limited classroom space), but in phase two (the construction work for which would be going on whilst the tiny new school was making its way through its first year in the bottom half of the building). For some students music is more than just a subject – it is a hobby, a social life. Not me, by the way – I am badly coordinated, unrhythmic and almost tone-deaf – but for some. This was another way in which Nic and I complemented each other: amongst his many talents is a musical gift and he was able to weave this (and a performance by the lone music student of our first year – an impressively accomplished pianist) into an assembly.

On Music – 12 October 2015

An assembly by Nic Amy

Shakespeare's play *Twelfth Night* is subtitled: 'Or, What You Will' (which is interesting in itself for its punningly self-reflexive reference to Shakespeare himself – he is the will (Will Shakespeare) in the 'What You Will'). Anyway, *Twelfth Night* very famously opens with the Duke Orsino's paean to love and music:

> *If music be the food of love, play on;*
>
> *Give me excess of it, that, surfeiting,*
>
> *The appetite may sicken, and so die.*[6]

The Duke is in love but also in love with music, and the two concepts are so often linked. 'If music be the food of love, play on' is a phrase that many of us will have heard before. Think about it: food is something that nourishes or sustains – and so music, Orsino seems to be saying, keeps love alive. Well, that must be true given the number of love songs which have been written throughout history. That said, the line is tentative. It starts with 'If'. It posits its own uncertainty with its opening breath.

Several of you will have noticed that it is also couched in my favourite mood (not quite a tense). 'If music be' is subjunctive: that strange mood of uncertainty and doubt; the nothing-is-fixed-and-definitely-not-what-it-appears grammatical form.

But if it *is* (you will note that my paraphrase slips out of the subjunctive as we try to pin it down – but there is no pinning down to be had, really) ... but if it *is*, then Orsino would have us 'play on'. What a wonderful idea: an ongoing celebration of love and music intertwined.

Although, of course, his argument is that: 'surfeiting [i.e. getting too much of it], / The appetite may sicken, and so die.' Have you ever had the experience of listening to a song so often that it starts to sound silly? For Orsino, the 'spirit of love' and imagination combine both 'quick and fresh': 'So full of shapes is fancy, / That it alone is high fantastical.'[7]

---

6   W. Shakespeare, *Twelfth Night; Or What You Will*, Act I, sc. I, ll. 1–3.
7   Shakespeare, *Twelfth Night*, Act I, sc. I, ll. 14–15.

But 'play on' is key. Play is to perform, to make new, to engage in a scholarly act of love. Great learning should feel like play. Great lessons should be full of fancy and the fantastical. Listening to music this morning made me think of the fancy and the fantastical in music. And it made me think just what a stupid question it is to ask: what is your favourite type of music? Music is *the* supreme art form because, like Shakespeare, it is ultimately un-pin-down-able.

Music is also a much more private activity than it ever was in the past. Back in the day, music was an almost exclusively public experience. But now, not so much. I want you to try to imagine an era before personal devices, before ubiquitous headphones, before constant access to your own bespoke selection of tracks. Actually, personal devices have been around for a long time. I remember getting my first personal stereo cassette player for Christmas in 1983 (well over thirty years ago). It was a red Sony. And I was also given my first cassette to play in it: a compilation of some of the top hits of 1983 called *Now That's What I Call Music*. I think the series is now on something like volume 91; however, this was the very first. And it seemed novel and cool and new. But, looking back, it was rather more drab than the memory suggests.

It was a double cassette which kicked off with the terrible Phil Collins song 'You Can't Hurry Love', and you kind of had to listen to that because with a tape player there was no shuffle; it was, to misquote *The History Boys* (which Year 13 will remember I love doing in assemblies), one variable song after another and always, of course, in the same order.

There is very little to miss about cassette tapes. Except, possibly, the mixtape. A Spotify playlist just doesn't cut it in the same way. But too much nostalgia there lies. Now, we are all constantly plugged in, and there are several things to consider.

One is the serious long-term threat to our hearing posed by being permanently plugged in. Seriously. The second is the physical statement – the body language message – of headphones. It is not just about the music. Consciously, or subconsciously, you are making a very clear statement by wearing headphones. We are all Londoners. We all use public transport. So we all know that one message we send out by wearing headphones is: 'Go away – I don't want to talk to you.' That can be reasonable; although, if we are walking around school with our headphones on, or even with the white wires from our Apple cables looped over our ears, then we are making the same statement in a context where that is not acceptable manners.

Sitting in a study area being plugged in might be making the statement, 'I want to work' or 'Do not disturb', which is often a pretty decent message to send out. And a lot of you will claim that listening to music helps you to concentrate, that you work better when you are listening to music. Hands up if this is you – who thinks they often work better when plugged in? I think that *can* often be true. But I wonder how that holds up in terms of real concentration, in terms of deep learning. If *you* argue that you work better when listening to music, I want you to think about this proposition. If they changed the rules around examinations to allow you to plug yourself in and listen to music when you were completing your history or your physics examination, would you? When you need to concentrate at your very hardest, would music really help? Or would it, at some level, prove a distraction?

I am not going to suggest there is a wrong or right answer to that question, but it is something for you to think about. Another thing about listening to music whilst you are concentrating on something else is that actually you are not really focusing and concentrating on the music itself. And like all great art, paying more attention enriches and deepens the appreciation of that art. How many times have you listened to your current favourite song? And does it get better the more you listen to it, the better you know it?

The same is true, of course, of your work. I am currently studying *Hamlet* with my Year 13 class, and one of my constant refrains (it is interesting how many of our metaphors come from music – to sing from the same hymn sheet, as in so many of my assemblies) is: you need to know the play really well before you can truly appreciate it. You need to reread it as often as you listen to your favourite song. Well, almost. When we really pay attention to whatever it is, we deepen and enrich our experiences.

'If music be the food of love, play on.' Playing is the key; music both the medium and the metaphor. Give me excess of it. Play on.

We played on with our fishing net, looking for teaching staff. By now the 'we' was neither royal, nor figurative, nor a generous recognition of the support we got from the sponsoring partners, but a real description. Riquelle Okakpu, who had been offering admin support from within the federation, was now a full-time PA and swiftly learning what that entailed. I was learning slightly more slowly: I had never had a PA before and wasn't entirely sure what I needed assistance with.

This difference in speed on the uptake continued, and once the school was up and running it was accepted that if you wanted an accurate answer to any question about the current running of the school, you would be best off asking Riquelle (my usefulness was consigned to questions of the future such as: will there be timetables printed by this afternoon?).

The staff who would be asking Riquelle those questions were assembled as the spring and early summer terms unfurled. Charlotte impressed us with an English lesson on Charlotte Perkins Gilman; Hafsa impressively solved the MFL problem by being equally clever in French and Spanish; Marisa, the Canadian geography teacher, would clearly address our sporting needs; and Tristan was a philosophy teacher with a built-in keyboard (not quite true, but he did have one installed in his classroom before we had finished putting in the desks) which further bolstered our music provision. In science we appointed Matthew the biologist, and found that Mav had both biology and chemistry up his sleeve (a very useful accomplishment), and therefore turned our 0.25 biologist and chemist problems into a single 0.5 chemist problem – one that was solved by the appointment of Chloe, fresh out of Oxford University and keen to have a training timetable and contract. A day of maths interviews (we had five excellent applicants, which boosted my spirits considerably) resulted in the appointment of John and Tom, and from a highly stimulating day of art we appointed Hania, who would also teach for a day a week at Harris Greenwich.

Economics proved a thornier issue than I had expected and physics was inevitably difficult. I spent an afternoon drinking Belgian beer with one potential physics teacher and emerged with a headache but no hire. Fortunately, Conor saw our economics advert third time around and we were able to get Yurij, the musical physicist (my concerns on the musical front were clearly going to be resolved), to join us from Canada.

We then turned our minds back to the student applicants who had been busily engaged with taking their GCSE exams. We didn't want them to forget about us or to get the impression we were in any way an intangible enterprise consisting only of a slightly deranged head teacher working out of an office in Croydon (the only part of that impression I could hope to dispel through the use of facts was the word 'slightly').

The answer was clearly an induction day to introduce the prospective Year 12s to the school and the kind of education they would be facing. The drawback to this excellent plan was that the school building (now officially announced and duly paraded across the front page of *The Independent* as a waste of £45 million[8]) was still a building site inside. There were no classrooms for them to see, no older students for them to get to know and the teachers who would be working with them were currently employed elsewhere.

Eventually I hit on the idea of a treasure hunt. We could get them into London, provide them with clues that would show them some of the exciting aspects of the location, test their brains, let them spend time with each other and, by holding it on a Saturday, maybe entice some of the wonderful staff I had appointed to join us. That this sounded like a good plan, despite the fairly terrifying risk assessment I had to work through, is both testament to the imagination that was going into this project and evidence of some of the challenges that faced us. Nic and I spent a day getting to know each other as we prowled the environs of the school, searching for useful clues and inventing challenges. We came up with a few different routes so that Westminster wouldn't be plagued with a band of students a hundred strong all trying to pile into the same phone box, and I negotiated with the abbey for the use of St Margaret's Church as a starting and dropping-off point.

The use of St Margaret's Church on Parliament Square, through the generosity of the abbey, has been a feature of school life that began with that treasure hunt and has continued throughout our existence. In the first year we had no school hall at all (it was filled with builders and their stores), but even when phase two was completed the room was not big enough to fit in the whole school – and the need to fit the whole school into the same space for an assembly was always thought crucial to the success of the project. Functionally, we use the church as a single room big enough for 650 (actually it could hold

---

8   R. Garner, 'London Sixth-Form Heads Unite to Urge Michael Gove to Rethink New £45m Free School', *The Independent* (31 March 2014). Available at: https://www. independent.co.uk/news/education/education-news/london-sixth-form-heads-unite-urge-michael-gove-rethink-new-ps45m-free-school-9226642.html.

up to 750 but the size of Steel House limits the school to the lower number), but it is, of course, much more than that. It is a beautiful piece of architecture – a Tudor building with Victorian decoration; it is a resonant piece of history – the site of Walter Raleigh's burial and Winston Churchill's wedding; and it retains a place at the centre of politics, hosting monthly parliamentary communions and with one pew permanently roped off for the Speaker of the House of Commons.

When they first entered the church in June 2014, the students were daunted, quiet strangers (mostly) to each other, and they listened attentively as I explained the plan for the day – they would set off in groups of four, stay within some set bounds, call my phone if there were any problems, meet up for lunch in Green Park and come back to the church at 3pm for debriefing and prizes. Then they set off, excited, perplexed and intrepid. (This is how I think of that first group of pioneering HWSFers, committing their future to a promise they didn't properly understand, at least partly because I wasn't sure how it was all going to turn out.)

My recollection of the treasure hunt is one of high nervous tension – taking responsibility for so many people I didn't know and then sending them out unaccompanied (except by each other) in Central London was one thing; taking responsibility for their enjoyment of the day and making sure they had a fun time was an extra layer of difficulty. It was a sunny June day when I finally set off from the Tothill Street Pret with Nic and Riquelle, having had a coffee and a regroup once the students had disappeared out of sight (the hope was that the coffee would calm me down – I don't think it worked). We strolled through St James's Park up to the rendezvous point at the Canadian Memorial in Green Park. As we arrived, collecting teams of students and teachers (there were enough teachers for two teams who competed energetically with each other) to make our way to the designated lunch spot, black clouds rolled over head. A few raindrops started to fall. We moved under the trees and Hafsa drew an umbrella from her bag (being prepared for all eventualities and unflustered by developments being amongst her accomplishments). The rain then started to pour down; the trees quickly lost their appeal as shelters; two students danced out onto the wet grass in their summer dresses relishing the experience; Conor stood shivering in t-shirt and shorts;

and our picnic quickly fell apart as the teams all decided to see if the built-up areas of London offered more shelter than its open spaces.

By the time they made it back to St Margaret's the students were soaked, tired and talking nineteen to the dozen. If I may adapt J. K. Rowling's maxim on the benefits of mountain trolls to social integration,[9] it seems that there are some things you can't share without ending up liking each other, and an umbrella between four through a summer storm is one of them. Prizes (including one for deciphering anagrams of ambition, perseverance, legacy) and speeches followed, and the first Harris Westminster community (not quite a school, we would have to wait for September for that) event came to an end. Or almost: as I dragged myself up Whitehall, coming down from a ten-hour emotional high, I got a phone call from a student who had left her Oyster card in one of the pews. Back to the church to wait for her and finally I could make my way home.

The treasure hunt itself was Nic's work – he had taken the notes of our day out and turned them into something quite brilliant, replete with anagrams, puns and wordplay. This joy in the use of language, playing with ideas and enjoying cleverness, was something that we both enjoyed and would have been part of school life whoever the vice principal had been, but it was lifted and emphasised by Nic.

As the school grew and developed, other members of the senior team added their voices to the ethos, brought their own slant and their own stories to assembly, and the shared understanding of the community that had felt so fragile when the treasure hunt picnickers had scattered gained depth and solidity. The next assembly was delivered by Fiona Templeton, who joined us in 2015 as head of humanities and was promoted later that year to assistant principal. She brought order to the UCAS process (a significant challenge for a school where half the students apply to university every year, with about half of those being 'early entry' – either Oxbridge or medicine), she encouraged us to assume that any problem could be solved through better planning and better frameworks, and she introduced us to the idea of failing better and to the words of Samuel Beckett.

9   J. K. Rowling, *Harry Potter and the Philosopher's Stone* (London: Bloomsbury Children's Books, 1997), p. 132.

Failure – 9 January 2017

An assembly by Fiona Templeton

Over the Christmas period, I spent time with my family and I got to see my 3-year-old niece again. We were playing catch, and time and time again she failed to catch the ball. Her hand–eye coordination is still developing and therefore this is not surprising. My husband, however, rather than indulging her by saying 'Well done' every time she failed to catch the ball, would tell her, 'That wasn't good, was it? Cup your hands and try again.' I asked him later why he had said this and he told me, 'She won't learn if she doesn't accept failure. If I teach her a technique and she practises it, she'll succeed.' He is right, of course, and Rosie (my niece) never once complained, cried or had a tantrum because my husband told her she was not very good. Instead, she listened and tried to catch the ball by cupping her hands. Her hand–eye coordination still isn't there but statistically she manages to catch the ball more often than before.

Failure is a word which probably strikes fear into your hearts and yet failure is one of life's most important lessons and is key to our evolutionary success. As toddlers you made mistakes all the time – for instance, your attempts in learning to walk would have seen you crashing to the floor numerous times. However, you wouldn't have simply given in with, 'Well, evidently I can't balance. I shall be happy crawling for the rest of my life.' The one thing you have as a toddler is perseverance – perseverance to never give up and to try, try again. My question to you is, if as toddlers you were so accepting of failure and learned from it, why are you so scared of it now?

Failure is something we have all encountered, even people you would consider to be huge successes. The Harry Potter series has sold 450 million copies worldwide and has been translated into seventy-five languages. Harry Potter's author J. K. Rowling perhaps isn't someone who would be considered synonymous with failure. A few years after graduating from the University of Exeter, she said: 'I had failed on an epic scale. An exceptionally short-lived marriage had imploded, and I was jobless, a lone parent, and as poor as it is possible to be in modern Britain, without being homeless.'[10] Writing was her

---

10 J. K. Rowling, 'The Fringe Benefits of Failure and the Importance of Imagination', Harvard University commencement address, 5 June 2008. Available at: https://news.harvard.edu/gazette/story/2008/06/text-of-j-k-rowling-speech.

escape, so when she could she would sit down for a few hours and write. She submitted her first three chapters to a number of publishers for them simply to dismiss her. However, she did not give up. She said, 'failure meant a stripping away of the inessential. I stopped pretending to myself that I was anything other than what I was, and began to direct all of my energy into finishing the only work that mattered to me.'[11] She never gave up, as easy as it would have been – the failure she received made her stronger and, if anything, improved her work. J. K. Rowling went from being a jobless single mother living off unemployment benefits to one of the bestselling authors of all time. But it didn't happen overnight. She faced rejection and constantly strived for success. She worked hard at her craft before anyone noticed her. That practice, along with strengthening herself against rejection, was what made her work unforgettable. The rest is history, as they say. So what can we learn from J. K. Rowling's story? I would like you to think about that for a moment.

'Anyone who has never made a mistake has never tried anything new.' These words are attributed to one of history's greatest scientists, Albert Einstein. Ironically, this attribution is almost certainly mistaken but it has stuck because, despite his international renown, Einstein was a failure too. It took him nine years to secure a job in academia. This was, in part, because during his years studying at the Zurich Polytechnic, his rebellious personality and penchant for skipping classes saw his professors give him less than glowing recommendations upon his graduation in 1900. He spent two years finding a job and ended up working at the patent office in Bern. Despite this situation, Einstein was able to use the time he had to perfect his research, which saw him publish four revolutionary articles in 1905, one which introduced his famous equation $E = mc^2$ and the theory of special relativity. While the discoveries marked Einstein's entrance on to the physics world stage, he didn't win a full professorship until 1909 – nearly a decade after he had left school. Making mistakes and failing may seem a bitter pill to swallow at the time, but it is all part of life's rich tapestry and perhaps some things happen for a reason.

My best friend from school was an exceptional English student. In Year 9 she gained the highest SATs score of the year group with a ridiculously off the scale Level 8. She got an A* at GCSE without trying. She achieved 98% at AS in English literature. She was a prodigy and everyone expected her to go to Oxbridge. She received an interview at Cambridge, later finding out she was placed in the Winter Pool. She ultimately became an Oxbridge

---

11   Rowling, 'The Fringe Benefits of Failure'.

reject. She went on to read English literature at Royal Holloway and after graduation secured a job in publishing. Within nine months she had been made redundant. Unfortunately for me and my friends, we graduated in 2008 and, for the economists amongst you, the year of the big financial crash. She became a waitress.

If she were a different person, she would have been resigned to her fate. However, she persevered and applied for the KPMG graduate scheme. She got in – yes, an English literature graduate training to be a tax accountant, not something you would expect. The graduate scheme was relentless: if you don't know, there are numerous exams to pass. If you fail them, you have one chance to resit otherwise you lose your job. In order to compete in this world, you need grit, resilience and the ability to reflect on your mistakes. My friend eventually passed and became a qualified accountant. After five years of training, working and failing, she realised that the wonderful world of accountancy wasn't her cup of tea. She now manages the BPP training for the KPMG graduate scheme and apprenticeships – a job she really enjoys. She has, however, never given up her love of English and is currently writing a novel as well as publishing more and more articles.

Now, my friend did not go to Cambridge University, despite being one of the best English students my school had ever seen, but she did not allow this 'perceived failure' to hinder her. She tried and perhaps things worked out for the best – after all, she met her future husband at Royal Holloway. For some Year 13s, you are anxiously finding out whether you have got into Oxford or Cambridge, and if you don't, that is absolutely fine. You have had an amazing experience; in fact, the label 'Oxbridge reject' has been worn as a badge of pride by some students, especially those at Bristol and Durham. I guess what I am trying to say is that don't let something which probably makes up 1% of your life's experiences shape the rest of your life. Perhaps everything does happen for a reason.

You all have dreams. When you are young, you think your career will be linear – a straight road. If anything, I hope these stories illustrate that the pathway to success isn't like that; it is a bumpy, twisty, steep road and one which will see you going down one-way streets and doing numerous three-point turns. Everything, even the unexpected, is an experience which makes life all the more interesting.

My cousin is perhaps an excellent example of this. She gained ten A*s and an A at GCSE and four As at A level, and also failed to get into Cambridge to read philosophy; instead she went to Durham where she gained a first class honours degree. However, her passion was always marine biology – the study of dolphins, to be exact. She got on to the KPMG forensic accountancy graduate scheme (clearly, I know a lot of people who have had some involvement with KPMG), but before she took up her place on the scheme she had a belated gap year during which she explored South America. There her future would change forever as she met her future boyfriend, a Norwegian oil engineer. On her return to the UK, she started work at KPMG and lived in London – all seemed fine. Except deep down she wasn't happy. She would visit the engineer in Oslo as often as she could and came to realise that this wasn't what she wanted. She did something incredibly brave: she quit her job, enrolled into the University of Oslo to study marine biology and moved to Norway. Now, many people might think that she threw away an amazing career and perhaps she is a failure. That was three years ago. Today, she is excelling at university, speaks fluent Norwegian and is on course to becoming a marine biologist.

Now to me personally. I have failed many, many times, especially when I was learning to be a teacher. You may have heard about a TV programme called *Tough Young Teachers*, following trainee teachers on the Teach First graduate programme. I was such a trainee (although I never appeared on telly). There I was in September 2009 standing in front of a class of teenagers in a challenging inner-city school in Elephant and Castle. I had no teaching experience, I didn't know the kids, plus I sound like someone who works for the BBC – what could possibly go wrong? Being squared up to by a six-foot student who was refusing to follow my instructions was a high point. Students talking over me, being told to f*** off and being called a 'beg friend' twenty times by one of my students when I challenged him wandering the corridors during lessons. It was tough – spending hours preparing a lesson only for it to descend into anarchy. I have had fights in my classroom, I have had a student projectile-vomit – all over the classroom floor – you name it, I probably encountered it. I could have quit, thrown my hat in and given up. Spoiler alert, I didn't. To make matters tougher, I was teaching a subject I hadn't studied in years – business studies. Not only was I learning to control ridiculously challenging students, but I was also teaching myself accountancy, production theory and marketing. Over time, slowly but surely, the students gained my trust and we started to bond. I hat student who squared up to me? By the end of Year 11 he had become one of my star students.

Even today I fail – perhaps a lesson I had prepared didn't go to plan. Do I repeat the same lesson over and over again? Of course not. I reflect. I tweak it. I make it better. I respond to feedback. I respond to my own criticisms. This is something you all should be doing on a daily basis, because without responding to failure we are bound to repeat it.

I have often said to students that if everyone was 100% perfect I would be out of a job – I expect you to fail in order to succeed, otherwise how would you ever learn? Failure needs to be destigmatised in our world and we need to embrace it. However, that means you need to be proactive in embracing it and doing something about it. You have had three weeks to reflect and take ownership of your learning. For Year 13, you should have really thought about your mocks but also how you are using your time to maximise your success. Yes, you may not have achieved the grade you wanted, but what are you going to do about it? One thing that all of these individuals had is resilience, and this is Resilience term. You are the master of your own fate to a certain degree (I admit I may be somewhat paradoxical by saying things happen for a reason), and if you want to change something, you will need to work hard at it.

We have ten weeks of teaching until Easter, thus this term is by far the most important. You will need to be resilient and you will fail many, many times, but that is OK! Failure is not bad if you learn from these mistakes and you ensure they don't happen again. In Japanese, there is a business term I rather like, *kaizen* – continuous improvement. You must reflect and you must take ownership of your learning. Devise a plan, break up your time, complete work ahead of schedule and then review it. Seize every moment because, as I have said before, we don't have time.

I will leave you with these final words from Samuel Beckett's *Worstward Ho,* which I think sums up what I am trying to say: 'Ever tried. Ever failed. No matter. Try Again. Fail again. Fail better.'[12]

Back in June 2014, we were still formulating the ethos and still trying to develop the depth we needed to hold a school together despite any rainstorms that might come our way, so I held a meeting with a group of students we called 'The Consultants' – volunteers from those who had been offered a place at the school and who wanted to have a

---

12   S. Beckett, *Worstward Ho* (London: John Calder, 1983), p. 7.

hand in its development. We met in a geography room at Westminster School (Steel House, of course, still being unsuitable) and discussed the dress code, the challenges they thought students would face coming to the school, the need for houses and house competitions, and what they were most looking forward to. That group was retained in the first few weeks of the school and then replaced by an elected senate with a president and vice presidents.

The senate meet with me every week, bringing concerns and questions and helping to interrogate the ideas, ethos and structure of the school. Ever since that first meeting they have been an important part of the school leadership: looked up to by the students, put on display to charm guests and integrally involved in decision-making (not that they make the choices themselves – I accept responsibility for those – but they provide advice and a point of view I would otherwise miss). By June 2014, then, many of the planks that underpin our ethos were in place, but there was still much to do, much to think about and much to develop – a subject for the next chapter.

Final Thoughts

- A leader isn't a leader without a team to lead – and much depends on the first follower. They are the one who will determine whether the vision remains forever an illusion or if it turns to reality – and to some extent, what shape that reality will be.

- The reason for building an ethos is that it frees others to build alongside you; attempting to control details is much more limiting than setting the mood of creation.

- If other members of the team are doing things you would love to do but don't have the skills to perform or the imagination to conceive, then you know you are winning.

- Sometimes, as with music at Harris Westminster, you can't see the solution – you can only build, leave a space and hope that it will be filled.

Chapter 3

Development of an Idea

The end of June 2014 marked one year of Harris Westminster Sixth Form – or, at least, one year of my involvement with Harris Westminster Sixth Form because as a real, functioning school it was yet to have its beginning. I was still the 'principal designate' but it was a year since I had sat in the Speech Day dreaming up words and it was a year since our tricolon of ambition, perseverance, legacy had come together, but there was a lot still to be done before I could dump the 'designate' and now just over two months left to do it.

In the summer of 2013, I'd had a series of meetings with all the relevant parties and at one of those the importance of houses to the Westminster half of the collaboration had been impressed upon me. Houses, in the sense of boarding houses, play a crucial role in the operation of Westminster School, and housemasters are some of the most important people in the hierarchy. We wouldn't have boarders but it was felt that we should still have these subdivisions of the school to provide a sense of belonging. This fell in with my own views: the school I was working at had a very strong house system with a competition that drove the social life of the school and enabled a huge amount of creativity. We would have houses – four of them – with heads of house who would be the pastoral leaders of the school and who would exhort their charges to compete with each other over an eclectic series of challenges. This left me with just the minor problem of what to call the houses, although I was sure that something suitable would come to mind.

A year on and I was still struggling. The houses at my old school had been named for their founding heads – an idea that I liked fifty years down the line but I felt would hang strangely on a new school. The houses at Westminster are named for the buildings in which the students live, and that wouldn't do at all. I considered naming them after London's hills or rivers but these seemed difficult to relate to – they lack personality. People then. House heroes who can represent and encapsulate the kind of community they aspire to be a part of, the kind of student they aim to develop. The trouble with heroes is that they are flawed – select someone you are inspired by now and you run the risk of scandal or society's changing views. It is also difficult to pick out a set of four: people don't come in fours, they are individuals, unless they form some kind of quartet, and then you are not just looking for exemplar individuals but an unflawed foursome.

This indecision had stayed with me for twelve months. I had consulted friends and family who had joyfully shot down my ideas without providing any satisfactory alternatives. Two years later, as I sat in St Margaret's Church listening to Nic giving this particularly equivocal assembly, my mind naturally tripped back to the difficulties of naming houses.

On the Role of Heroes – 18 January 2016

An assembly by Nic Amy

My theme for today is heroes. Or, more accurately, my assembly is a warning to beware the urge that we all feel to identify with heroes. Or, more accurately still, it is an exploration of symbols and the power and dangers of symbolism. Or, perhaps, it is a meditation on the difficulties of making decisions. I am not really sure because, as with so many things, I am not really sure what I think.

The assembly features a cast of heroes and villains: the nineteenth century imperialist Cecil Rhodes; the Egyptian pharaoh Ramesses II; the narrator of *Heart of Darkness*, Charlie Marlow; and the director of Liberty, Shami Chakrabarti. That said, I am going to encourage you to think of none of those as either heroes or villains. It is an assembly which starts in southern Africa, which moves to Oxford, which (perhaps inevitably) quotes some poetry and which ends up on a cold Tuesday afternoon in the hall at Harris Westminster Sixth Form. But it has to start somewhere, and today the assembly starts in the southern African country of Zimbabwe.

I have never visited the Republic of Zimbabwe. Perhaps some of you have been lucky enough to do so. It is a landlocked country located in southern Africa, between the Zambezi and Limpopo rivers. It borders South Africa to the south, Botswana to the west, Zambia to the north-west and Mozambique to the east and north-east. The capital and largest city is Harare, although that capital used to have a far less African and much more British sounding name. It was named after the Wiltshire cathedral city of Salisbury. In fact, until 1980, Zimbabwe itself wasn't called Zimbabwe. It was named after a nineteenth century British imperialist: Cecil Rhodes. It was called Rhodesia. 1980 is, of course, within my – if not your – lifetime.

Let us spend one minute on Rhodes. Cecil John Rhodes (who lived between 1853 and 1902) was a British colonial era businessman and mining magnate. He was an advocate of British colonialism and the founder of the southern African territory of Rhodesia (now Zimbabwe and Zambia), which was named after him in 1895. South Africa's Rhodes University is also named after him. He set up the provisions of the Rhodes Scholarship which is funded by his estate. It is an amazing scholarship which has enabled some amazing people (including many world leaders) to study at Oxford – that list includes the former US president (and possibly the next (or first) First Gentleman of the United States) Bill Clinton. And, like everything else I am mentioning in this assembly today, it is not without its critics, not least because of its association with Rhodes.

Despite this apparent education altruism, Rhodes is a problematic character. He was a committed colonialist and shared some of the worst opinions of those who propagated such values. I am not going to take you through a potted history of the worst things that Rhodes said or did (or, indeed, why some people still hold him in high esteem), but I hope that some of you will read about those things for yourself. Nevertheless, he was involved in imperialism and he did many terrible things.

Even Charlie Marlow (Conrad's flawed narrator of *Heart of Darkness* – which many of you will know) is able to acknowledge that: 'The conquest of the earth, which mostly means the taking it away from those who have a different complexion or slightly flatter noses than ourselves, is not a pretty thing when you look into it too much.'[1] This is not exactly biting criticism and it is deeply ironic. However, it also shows us that a late nineteenth century employee of imperialism was able to stand back and reflect on the nefariousness of the endeavour in which he was engaged.

---

1   J. Conrad, *Heart of Darkness*. In *Youth: A Narrative, and Two Other Stories* (Edinburgh and London: William Blackwood, 1902), ch. 1. Available at: http://www.gutenberg.org/ebooks/526.

There is an awful lot of hogwash talked about judging people 'by the values of their age' as if the fact of having been born in 1853 or, indeed, 1791, disqualifies you in some moral sense from realising that violence or theft or cruel and unusual punishments are inexcusable. Anyway, colonialism has left a terrible historical legacy and Rhodes is one of the most powerful symbols of that legacy. Our story moves on to the present day. In March 2015, a prominent statue of Rhodes on the main campus of the University of Cape Town was vandalised with human excrement, giving rise to a student-led campaign called Rhodes Must Fall, which drew attention to what the activists considered the lack of systemic racial transformation in South African institutions after apartheid. The university's management took the statue down for relocation on 9 April 2015, and thus a movement was born. #RhodesMustFall. Protest for the age of Twitter. And now the story moves to Oxford.

Oxford University is, rightly, considered a symbol of great intellectual achievement, of scholarship and of freedom of thought and speech. It is a collegiate university: students belong to a number of different colleges, all of which have long, and not always entirely glorious, histories – especially when you follow the money. Anyway, Oxford is a kind of beacon and for this reason it is often, rightly, held to the highest standards. One of the colleges at the University of Oxford is called Oriel. A statue of Rhodes adorns the frontage of Oriel College – and in 2015, partly in response to the events in South Africa, a group of students demanded the removal of his statue, stating that it symbolised racism and colonialism.

On one level, this is very simple, isn't it? In one sense, of course, it symbolises racism and colonialism. So rip the statue down, no? What do you think? I think this is a really interesting debate. If you are interested, go online and see just how passionate people are on either side of the argument. It has been my privilege to debate this issue with a number of you last week. Free speech and debate and, of course, knowledge, are such privileges. But I am not going to offer you an opinion on one side or the other. Partly because I am not sure what I believe, but also partly to warn you against taking sides without really thinking through the issues and jumping on a bandwagon based on prejudice, or dislike of the people who hold the opposite view, or a misunderstanding of history or the relationship between symbols and actions. Because symbols can work both ways: one person's celebration of colonialism can be another's memorial for the victims. But even that is a far too simplified and potentially patronising view.

Just next door, Westminster Abbey is one of the great national monuments to figures from British history. To wander past those memorials is not only to be reminded of great achievements but also to recognise that individual human beings are often deeply flawed. If we cherry-picked which of the Westminster Abbey memorials must fall based on the logic of the Rhodes arguments then that monument would be radically denuded. Equally, a morally relativist approach can blindfold us to atrocities. Lest we forget. Statues are problematic symbols. But they are symbols, and the meaning of a symbol can be turned on its head.

The romantic poet Percy Bysshe Shelley wrote a famous sonnet called 'Ozymandias'. In it he tells the story of a traveller who has returned from a trip where he has seen the remains of a statue of Ramesses II, or Ozymandias, in the desert. But Ozymandias is long dead. Now, the statue is a memorial not to the greatest of power or the terrible rule of the pharaoh, but rather an homage to power's ineluctable temporariness.

> *I met a traveller from an antique land,*
> *Who said – 'Two vast and trunkless legs of stone*
> *Stand in the desert. … Near them, on the sand,*
> *Half sunk a shattered visage lies, whose frown,*
> *And wrinkled lip, and sneer of cold command,*
> *Tell that its sculptor well those passions read*
> *Which yet survive, stamped on these lifeless things,*
> *The hand that mocked them, and the heart that fed;*
> *And on the pedestal, these words appear:*
> *'My name is Ozymandias, King of Kings;*
> *Look on my Works, ye Mighty, and despair!'*
> *Nothing beside remains. Round the decay*
> *Of that colossal Wreck, boundless and bare*
> *The lone and level sands stretch far away.'*

Time has torn this statue down. If a group of angry students had had it taken down it wouldn't have had the opportunity to stand (or crumble) as an ironic symbol of power's evanescence, its fleeting transience in the long march of history. But Rhodes is probably still too close; perhaps he should go. And students certainly have the right to be angry. And you have the right to be angry about my argument in that previous paragraph. Yes, it was deliberately emotive. You will make up your own minds.

But what this whole question presents us with is actually an opportunity to celebrate free speech. We can have this debate. The authorities at Oriel will make a decision but they will be influenced by argument, by debate, by the clash of strong views. And that statue might, ironically, end up becoming a symbol for free speech. Although, that too might be rather naive of me. Let us think before we tear down our statues. Iconoclasm is a dangerous game, but then Rhodes is no icon. And perhaps that is part of the problem – our obsession with heroes and figureheads. 'Who are your heroes?' is probably the wrong question. It is a way of thinking predicated on *ad hominem* logic.

'What are your values?' is probably a much better question. And which values do great figures from history espouse? And should we remember these even when they are distasteful? Because if we don't learn from history then we are probably doomed to repeat it. Once the dirty, flawed politics of personality are inveigled into any debate, we stop thinking as clearly and as logically. That statue is a terrible reminder of the past. But it has given us pause to think about that past and to consider how we can make the world a better place going forward. In that sense, at least, it has performed a positive action. Knowing about Rhodes is probably better than not knowing about him, so the statue is able to facilitate something good.

It has given us an opportunity to reflect that we are (relatively) free, and sometimes by reflecting on the errors of the past we can move towards a celebration of equality in the present and a rejection of prejudice and oppression in all forms. Assemblies this term will take this as their theme. In Westminster Abbey on Wednesday, amongst all those memorials, many of them deeply problematic, Mr Handscombe will talk about assemblies over the course of this Resilience term and invite some of you to contribute. In the meantime, and on the subject of free speech, it is wonderful to be able to remind you that our lab speaker tomorrow is Shami Chakrabarti, the director of Liberty, the British civil liberties advocacy organisation. She is an amazingly powerful advocate for freedoms for all and I commend her talk to all of you without reservation. Why not sign up immediately after this assembly? Rhodes may or may not fall. History won't judge us on whether or not the statue stays standing, but it will judge us on our values and our actions, and on the legacy we leave for a better tomorrow.

In the end I gave up on the decision. We held an induction day for staff and invited applications for the post of head of house, with interviews taking place over lunchtime (the morning was filled with my attempt to articulate the vision and ethos of the school, the afternoon was spent with Westminster teachers thinking about how the subjects would get taught). Once we had chosen our four (Hafsa, Marisa, Tristan and Tom) we told them that their first task was to decide upon their house hero with two rules: they must be linked to London (giving some kind of coherence) and they must be dead (and thus unlikely to cause any new scandal). Fortunately for me, all four new heads of house rose both to this challenge and the subsequent one of choosing house colours. After a little horse trading on the latter we ended up with Turing taking Cambridge blue over Wilberforce who settled on Lincoln green, Somerville had pillar box red and Garrett laid claim to Merton magenta (as far as we know, the only link between Elizabeth Garrett Anderson and this particular shade is that Hafsa wished to honour her old college and knew that I, as a fellow ex-Mertonian, would be unlikely to object).

At the end of our day I offered to give a tour of the school, and there is a photograph of the fifteen of us peering gingerly around one of the doors, wearing hard hats and reflective jackets, in the middle of what is evidently still a building site. They have since told me that they saw no hope of having a school to teach in before September. We had an ethos, we had middle leaders, we had a pastoral structure and a plan for teaching, but we didn't have a school – not one that we could safely introduce 150 students to, anyway.

The builders were working hard to meet the deadline we had imposed. One meeting sits clearly in my memory: it was when they presented, with a degree of pride, a huge chart that set out all the tasks and dependencies that would, with skill and diligence, lead to the project being completed by the third week of September. My reaction was not what they were hoping for: the third week of September was no use at all – by then the students would expect to be firmly settled in their school. If we didn't have classes for them then they would go somewhere else. 'The beginning of September or we may as well put it off to 2015,' I said. Arms were twisted, overtime was agreed upon, the chart was rewritten and I agreed to a completion date of 3 September. We all crossed our fingers and hoped for the following wind we needed to get the classrooms ready before the students showed up.

Whilst the pipes were laid (it turns out that a great deal of building – or, at least, of renovation – is installing pipes; terribly necessary to the functioning of a school but not terribly exciting to watch (although on that score I needn't have worried – the paint would still be drying when we took occupation)), I took advantage of the hiatus and of the sunshine to have a holiday. Ten days off, or almost so – restricting myself to checking emails twice a day – lying in the sun and reading books.

The rest was necessary: it had been a busy twelve months and it wasn't going to get any less busy. Throughout September, Nic, Paul and I would meet in the morning, look at our schedule and wonder if there was anything that we hadn't done before, that we needed to make up rules for. This sense of making things up as we went along was very strong. What kept us going was the idea that we had already made the important decisions about direction and purpose and all that was left was the detail. One example of this was on the first day when we realised that we needed to give the students some ground rules. Generally our plan was to expect them to behave decently and to correct them if they went wrong, but it suddenly struck us that we could save ourselves some time by being direct about a few specifics, so I went around all the tutor groups and explained the basic expectations of communal life at Steel House. Three years later, they were still forming the basis of my opening assembly of term.

A Metaphorical Violin – 6 September 2017

Good morning and welcome back! It is great to see you all, relaxed and ready to go after a well-spent summer, full of enthusiasm and wondering what the year has in store for you. Well, I can't tell you everything that lies ahead – the joys, challenges, excitements and heartbreaks – but I can tell you a bit about what you can expect from the assemblies. One a week for thirty-four weeks, and an extra one, like this, in the abbey every month, means that in total you will have forty-four or so whole school assemblies plus about eight with your house.

From these I hope you will learn something – that is their main purpose, to learn something that you might not otherwise have come across. And I heartily commend to you the practice I adopted last year of writing notes in assemblies: not copying what was said word for word but listening with a pen in my hand ready to write down anything I particularly wanted to remember, look up or think about. As well as offering you gobbets of knowledge, we will be offering advice – as I have already done this morning – and the most frequent piece of advice will be this: read more. It is good advice – reading makes you clever – and we will expand on the idea, letting you know when you should read and giving suggestions on what to read, a process that will start right now.

You see, there is a book that I would love all Harris Westminster students to have read before they leave the school; a book that I think all Harris Westminster students should read before they leave the school. It is on the shelves of the library and I have tweeted about it, but given that it has never been borrowed, I guess none of you have yet read it. It is *As I Walked Out One Midsummer Morning* by Laurie Lee, who is better known for the description of his early twentieth century Gloucestershire childhood in *Cider with Rosie*: a book that is well worth reading and whose title chapter tells of … Well, maybe it is best that I let you read that particular episode for yourself and move on to the sequel which describes him as a young man, a late teenager of about your age, leaving the Gloucestershire village that has been his entire world and walking out across the countryside with a pack on his back containing 'a small rolled-up tent, a violin in a blanket, a change of clothes, a tin of treacle biscuits, and some cheese'.[2]

There is something amazing about the simple act of walking out. In another wonderful book, *The Lord of the Rings*, there is a poem called 'The Road Goes Ever On' which recurs, repeated several times, always slightly different but always with the same theme that when you step out onto the road outside your house, you are embarking on an adventure in which that same road could lead anywhere. Roads all join up, you see, and the boring suburban street is the same as the country lane, the same as Whitehall, the same as

---

2   L. Lee, *As I Walked Out One Midsummer Morning* (London: Penguin, 2014 [1969]), p. 12.

the M1. The English Channel poses a problem but not an insuperable one because when Laurie Lee walked out that midsummer morning, he went first to Southampton and then to London and then, via ship, to northern Spain from where he set out to walk alone across the Iberian peninsula.

This morning we are setting out on a new school year and ahead of us lie choices and opportunities, and the decisions we make when we get to these junctions will determine our experience. For those of you in Year 12, you are actually setting out on two years of experience, two years of opportunities and choices. The amazing thing about travel is that the more you choose to take an unfamiliar path, the more you take a chance and step into the unknown, the more choices and opportunities come your way. For those of you in Year 13, things are even more exciting: UCAS choices are upon you and you are planning the next adventure: one that will take you three years to complete. The plans you are making now are directed by the choices you made last year (I hope the Year 12s are listening) and, even more than that, the paths that will actually be open to you in August will be determined by the choices you make over the weeks to come.

Back to Laurie Lee and the walk across northern Spain. He writes about it very nonchalantly – in fact, he writes beautifully, as you would expect from a poet, and the book would be worth reading because of the way he uses language even if it weren't for what we can learn from the content. The walk across northern Spain is not, however, something that you just do. It is not like a ramble across southern England: the mountains of Cantabria are well over 2,000 metres high and to set out into the unknown on your own takes a kind of adventurousness that is poetical if not entirely wise. There is something epically romantic about this enterprise – I see the author as a sort of Warrior Poet, stepping out fearlessly to face the unknown. The unknown was far from friendly, the walk far from easy – in one episode he got sunstroke and stumbled for miles, really rather ill, until he blundered into a small village cafe and had pity taken on him. He ends up in the middle of the Spanish Civil War and is rescued by a British gunship.

I see you as Warrior Poets – walking out into the unknown this late summer's morning, but I hope you will be wise ones and take a map, a hat, plenty of water and some sunscreen. Even with those precautions you shouldn't expect the going always to be easy – there will be difficulties along the way but I hope you won't turn back. Part of the ambition that we have at the centre of Harris Westminster is the belief that we can do big things, that we can have big adventures, that we can overcome big difficulties, and you don't do that by giving up or turning back. Laurie Lee didn't turn back. Once he had recovered from his near-death experience he carried on through the towns and villages of central Spain. There were no more moments of such physical danger, but the low point of the book is not as he staggers over the crest of the hill with his brains cooking gently inside his skull, but a little later when his violin, its glue weakened from heat and rough treatment, finally falls apart. The violin, you see, was his security: whenever he came to a town he would pull it out and busk in the main plaza and the well-frequented side streets. With his violin he was confident he could earn enough to buy food and shelter, but with the violin gone he lost confidence and was on the verge of turning back. Compared with that moment of loss, being accidentally shelled by a confused destroyer pales into insignificance.

The question at the heart of the book is, how did a young man from rural Gloucestershire have the courage and confidence to walk out from the security of his family to face the wide world? The answer is that he had a violin. I want you to have the courage and confidence to face the wide world, to dream huge dreams and then to look your ambitions squarely in the face and to go out there and grab them, and so I think you will need a violin, at least a metaphorical one. This is, I think, the heart of Harris Westminster. Joining us here is not quite walking out one midsummer morning – you are still living at home, still supported by your family – but it is quite deliberately looking forward to following that great road into the unknown. To have the confidence to do that you need to have confidence in your own self-sufficiency. Many of the opportunities we offer are opportunities for you to practise, to see what you can do, to find out what skills you have or can develop, but you also need a metaphorical violin and what we offer you is an academic education and qualifications at the end.

Those pieces of paper are not the most wonderful bit of Harris Westminster. The best part of Harris Westminster are the amazing things you will learn and the opportunities and adventures you will have here – but the qualifications are a little piece of magic. If you work hard and get nice letters on pieces of paper, they will become the metaphorical violin that will give you the confidence to take risks, to walk out into the unknown. They are not worth prioritising above opportunities for learning (there is no point having a violin if you don't get used to taking it out of its blanket), but they are worth every last ounce of your energy, every half hour you can find to spend in the library, every missed episode of *Bake Off* that they cost you.

That is today's advice — and should I have lost you with my extended metaphors, I will provide you with a summary. But before I do, I will step out of advisory mode because there are a small number of things about our scholarly life that go beyond good advice and are quite serious rules, so if you have been dreaming of adventures or enjoying the glorious vaulting above you, listen up.

Rule number one, in true Dumbledore mode, is that the basement is out of bounds to any student who does not want to die a horrible death. We have no three-headed dog but it is not nice down there — by all means park your bike in the racks but don't loiter and don't go exploring. The same goes for the alleyway down the back of the school that leads to the basement, which is not a place to hang out, and the stairlift up to the eighth floor, which is not a toy.

Rule number two: I believe that you are all too intelligent and sensible to smoke, and I wish to continue believing this, so should you be secretly making bad decisions in this area, please conduct your filthy habit away from the school. Not on Tothill Street, not on the roads that go from Tothill to Victoria Street, not on the Barclays corner and absolutely not in school.

Rule three is that occasionally I like to go to the pub and have a quiet glass of lemonade, and I am sure that many of you do the same. However, when I am drinking my lemonade I do not like to come across students, and so I am telling you now that the pubs within 200 metres of Steel House are my pubs — the rest of London is full of pubs, those are your pubs. Feel free to enjoy a quiet glass of lemonade in your pubs, but please don't come into mine.

Rules four, five and six are very straightforward: come to school every day unless you are in hospital or vomiting, be on time — even a minute late is an incredible level of rudeness when getting up half an hour earlier would have got you here in plenty of time — and follow the school dress code, which means wearing a jacket every day, except the most bakingly hot days of summer when you can come to school in just a shirt if you are sure you won't get cold.

Six rules and we will get along just fine, but that advice? The advice is to read, to read *As I Walked Out One Midsummer Morning*, to take opportunities that come your way even if you are not sure how they will end up, to wear a hat when hiking, and to work hard now so that your opportunities will be better later and so that you will have the security you need to take them. In future assemblies you can expect more advice but I am unlikely to add to the rules. Thank you.

Assemblies always have to perform a variety of tasks – in fact, it is clear that any given assembly is almost certainly overburdened with tasks: they are a precious resource and there is so much that can be done in a whole school assembly that can't be done as well elsewhere. In this assembly, for example, the six rules are slipped in as an afterthought to the main theme – but what is that main theme? The final piece of advice is to read, and this advice is echoed throughout the piece: we start with Laurie Lee and his first two autobiographical books (there is a third, dangled tantalisingly out of sight, for any diligent student to follow up afterwards), swing through *The Lord of the Rings* (possibly inevitably – it is a favourite and rich in potential) and then return to *As I Walked Out One Midsummer Morning* (a title that I covet exceedingly) before flirting briefly with a J. K. Rowling allusion. Reading is not just an exhortation at Harris Westminster, it is a shared passion – we have no truck with those folk who don't have time for it, who don't see the point or who just can't be bothered. The literary allusions in assemblies are not posturing or pretentious, therefore; they are crucial to living the message. By talking about books students have never heard of (as well as ones they have) we are recommending, opening doors, navigating library shelves and, most of all, showing that there is always more – more to read about, more to think about.

This assembly also introduces the idea of the metaphorical violin. Sometimes ideas are introduced in assembly that then get carried through into school life and echoed in the developing vernacular (Beckett's 'fail better' is one such phrase); sometimes they are thrown out as ephemera to be enjoyed on that day and then forgotten (Nic's delight in the subjunctive in 'On Music', for example); sometimes they are big ideas to be reflected on, debated, argued with, internalised (the role of heroes is one such); but this one, I think, was a private meditation on the functioning of the school. The metaphorical violin has stuck with me as a crucial idea in leading Harris Westminster, even if it has been forgotten by all of those who were in the abbey that day. Our challenge is not just providing students with knowledge but also with the confidence to use that knowledge – for some of them, filling in the application form for an elite university or setting their sights on a prestigious career is as much of a step into the unknown as Laurie Lee took that midsummer morning.

The first step into the unknown was taken by the students who had received offers to join Harris Westminster in September 2014. When Nic, Paul and I met that morning to discuss the way ahead, a question came up that I had never paused to consider: will they show up? I had never doubted it until that moment, never allowed the thought to cross my mind that after months of ethos building, recruitment, builders and policies the students themselves might, at the last moment, decide they had a better offer. I left that meeting at 8.30am with knees shaking and went out into the street to take the air and get myself ready for a 9am start. Gratifyingly, I found a small queue had already begun to form; by the time we were ready to admit the students it snaked around the block and we had a completely mad hour and a half of organising timetables, linking up students with their tutors, showing them to form rooms and explaining what the week ahead would look like. At 11am, they went into their first Harris Westminster lesson (it already being an established precept in the school that valuable as non-lesson activity was, you could have too much of a good thing and that if you weren't learning you were probably missing out). Then, for the first time in over a year, I sat down and relaxed: Harris Westminster was happening in real life and not in my brain; Harris Westminster was happening and I didn't need to do anything in that moment to sustain it; Harris Westminster was happening in those classrooms and with those amazing teachers; and the way it was happening was determined by the ethos we had developed.

Those first students are now university graduates, adults shaping their own lives and their own futures, and the biggest question for them when they come back for alumni events is, 'Are the students now better than us?' It is a nervous question – one that they think they know the answer to because they can see that results have improved year on year and that competition for places has become more fierce – but one with a complicated answer because, important though academics are, they are not everything and that first cohort were unique in the history of the school in the risk they took, stepping out into the unknown, trusting their future to an institution without a past, believing entirely in the ethos. They were driven by ambition, a knowledge that they wanted more (or at least different) than they had been offered elsewhere, a hope that things could be better.

Big City Ambition – 17 September 2018

This morning's assembly is the result of combining my notes from Mr Grant's assembly on Friday, a paragraph from the book I am currently reading and some thoughts from the greatest thinker of the modern age. Over the next fifteen minutes or so I will stitch these elements together to say something about two pieces of Harris Westminster jargon, two words that we use to mean something particular and that we thus find particularly meaningful.

I will start with the thinker who, as a young woman, found herself on the wrong side of a group of bullies – and her response, to one in particular, is instructive. In a short piece of writing, she addresses some damaged classmates who were bullying her, explaining the impact their words and behaviour have on her before exploding into a defiant statement of purpose – her purpose to someday live in a big old city whilst they remain small and mean and pointless. I hope that none of you feel like that – I hope that if you did you would tell me. I hope that none of you ever make someone else feel like that.

Being at Harris Westminster places us in the enormously privileged position of having almost 600 amazingly interesting people with whom to share our days. Each one of you has passions and interests that make you worth knowing, and I hope that each one of you will find others to share those passions and interests. Some of mine that I hope you will share – although I would be equally happy to find you had your own to share with me – include: Diplomacy, a board game we play in the map room at 4.30pm on Fridays (if you missed last week, don't worry – find the map room and come along) the Last Night of the Proms, which was on Saturday and you can still enjoy the world's largest music festival on iPlayer; and Tim Vine, who has a new Radio 4 show, and if I can work out how to listen again I will be incorporating his puns into my life. Sharing passions and interests is a joy – it means that we need never feel alone, it means that we need never put each other down. But I digress, because the point is not the bullies who made our philosopher's life difficult but her response to that difficulty. What kept her going, you see, was the promise she made herself, her long-term goal, her ambition. You can't break me because 'someday I'll be living in a big old city'; I'll make it out of your small-town mindset; I'll be a success. An ambition is a powerful thing: it can keep you going when times are tough and give you something to aim for, and that is why the first word in the Harris Westminster lexicon, the top word in the list on the red wall in our entrance, is ambition.

We are people of ambition. We want more than we have right now. We throw ourselves into our opportunities, holding nothing back because we are stretching for something beyond our reach. We know that if we play it safe we will get nowhere, that if we keep one foot in our old habits we will end up only with what we started with.

Ambition is more than a pull to get us through hard times, although it can, used correctly, turn hard times into great times. To illustrate that I turn to my current novel – Mary Shelley's *Frankenstein*, a book, by the way, conceived whilst on a rather free-wheeling holiday in Switzerland with a couple of poetry's wilder boys: Percy Bysshe (that is Mary Shelley's husband) and Lord Byron. What they got up to when they weren't writing gothic novels is a story for another day. You may have noticed that I haven't told you the identity of my philosopher – this is deliberate, I will let you in on the secret later, but I am hoping that some of you will guess, either because you recognise some of her sayings or because you have paid attention in previous assemblies and know something of my tastes. Part of the game in assemblies – and you will quickly learn that one of my tastes is a fondness for games – is that I will occasionally make oblique reference to some other body of work and see how many of you pick up on it. You get a point for each one you spot. As an incentive this year, I have decided that points can be exchanged for extra credit which is interchangeable with regular credit – a purpose for which I am yet to find.

Back, however, to *Frankenstein* and the title character, one Dr Victor, who has been taken by ambition to university and has come to the conclusion that science is where the action is at. This is what he says:

> *From this day natural philosophy, and particularly chemistry, in the most comprehensive sense of the term, became nearly my sole occupation. I read with ardour those works, so full of genius and discrimination, which modern inquirers have written on these subjects. I attended the lectures and cultivated the acquaintance of the men of science of the university, and I found even in M. Krempe a great deal of sound sense and real information, combined, it is true, with a repulsive physiognomy and manners, but not on that account the less valuable. In M. Waldman I found a true friend. His gentleness was never tinged by dogmatism, and his instructions were given with an air of frankness*

and good nature that banished every idea of pedantry. In a thousand ways he smoothed for me the path of knowledge and made the most abstruse inquiries clear and facile to my apprehension. My application was at first fluctuating and uncertain; it gained strength as I proceeded and soon became so ardent and eager that the stars often disappeared in the light of morning whilst I was yet engaged in my laboratory.

As I applied so closely, it may be easily conceived that my progress was rapid. My ardour was indeed the astonishment of the students, and my proficiency that of the masters.[3]

I am charmed by the two teachers – the repulsive M. Krempe who is nonetheless often right and the delightful M. Waldman who smoothed the path of knowledge. I am also struck by the way in which the study of chemistry, originally merely a means to an end or a source of Waldman-driven amusement, becomes a joy in itself, and so Frankenstein dedicates more time and energy to his studies, finding, as he does so, that his enjoyment increases in equal measure. I hope that you will find your studies so, and if you do not then I suggest you follow this example and work harder at them – like the eponymous hero of *Frankenstein* (and I should apologise at this point for not taking the opportunity earlier to use the word 'eponymous' which, as well as being a rather good REM album, is a delightful word for the character named in the title), you will find that the harder you work, the easier it becomes and the more you enjoy it.

This is the heart of scholarship – the second of today's pieces of jargon – and we describe scholarship as knowledge that is extensive and exact and thinking that is critical and scrupulous. I hope I have added a little to the extent of your knowledge today, but it is with the idea of thinking scrupulously that I will close.

In Mr Grant's assembly he mentioned, with mathematical aplomb, the Cauchy–Schwarz inequality. I suspect that few of you would have been familiar with this mathematical gadget and I choose, therefore, to believe that most of you will have googled it on your way back to school. For those few who didn't, I shall just say that it states that the area of a parallelogram with fixed side lengths and varying internal angles is maximised as a rectangle. It is one of an amazing array of mathematical theorems, equations and other wonders

3   M. Shelley, *Frankenstein; or, The Modern Prometheus* (London: G. and W. B. Whittaker, 1823), ch. 4. Available at: http://www.gutenberg.org/ebooks/84.

that are named after Baron Augustin-Louis Cauchy. He is the eponymous mathematician (and let nobody say I leave a *hapax legomenon* undisturbed) behind the Cauchy distribution, Cauchy sequences, Cauchy surfaces and the Cauchy product. He is responsible for a wonderful theorem which states that the integral of a continuous function around a closed loop in the complex plane is always zero, and is definitely one of my top three favourite barons.

He achieved all these mathematical wonders by adopting a thoroughly scrupulous approach to mathematics. Previous mathematicians, such as Euler, had engaged with new ideas by applying old methods, and in response to the question, 'But does that still work in that setting?' had waved their hands and said, 'I dunno – probably.' Cauchy, on the other hand, refused to take any steps that were not rigorously justified. He took care with each line of his work that it followed logically from the previous one, and as a result his proofs were all watertight. This is scrupulous thinking – a scruple is a tiny unit of weight, just over a gramme, and to be scrupulous is to take care of tiny issues, not to sweep unknowns under the carpet, not to let great ends justify shoddy means, not to wave one's hands and say, 'I dunno – probably.' Being scrupulous is a key part of being a scholar. It means that other scholars can trust your work because they know that you will have been harsher with it than anyone else would, and it means, therefore, that your conclusions will carry more weight than anyone else's.

And, talking of conclusions, you will be wanting to know what happened to that philosopher: did she achieve her ambition? Well, I am glad to tell you that she did – she made it to New York. She is now known to the world as Taylor Swift. And there in the Big City she found a kaleidoscope of people and noise; she found that the city of her ambition had been waiting for her. And so too with your ambitions. They may seem far away and obstructed by obstacles, but they are there waiting for you. Waiting for you to get there, waiting for you to be the right kind of person to take advantage of them, waiting for you to learn what you need to know, and when you get there they will say 'Welcome'. In the meantime, let's go back to school.

As well as providing a meditation on ambition, this assembly links into a rich and vibrant community of scholarship in which Mr Grant's assembly of the previous week is picked up, given a new spin, tied into one of poetry's 'wide boys' and passed on to a great philosopher. (The joke being partly that nobody else considers Taylor Swift to be one of the greatest philosophers of the age, and partly that I really do: we can examine 'trivial' pop music with the same scholarly intent that we impress upon poetry or mathematics.)

The idea of scholarship – of learning that is extensive and exact and thinking that is scrupulous and critical – is one that has developed through the school's existence. We had no particular sense of the word back in September 2014, but it has become so much a central plank of our community, not just an idea but a way of life, that it deserves an entire chapter to itself.

Final Thoughts

- Sometimes the perfect answer won't come and the solution lies in interesting imperfections.

- People can only ever be imperfect pictures of ideas and values.

- If you are usually accommodating and reasonable then you earn the chance to be unreasonably demanding occasionally. Use it wisely.

- Sometimes the problems you have in year one are still the problems you have in year four as you seek better solutions. That is OK.

Chapter 4

Scholarship

Remembrance term of 2014 occupied four calendar months but felt much longer. There were so many new things to be worked out, things done for the first time where we were guessing as to what would work and knowing that our guesses would shape the future (the idea of the 'first annual ...' became a bit of a joke between students and staff as we wheeled out our latest wheeze dressed up as though it was, or at least one day would be, an ancient and venerable tradition). We had our first exeat having worked three Saturdays in a row and wondered how we would spend the glorious half-holiday; we had the first half-term break and sent students off with the instruction to read, rest and revise in equal measure; we had our first Christmas tree and our first Christmas Jumper Day; and then we crawled, exhausted, into our first proper vacation.

In the second half of term we had our first Remembrance Service – the first time we had been together as a school in Westminster Abbey. To my delight, I had discovered that the evening of 11 November was an empty one in the abbey calendar and we had been able to lodge ourselves there for a special service (made possible by the kind offices and generosity of the dean and chapter). Students and staff were expected, parents and guests were invited, and the students selected as ushers for the evening glowed with pride as they welcomed the congregation to their seats. I processed with the dean, knees trembling, just remembering to avoid banging my head on the mace carried by the verger ahead of me. There were hymns and prayers, an address from the dean and the act of commitment – the whole school community remembering their pasts and committing to a better future – and then the first student president, Hajar, laying a wreath on the grave of the Unknown Warrior. A fledgling school creating history in a 750 year-old abbey; it was, as the dean remarked, a moment.

The morning after term ended, I was up at 2am to get a taxi to St Pancras Station from where Harris Westminster's first foreign trip would depart. Sixteen students, the French teacher Hafsa and I climbed aboard the first Eurostar of the morning to spend the day in Paris. The students were incredibly excited and we had left enough time that even those who cut their arrival fine made it onto the train. Hafsa had planned everything with military precision and the weather remained, if not exactly fine, then at least not awful for early December; all I had to do (at least, all I remember doing) was to count to sixteen over and over again to make sure we didn't lose anyone. By the end of the day we were absolutely shattered: half of us slept throughout the journey home; the other half traded word puzzles and maths problems until we got back to London.

Resilience, therefore, had a lot to live up to – a feat that it achieved through a staff INSET day just before the February half-term (the first annual February INSET day, in fact). INSET is teacher jargon for a professional training day and on this one we were set off by a presentation from the Westminster School head of science Kevin Walsh, who spoke about the Westminster approach to learning. As an illustration he used a fried egg: the egg is the learning that takes place in a sequence of lessons, the yolk is the syllabus and the egg white is the other stuff – the parts of the subject that are no less fascinating for not being examinable. Along with this idea, we adopted his definition of scholarship (I have not heard it used by anyone else in Westminster and suspect it was invented just for this session): for a reader who has followed the chapters of this book in order, the words extensive, exact, scrupulous and critical will be familiar – for us on this day they were new. This quadricolon (like a tricolon, but one more) was exactly what we needed to push our teaching and learning forwards. The question was simply how we would get the message over to students, and the answer was through a series of assemblies.

Extensive and Exact – 16 March 2015

Last week I quoted to you some of the wisdom of my favourite pop songs. This was not universally well received. I will not say that my learning has been called frivolous and plebeian, and nor will I tell you exactly who it was that told me that looking for wisdom in popular culture is like looking for lunch in a rubbish bin – you might find something but it is unlikely to be healthy. Anyway,

I am not one to turn down a subtle hint, especially when it is wrapped around a brick and hurled through my window, and so this week I bring you Socrates – of whom it was said, by the Oracle of Delphi, that no human was wiser. A well-known saying of Socrates is 'I know that I know nothing'. What is less well known is that Socrates probably didn't say that at all. For one thing it is nonsense, a paradox; for another, we have none of Socrates' writing and our best source, Plato, seems likely to have made up quite a lot of what he attributes to Socrates; and for a third, not even Plato claims that Socrates said this. If we wish to be exact, which I am sure you all do, then we can say that in Plato's *Apology*, the character Socrates says:

> *I am wiser than this man, for neither of us appears to know anything great and good; but he fancies he knows something, although he knows nothing; whereas I, as I do not know anything, so I do not fancy I do. In this trifling particular, then, I appear to be wiser than he, because I do not fancy I know what I do not know.*

Of course, if I was being over-scrupulous I would point out that even this is inaccurate as Plato wrote in Greek, of which this is a translation of dubious provenance (Wikipedia).[1]

For all that, the knowledge that even the widest scholarship is a drop in the ocean is considered wisdom: we should know our limits. OK, we should know our limits, but then what do we do with them? I put it to you this morning that there are two things we should do that are, on the surface, contradictory but are, in fact, complementary. We should know our limits so that we do not overstep them but also so that we can expand them.

My wife is a doctor – and in medicine the first, primary and crucial rule for knowledge is that you should never claim to have knowledge that you do not have: if you are asked to make a judgement for which you do not know the answer, you should admit your deficiency and defer to someone else rather than make an educated guess and risk harming the patient. This approach is exemplified in one of the many exams that doctors need to pass: the MRCP – Membership of the Royal College of Physicians. This exam has two parts, and the first is a long multiple-choice paper to test your knowledge of outlandish and obscure diseases. When revising for this my wife made a set of file cards with one disease she needed to learn about on each card. She would then carry the cards around with her and try to learn them, after which I was called

---

1   See https://en.wikipedia.org/wiki/I_know_that_I_know_nothing.

upon to test her. I remember walking to the pub for a Friday evening lemonade asking questions about ulcerative colitis, lupus and acute pancreatitis. By the time she took her exam, I felt I could bluff my way quite well through the questions because as I had been testing her, I had also been testing myself and trying to extend my knowledge.

Actually, though, impressive though my knowledge of obscure ailments may have been for a non-medic, I would not have stood a chance in the MRCP because the questions are designed to catch out bluffers and the whole thing is negatively marked, which means that if you guess wrongly you lose as many marks as you would win by guessing correctly: a bluffer can expect to end up with a negative score. In medicine it is important to know your limits and not to stray beyond them, and it is important to be exact. It is also, by the way, important to have good revision habits and I commend to you my wife's approach. Putting information on index cards is an excellent way of processing it, of making sure it passes through your brain. Then, more importantly, taking those index cards with you and testing yourself on what you know is an excellent way of identifying those facts you find difficult to memorise. Finally, repeating this process is an excellent way of making sure that they do all get memorised. It really works – she passed her MRCP.

Knowing your limits is also important in climbing, if I may draw on a recurring metaphor. Until recently, my climbing had all been of the tree in the back garden or rock piles whilst out walking variety, and I had been very careful to stick within my limits for fear of falling off and going splat. I was very clear about what I could achieve safely and when I should make my way back to terra firma. One of the joys of climbing with ropes and harnesses is being able to test those limits, having the opportunity of stretching right out in the hope of getting a handhold and knowing that if I missed it I would dangle inelegantly rather than fall to my doom. I have discovered that I can actually achieve things I would previously have thought beyond my limits, but should I go back to the trees and rock piles I will need once more to be aware of and stick to what I am sure of.

Having the opportunity to extend the borders of your knowledge is the great delight of learning and you should not put artificial boundaries on what you wish to learn: a scholar's learning is extensive as well as exact and there is scope to be an expert in one area whilst maintaining a bluffer's modicum in several others. The importance of this was discussed by Flanders and Swann, a duo from the sixties whose works will feature heavily if I ever run a cultural perspectives course on the history of the comic song. Michael Flanders was the wordsmith and proud possessor of an exceptional beard, and he explained to his audience that the problem with modern life is that we (ordinary people) can't talk to scientists 'because we don't understand science; [and] they can't talk to us because they don't understand anything else, poor dears'.[2] This monologue was, by way of introduction to a song on the laws of thermodynamics, an odd topic for an odd song – a combination that was the Flanders and Swann speciality. The first law is that heat and work are the same, and the second is that heat won't naturally travel from a cooler body to a hotter one.

Those two laws of thermodynamics are of enormous importance: not only do they form a framework within which the rest of physics can be understood but they also explain many aspects of ordinary life – not least why it is that no matter how careful I try to be, my desk just gets less and less tidy until I lose my patience and spend an hour putting things away in files. My father, who is a great man as well as being accidentally related to me, has written a book on business leadership based on the principles of thermodynamics. He is at heart and by training a scientist: he rephrases the first law as 'you can't have something for nothing' and the second law as 'you can't have it just any way you like', and uses these principles to suggest how businesses should approach innovation.[3]

It is easy for us to get pigeonholed and to end up, as Flanders describes, in academic ghettos of people who can't communicate, but there is, as my dad's book suggests, power in stretching across disciplines, in allowing ideas from one field to fertilise another, and in order to achieve that we need to extend our knowledge. Flanders and Swann might sound as though they are institutionalising these ghettoes but actually their silliness crossed all boundaries with songs not just on the fundamental laws of physics but also the habits of certain flowering plants, the predilection of the hippopotamus for mud and the history of the tune 'Greensleeves'. To learn more you will need to come to my cultural perspectives course, if I get around to writing it – it will be wonderful.

And so we return to Socrates – or at least Plato's facsimile thereof – for in Plato's *Theoetetus* the Socrates character says, 'this feeling of wonder shows

2   M. Flanders and D. Swann, *At the Drop of a Hat* (first performed in 1956).
3   R. D. Handscombe and E. A. Patterson, *The Entropy Vector: Connecting Science and Business* (Singapore: World Scientific, 2004), p. 15.

that you are a philosopher, since wonder is the only beginning of philosophy'.[4] Again, I can only give you a translation because my classical Greek is non-existent, which is a beautiful illustration of mechanics and purpose. If I were to study Greek I would spend the first few years learning vocabulary and grammar, making index cards of verb forms and endings and testing myself on them as I supped my evening lemonade. But as my knowledge of the language grew, I would be able to read Plato's writings, to make out his meaning – if my learning was sufficiently exact, of course – and then, to enable my purpose of being able to understand exactly what he meant and to enjoy his crafting of a phrase rather than relying on someone else's translation.

We each have fields where our knowledge is deep and exact and where this gives us the power to unlock new mysteries and to explore arcane wonders that are inaccessible to the non-scholar. This is amazing, but also amazing is the breadth of the world, of all the things that other people have studied and the wonders they have unearthed, and we should ensure that our learning is extensive and reaches out into other fields. In both areas, however, we will do well to cling to the non-quote of imaginary Socrates because no matter how deeply we study we will never sound the depths of the subject, and no matter how widely we read there will always be things of which we know little. We should aspire not to knowing nothing, rather to having extensive and exact scholarship, but we should know that all our learning makes but a molehill on the side of the great mountain of universal knowledge. There are always more wonders to find.

That final idea, that there are always more wonders to find, gets to the heart of the academic ethos of Harris Westminster – what we now call scholarship. It encapsulates the rejection of seeing the syllabus as a limit (instead we consider it as a basic minimum to be built upon) and of allowing yourself to be pigeonholed as a scientist or not. It is not, however, the phrase we use now, because this idea was picked up and developed further by one of the students.

As part of the Remembrance Service, before the student president lays the wreath, one of the vice presidents gives a reflection on their experience of Harris Westminster. These addresses are great moments

---

4   Plato, *Theaetetus*. In *Plato in Twelve Volumes*, Vol. XII, tr. H. N. Fowler (Cambridge, MA: Harvard University Press; London: William Heinemann, 1921), 155d.

both for the individual concerned and for the school as a whole – an annual moment to pause and reflect honestly on the challenges and privileges of developing scholarship. In 2016, Lamya gave the reflection, and explained that at her previous school she had been used to asking whether she was doing enough – studying enough, volunteering enough, participating enough – but that when she joined Harris Westminster she had come to the painful and transformative reflection that 'enough was never enough'. This phrase is a marvellous repackaging of the heart of scholarship because it captures both the dispiriting experience of realising that there is no fixed body of knowledge to be acquired, no goal to be attained, no point of relaxation on the horizon; and the wonder of rejecting the question, the joy of knowing there will always be new worlds to conquer. As Lamya discovered, being a Harris Westminster student is not easy – the prize for working hard enough to get in is being given more hard work to do. It is not meant to be easy: as I was told when finding things particularly difficult in our first year, 'If it was easy everyone would be doing it.' Our goal of changing trajectories and rejecting limits inevitably requires more from the students than their peers are doing elsewhere and more from the school than could be achieved if we simply copied what was being done in other institutions.

One of the things I didn't realise before starting Harris Westminster (a failing that demonstrates a shocking level of naivety) was quite how much of a disadvantage being disadvantaged is. I had thought that if we created a school where opportunities abounded and were free, where scholarship was expected, where high standards were encouraged and expected, that this would be enough, that the basic barrier for these students was access to uncompromisingly academic education. For some this was true: for some, all we had to do was build the institution, create the ethos and they leapt at the chance, fitted in with the culture and swam with the tide. For others, however, there was a great deal of unlearning to be done: unlearning the habits of keeping your head down and not revealing cleverness, unlearning the expectation that opportunities would be only for better-off students, unlearning the attitude that school was a game where the object was to do the minimum required to avoid the teacher's attention. For a third group there were significant practical challenges to be overcome: whilst free bus travel is provided to sixth formers through the largesse of the mayor of London, the tubes and trains (much faster and more efficient for travelling the large distances some students grappled with) must still be paid for, and whilst the councils provided (in our experience) an excellent service of emergency housing for those who needed it, a single room shared between a family with small children is hardly conducive to effective A level study. We addressed the practicalities as best we could through travel bursaries and long library opening hours (although one of my ambitions remains to raise enough money to be able to increase both of these provisions) and found that our focus on ethos and the development of the school community was the best recipe for the intangibles.

Our counter-cultural ethos of not focusing on exams, of expecting students to look for the maximum achievable rather than the minimum required, of dressing up on Fridays (bow ties are de rigueur for the end of the week) rather than dressing down, of treasuring things that made us unique rather than comparing ourselves with the common denominator, is part of the provision for disadvantaged students whose expectations and ambitions have been oppressed by circumstance. It is something that we can't relax without reducing this provision – a fact that forced us into some hard thinking when the season of external examinations came round: how do scholars who have refused to acknowledge the arbitrary impositions of examining boards react to the approach of assessments that will lead to important qualifications?

Examinations – 22 April 2015

An assembly by Nic Amy

OK, so this is what this assembly is going to do today. This is its meta-fictitious structure, if you like: firstly, it is going to quote a bit of text. A quite tenuous bit of text and one which the speaker (that's me) has been reminded of recently for reasons unconnected with the assembly. The starting with a text thing is a symptom of the speaker's (that's me) ongoingly problematic relationship with the sermon and a passion for exegesis. But let's leave that.

It will then muse for a while on time. The passing of time. It is an obsession of the speaker's (that's me) which comes up again and again in his assemblies.

This is his twentieth this academic year. He is obsessed with Shakespeare's sonnets too, and there the problem probably lies.

He will then do what a student of comedy would call a call-back (except this one won't be funny) and refer to a previous assembly (as is his wont). I am going to stop talking in the third person now – it is just too weird. Back to a more normal I. The reference back to a previous assembly will be in there either (1) to underline the theme of the passing of time, (2) to reuse material that I have written before, (3) to check whether you have been listening in the past or (4) because I am obsessed with intertextuality. Or all four. I will let you decide.

Then I will tell you a personal anecdote. This will be a bit egotistical, so I apologise in advance. But all the rhetorical handbooks advise you to make your speeches personal. And I will this time. Then I will make another tenuous and forced segue (or link) to force a questionable analogy upon you which should make you groan but will, hopefully, drive home a slightly pedantic point which at the very least has the value of being timely.

Then we will have one final call-back (to show I am consistent if nothing else), one final piece of advice (a kind of trump card, if you like) and then an exhortation to you all to get back to work. So, that is a somewhat sceptical overview of the assembly. And, to be honest, I hope you are a bit sceptical – enough, at least, to recognise the structure even if, ultimately, you quite like it. And I hope you do.

So, I start this morning with a wonderful novel by Arundhati Roy called *The God of Small Things*. She is talking about being young, about the 'early amorphous years' of childhood, and describes how the twins at the centre of the novel move from the innocence of youth to the experience of great maturity via their appreciation of 'Edges, Borders, Boundaries' appearing like a 'team of trolls' to limit their lives.[5]

It is a great piece of writing. I like the simile of the team of trolls. Trolls hide under bridges and police boundaries. Things are in their place. Terms are defined. That is kind of where we are now, with examinations on the horizon. (Roy goes on to describe how 'Their lives have a size and a shape now.'[6]) And it is so different from those early amorphous years. Amorphous means without shape, not yet fully formed.

5   A. Roy, *The God of Small Things* (London: HarperCollins, 2017 [1997]), pp. 2, 3.
6   Roy, *The God of Small Things*, p. 3.

I can't help being reminded of our very first few days and weeks in this school when nothing really did have a shape. And life does, definitely, and for all of us, have a size and a shape now. But to go back to then. Let me take you back to 23 September – seven full months ago – well over half a year. This is what I said to you then:

> Today I am going to tell you about two of my ambitions. Two with a similar timescale: this year. And two ambitions which I suspect I might not achieve. They are ambitious, after all. But I am going to tell you now so that in the long dark recesses of Resilience term you can ask me how I am doing and – hopefully – encourage me. And I might just make it. The first is to read Charles Dickens. All his books, from the first to the last. Over the next few weeks and months, please ask me how I am doing and do read some of the wonderful novels yourselves. The second ambition is even odder. I want to complete a bicycle race on Easter Sunday next year called the Tour of Flanders. It takes place in Belgium, lasts for several hours and involves a gruelling route including lots of very steep cobbled hills. But I do have seven months.
>
> So, next year, I may complete both the Tour of Flanders and the whole of Dickens. Or one. Or neither. But I will almost certainly be in control of my destiny. The decisions I make will shape whether or not I realise my ambitions. And the decisions you make will shape whether or not you too realise your ambitions. You don't have to share them (certainly not with the whole school) but do know what they are. Think about them now. What are your ambitions? What do you want to have achieved by the end of this year?

That was then. This is now. It certainly feels different from the first or second terms, doesn't it? Can you remember what you felt like then? Can you remember what you thought your ambitions should be back then? And to mine? Well, the Dickens is still on, but on the back-burner – it is my long-term goal. In your terms, it is my 'getting to university'. I have extended its scope. But I did complete the Tour of Flanders over the Easter weekend. In the rain, the 127 kilometres over the cobbled hills of Belgium took me four hours and two minutes. And, yes, I wish I had done more training so I could have been a bit quicker. But I did it.

Watching the amazing professionals race over the same course on Easter Sunday made me think about the many parallels between preparing for a professional cycling race and preparing for an examination. I wish I'd had three more weeks' preparation for my sportive. But three weeks is what you have for your ASs. And if I'd had three more weeks, this is how I would have used them.

So, here is my professional bicycle racing/examination preparation extended analogy. Because it is often a good idea to think and behave, as far as possible, like a professional.

The first thing you need to do is to put in the hard winter miles – the training in the cold of January and February – but the good news is that you have done that. You have been learning hard all year. You have got to train but you have also got to rest. Many top sportspeople (Roger Federer, for example) advocate ten hours' sleep a night. On the big stage races, such as the Tour de France, some of the top cycling teams have a van with special, personal mattresses for their riders and they employ someone each night to swap those mattresses for the default ones in the hotel. That is how seriously they take sleep. In addition, all the professional teams employ nutritionists and spend huge amounts of money ensuring that their riders are always hydrated. So, you should:

- Aim to sleep at least eight hours a night. Don't look at a bright screen before you go to bed and, if possible, take a shower, drink a small glass of warm milk and make sure your bedroom isn't too hot (16–18 degrees Celsius is ideal). Eat sensibly over the next few weeks and always make sure that you are properly hydrated. If necessary, carry a water bottle.

Cyclists are individuals. Often maverick. Often with huge egos and personalities. Just like some of you. However, they are also closely guided by what their team boss or director sportive (DS) tells them to do. The DS makes a very clear plan and the cyclists are expected to stick to it (in fact, even during the race, the riders will have a radio and an earpiece and the DS will be telling them what to do). So you should:

- Make a very clear plan with your teachers and stick to it. Check with your teachers that your revision cards are accurate and really do contain the right information. And, in the examination, imagine your teacher's voice in your head. What would they be telling you to do? Listen to that sage advice and follow it.

The training programme before a race looks very different from that in the winter. There is more focus on speed, on working at the intensity of race pace and ensuring good quality recovery. So, you should:

▦ Take off ten minutes for every hour of revision time. But make sure that the other fifty minutes are flat out or at 'race pace'. And in silence and properly focused.

All the teams will recon the courses before a race. Again and again. They will ride out over the exact terrain of the race so that they know exactly what to expect. So you should:

▦ Complete timed essay plans, timed essays and practice questions over and over again. If you have completed all the past essay questions before the examination, you are far less likely to be thrown by anything the examiner might set this time.

In fact, in training for a particular event, cyclists will go out and, in particular, do the hardest parts over and over again. In a race like the Tour of Flanders, the really tough bits, the bits where the race is decided, are the steep cobbled hills. In training, therefore, they will rerun those key bits, training behaviours to come naturally to them in the race (it is their muscle memory). So you should:

▦ Practise the hard bits over and over and over again (making sure that you get feedback from your teachers or from the mark scheme after each practice attempt). That way your brain muscle memory will be expecting the tough bits of the examination and will be ready for them.

All the top teams use data obsessively. They know exactly what has happened in the past, where and what was successful. So you should:

▦ Know your way in detail around the examination boards' websites. Know exactly what each element of the examination expects and how it is assessed. Know all of the past questions that have been set and know the mark schemes and examiners' reports.

One key way in which the teams use data is to obsessively review past performance: they keep going back and seeing where they could be better. They keep checking. So you should:

- Check obsessively. Here are three ways you can check. (1) Reread the question – have you answered all parts in full? (2) Do your answers make sense? (For example: elephants don't weigh 2 kg, percentage weight loss after diet can't be 250%, no one runs at 85 miles per hour.) (3) Check your calculation – can you do it in a different way to help check? Can you estimate without a calculator?

One of the cycling teams, Team Sky, under Dave Brailsford, has famously talked in the last few years about marginal gains. Where can you make those little improvements? What small things can you change? Can you use all of your time even better? So, you should:

- Have your revision cards with you all the time and stick up key facts in important places at home. One of your teachers even suggested laminating a sheet of the most important things you need to learn and sticking this up in the shower!

All good cycling teams work with sports psychologists – keeping their cyclists' eyes on the goal, on the big picture. So you should:

- Keep your mind open. If you have planned properly you should still be going to the lab talks. If you know your stuff, it is there that you might hear the thing that inspires you and makes the difference between a B and an A.

Preparation is key. Cycling teams employ hordes of mechanics, drivers and supporters to make sure the riders arrive at the start line ready to give themselves the very best chance possible. So, you should:

- Ensure that you get into school with plenty of time before an examination (at least forty minutes before the examination starts) and that you have all the right equipment: a black pen (it must be black and it should be one that is easy to write with and that you are used to writing with – I would use a fountain pen – seriously!), a sharp pencil and anything else you need, such as a calculator, rubber, ruler and so on. Bring them in a clear, see-through pencil case.

If you think back to the end of last half-term you will remember I was advocating the mantra: learn it, practise it, answer it. A few of you still have some learning to do. You know where. Just do it. Other than that, it is all practice and answering from here on in.

I started this assembly with a prequel. An exhortation to consider the structure of the assembly. To be metacognitive. And I return to that idea for my last piece of advice about revision and examinations. Think like the examiner. Imagine what it is like to mark a paper. You are faced with a four-mark question. How does the student make it as easy as possible for you to give them four marks? Think: four marks. Right: so they need four bits of information all neatly and clearly set out and all answering the question. So, for four marks:

Firstly … this is the case … tick.

Secondly … this is the case … tick.

Thirdly … this is the case … tick.

Fourthly … this is the case …tick.

Four marks. Move on. And use the first, second, third and fourth markers or use bullet points. But know what you need to do to get the marks and help the examiner to give you those marks. Make it easy for them.

Go back to school, please, and prepare for glory.

With two assemblies a week, the quantity of communication through this medium in that first year of Harris Westminster was quite extensive – and it needed to be because although the ethos message was inherently quite simple (learning *really* is amazing), it is not accessible via a standard approach. It is like a mountain, one side of which is a grassy slope but on the other is an inaccessible cliff face. If you approach the climb from the right direction, if you allow yourself to believe that learning is amazing, that being both extensive and exact is desirable, and that examinations are a celebration of how much you know, how hard you have worked and how clever you are; if you have internalised those things, then switching from exploratory mode to exam practice is just a question of details to slot into place. If, however, you approach the problem by asking, 'What do I actually have to do?' then you have to remember what Nic has said through his previous nineteen assemblies and then augment that advice with the ten bullet points from this one.

The practice of referring to previous assemblies, either directly (as in 'Examinations' above) or more obliquely, was on one hand part of the academic (and possibly self-indulgent) game that Nic and I played with each other, offering sly nods to what the other had said (or emphasising something we felt had been inadequately recognised) and, on the other, part of the process of reinforcement, of the repetition of ideas, of nudging students uncompromisingly up the slope.

The challenge of balancing the big picture against the detail is one that is an explicit part of the Harris Westminster curriculum: it is written into the assessment policy (fruit of the summer of 2014) and has come up several times in assemblies already quoted – most notably in 'Beginning' where we started. In our view, every subject has a purpose, a *raison d'être*, a way of thinking that makes it more valuable a pastime than, say, numismatics: mathematics is learned in order to solve problems; history to learn from the past; art to challenge the way we see things. Every subject also has a body of knowledge and skills that are required to achieve that purpose: maths has theorems; history has dates, events and characters; and art has techniques and styles that must be learned and practised. Every half-term students receive a grade in each subject for purpose (how well they have got to grips with the big ideas and challenges) and for mechanics (how well they have acquired the nitty-gritty knowledge they need to apply). They also receive a grade, on the same basis and scale, for response (how well they act on feedback, how effective their effort is in improving their learning), and these three grades are what is reported to parents and what is used by the school to understand and support their learning.

Mechanics and purpose is not, however, only a useful tool for understanding academia: it is a framework for approaching all kinds of learning. The paragraph before last, for example, could more simply be expressed within the jargon of Harris Westminster as: 'The purpose behind the school ethos is easily expressed and understood but the mechanics that lead to it are many, and selecting the right one at any given time is non-trivial.' Trying to do purpose with mechanics will get you a C grade but it won't get you to the top; to do that you have to embrace the challenge holistically.

This is not normal. Scholarship is not a normal quality. And so, in introducing the idea, we have had to transcend the preconceptions of school, of being a student. We have ambitions – for ourselves, for the school – that are not normal. We are working hard and investing energy to reach those ambitions, and so we have to avoid comparing ourselves with 'normal'. 'Enough is never enough' reminds us that the only sensible comparison to make is between where we are now and where we want to be, but in Resilience term of 2015 Lamya was still in Year 11 and I had to find another way of expressing this idea.

Pantagruel's Labours – 20 February 2015

There is a *Calvin and Hobbes* cartoon I know well which takes as its setting a Saturday morning with the eponymous heroes musing over their breakfast cereal on the extent to which a kid's understanding of normal is determined by their family. At which point, Calvin's father comes into the kitchen rejoicing in the 'crazy hedonism of weekends', having got up before the crack of dawn to go for a long run which he plans to follow with plain porridge. 'I think we'd know normal if we saw it,' mutters Hobbes laconically.[7]

If you have not read *Calvin and Hobbes* then I commend them to you. They are as full of wisdom as either Calvin or Hobbes and much more readable than either. One of the things I mistook for normal growing up was a copy of *Whitaker's Almanack*. This marvellous book is published every year and contains a digest of the year just gone, together with a calendar of events for the year ahead and a vast collection of facts and figures relating to the UK particularly and the world more generally. If you get a copy every year you will have in your house an up-to-date compendium of everything you might need to know – a single go-to resource for any fact you might want to check. When I was growing up, before Wikipedia, if you can imagine, this was even more marvellous than it is today. We didn't, however, get a copy every year. We had one copy, 1985, a beautiful thing, hardback in green and gold, and purchased second hand at a jumble sale in 1988. This kind of behaviour passed for normal in the Handscombe household, but what got my sisters saying, 'I think we'd know normal if we saw it' was that I read it cover to cover and then reread it to be sure I had extracted every useful fact from its pages.

7   See https://www.gocomics.com/calvinandhobbes/1993/03/13.

Secretly, I reread it more often than that, just for fun – because it was fun: not the bizarre, immediate history of 1984, nor the retrospective foretelling of 1986, but the strange collection of facts that were considered worth recording. There was a list of all the constituencies in the UK with the results of the 1983 general election, the candidates, parties and votes – the relevance of this information to me was somewhat dented by the 1987 election. There was a list of the ranks of officers in the army, navy and air force – from which I can tell you that a major outranks a lieutenant but a lieutenant general outranks a major general. There was a list of the coinage of the UK, its value, manufacture and the conditions under which it is legal tender, from which I learned that the bronze penny could be used to settle debts only up to 20p. Nowadays, of course, the penny is copper-plated steel which means you can win a lot of bets on whether a penny is magnetic: you can guarantee a win by having one in each pocket, dated either side of 1991 (when the change was made).

The disadvantage of *Whitaker's Almanack* was that in order to happen across such gems as these one had to trawl through pages of boring lists that even I could tell were out of date as soon as they were written: holders of certain posts within the royal court, for example. Since 2002, however, there has been a rival reference tome which combines the eclectic breadth and unwarranted detail of *Whitaker's* with a slimness of tome obtained by ruthlessly removing anything remotely boring. Behold *Schott's Original Miscellany*, containing the text of the Riot Act, a list of curious deaths of Burmese kings and a description of the Glasgow Coma Scale. It also contains a piece of text entitled 'Pantagruel's Labours' – an extract from a story by Rabelais about two giants – in which the elder giant addresses the younger thus:

> I intend and insist that you learn all languages perfectly, first of all Greek, in Quintilian's method; then Latin, then Hebrew, then Arabic and Chaldee. I wish you to form your style of Greek on the model of Plato and of Latin on that of Cicero. Let there be no history you have not at your fingers' ends, and study thoroughly cosmography and geography. Of liberal arts, such as geometry, mathematics and music, I gave you a taste when not above five years old, and I would now have you master them fully. Study astronomy but not divination and judicial astrology, which I consider mere vanities. As for civil law, I would have thee know the digests by heart. You should also have a perfect knowledge of the works of Nature, so that there is no sea, river, or smallest stream, which you do not know for what fish it is noted, whence it proceeds, and whither it directs its course; all fowls of the air, all shrubs and

trees whether forest or orchard, all herbs and flowers, all metals and stones
should be mastered by you. Fail not at the same time most carefully to peruse
the Talmudists and Cabalists, and be sure by frequent anatomies to gain a
perfect knowledge of that other world called the microcosm, which is man.[8]

As we start a new half-term I am tempted to set such a task for you, and I
am only held back by the completely unreasonable impossibility of completing
such a labour. There is simply too much in the world to know it all – even
in mathematics, which is surely the narrowest of subjects; it is said that the
last person to know it all was Gauss, and he died in 1855. This approach
to learning, of wanting to learn everything, of looking for both breadth and
depth, is exactly the Harris Westminster way – we should probably get copies
of both Schott and Rabelais for the library.

In the week before half-term, I gave an interview to a journalist from *The
Times*, and she asked how the success of Harris Westminster will be judged.[9]
I gave her a very complicated answer because our success, and yours, will, of
course, be judged by A level results (and even AS), but actually that isn't the
real measure of success. We started Remembrance term by thinking about
what success for each of us looks like, and I think that something along the lines
of being able to choose a job that you can do well, that you enjoy, that allows
you to improve the world and that pays well enough would be a reasonable
measure for you, and so that should be our measure also (although it is harder
to quantify). A level results are part of that but they are not the whole answer.
Your A levels will stay with you forever, and if you do well they will help you
to get an interview but they won't get you the job. That will depend on a
wide variety of complicated things, and to help you understand what those
are we have lined up a lab speaker for next term on the provisional title of
'Things that you need to know to get jobs but that they don't teach you at
school' – we are working on something snappier. Part of the difficulty is that
you don't know what you will need to know, and so whatever you learn
there is a chance that it won't be relevant. What is true, however, is that
the most interesting jobs go to people with three types of learning: they are
experts in their chosen field – they know more about whatever it is than
the competition; they are generalists, in that they know a bit about a lot of
different things and are interested in making links across disciplines; and they

8   F. Rabelais, 'Pantagruel's Labours', in B. Schott, *Schott's Original Miscellany* (London:
    Bloomsbury, 2002), p. 41.
9   H. Rumbelow, 'Could Harris Westminster Be the Most Elitist School in the Country?'
    The Times (16 April 2015).

are really good at learning – if they don't know something they need to know then they can find it out.

On the Friday before half-term, whilst you were busily resting, reading and revising, we teachers had a training day at school in which we thought about scholarship, what it is and how to develop it. When you started here we had to decide whether to call you pupils or students and, as you know, we plumped for students – people who study (pupil, by the way, comes from the Latin for little boy). As you move through Year 12 and into Year 13, however, we want you to stop being students and to start being scholars. Scholarship, according to our definition, is learning that is extensive and exact and thinking that is scrupulous and critical. It is broad and deep, it is careful and incisive. We talked a lot about different ways to help you become scholars, and you will hear more about these over the coming months, but there is one word I want to emphasise today from that definition, and it is *critical*. I want you all to try to be constructively critical in your learning, which means to ask hard questions, to listen carefully to what you are being told, to question the assumptions behind what is asserted, to ask the questions that your teachers don't want you to ask. In the case of this assembly, the critical thinkers will be asking, 'But why should we want to be scholars – are you assuming we want to become academics?' The answer to that question is no, I am not assuming you all want to be professors, but that extensive and exact learning – broad and deep and scrupulous and critical thinking that engages and uncovers new knowledge – is exactly the kind of learning and thinking that you need to have to take on the interesting jobs, the top jobs, the influential jobs, the jobs I hope you will have in ten or twenty years' time. Those jobs and that future are how we want to measure success – exam results are only the first step. I started by quoting, 'I think we'd know normal if we saw it.' Well, I have seen normal, I have seen ordinary and I am not interested. I think that each one of you has the capacity to be extraordinary, to do something magnificent with your talents, and I suggest that the first step is to follow Gargantua's advice to Pantagruel in purpose, if not mechanics, and to become a scholar. Learning is amazing.

Resilience is the term of the hard yards, the long practice cycles from Nic's extended analogy. It is, to my mind, the most amazing of the Harris Westminster terms because it is the most ordinary, the most archetypal. It is the term of long hours in the library, the term of grinding through the syllabus and completing coursework, the term in which the greatest strides in learning are made. It is also a term in which the extra things are driven by students; teachers are focused on their subjects and leadership on admissions for the next academic year. The big set piece of the term is not a service in the abbey but a collection of plays directed and acted by students – house drama. In 2015, each house selected a scene from Shakespeare and we gathered in Westminster School's theatre (a wonderful location) to see them acted. The winning piece was *Othello* performed by Somerville (who captured the house cup and took a lead in the total number of house championships won that they have yet to relinquish), but the abiding memory is of Wilberforce's performance of *A Midsummer Night's Dream* in which Bottom became an ass with the donning of a pair of novelty ears (both costume and props being severely limited by the rules of the competition). A moment of comic genius to round off a hard term.

Final Thoughts

- Education is fundamentally counter-cultural: the idea that we should work without immediate pay-off is inherent. Schools should embrace this.

- A school ethos should be a shortcut for students (and staff): if they are behaving in ethos then they should be doing the things we want them to without them memorising a list.

- There are times for making things explicit as well as implicit; purpose as well as mechanics; bullet-pointed brass tacks as well as literary assemblies.

- Communities need routine and set piece celebrations. A school calendar needs to balance both.

- Being disadvantaged really is a disadvantage – one that impacts on many areas and in many ways. Being determined to overcome it is not an easy ambition to achieve; if it were then everybody would be doing it.

Chapter 5

Important Messages

One of the things we have found difficult to get right is personal, social, health and citizenship education (PSHCE) – the things that students need to learn in order to be functioning adults but which are rarely tested in formal examinations. This includes things like sex education, drugs and alcohol information, self-care advice, finance and careers. These are clearly important and are covered by our ethos of 'learning is amazing' (after all, examinations are not amazing but learning skills that will make navigating the adult world easier certainly is), but they are not the passion of any of the staff. We can find experts in quantum computing, Viking history and even the musicianship of grime, but these more useful and even applicable areas of knowledge can be difficult to get enthusiastic about.

We have a PSHCE programme prepared by the heads of house and delivered by tutors to form groups which covers the important content. We have a sex education expert who comes in once a year so the students don't have to listen to me talk about the subject (I tried it once and received very strong feedback that whilst they wanted to learn about sex, they didn't want to learn about it from me – I have tried to be stoic about the rejection), and we have, through our guest speaker slot, an incredible assortment of employment advice and examples from people from a wide variety of careers. To supplement this, particularly when we have wanted all the students to receive the same message, and because we don't want PSHCE to be dismissed as unscholarly or non-core, we have sometimes included this kind of content in our assemblies. Inevitably, it would be mixed in with some poetry or philosophical musing: the trick in this case is to get the message across sufficiently clearly that it stays with the students without sounding like you are preaching or patronising them.

Tread Softly – 12 November 2014

An assembly by Nic Amy

Today my theme is legacy. Our legacy is what we leave behind, the footprint we leave for the future. And I want to consider a particular aspect of legacy today to fit in with our PSHCE programme this half-term, which is considering our futures, particularly our academic futures and the choices we will make over the next few months.

There will be a fair bit of poetry in today's assembly. There never needs to be an excuse for that, of course. But I want to make sure that there is plenty of beautiful language as a reminder that what we say, write and record for the future should be beautiful rather than ugly.

I start with the great Irish poet W. B. Yeats. Some of you know him through his poem 'The Second Coming', which contains the line 'Things fall apart', which in turn gives its name to the novel by Chinua Achebe, which many of you have read. Anyway, in his poem 'Aedh Wishes for the Cloths of Heaven', Yeats writes these lines:

> *But I, being poor, have only my dreams;*
>
> *I have spread my dreams under your feet;*
>
> *Tread softly because you tread on my dreams.*

Treading softly is a wonderful metaphor. Consider your dreams and consider your footsteps. Take them carefully, mindfully, softly.

Remembrance has been the theme of the moment. And yesterday, on the eleventh day of the eleventh month, we all experienced a sombre and resonant moment of collective memory. But as the dean said in his powerful address, one of the most important reasons we remember is to shape a better future going forward, and as he reminded us, those who do not remember the past are doomed to repeat it. But shaping that future is also about constructing a reputation. And reputations are both personal and institutional. The two are inescapably intertwined.

It doesn't do Yeats' metaphor about treading softly justice, but one of the things I want you to think about today is the concept of a digital footprint, because the online world gives us a new canvas and a new range of issues to consider. You will baulk at the word 'new'. It is not new: you have lived your whole lives in the era of the internet, of online communication, of social media. However, it is perhaps worth pausing for thought and considering that some of us (who aren't actually that old) when we were teenagers – your age – grew up in a world where none of this technology existed.

When I was at school the very idea of a mobile phone would have seemed extraordinary, magical, improbable – the stuff of science fiction. But that is now our everyday reality. Things change and they change remarkably quickly. And although some things change at lightning speed, sometimes attitudes and values struggle to keep up. And we need to be aware of this sometime tension. I want to explore with you what the education writer Michael Fullan has called the 'power and peril' of technology.[1]

It is nice to take these together: the power and the peril. And, as always, it is worth remembering what Spider-Man says because superheroes are almost always a useful source of wisdom. Spider-Man tells us that: 'with great power comes great responsibility'. And digital technology certainly gives us great power and we need to harness that to best possible use.

In a really interesting recent book *The New Digital Age*, Schmidt and Cohen – who are two key leaders at Google – argue that your generation will be the first to have an indelible record,[2] and that alongside sex education you should, and will, be taught about privacy and security online. Shaping your online identity and reputation management, they argue, will be the 'new normal' and this will even filter down to the names parents decide to give their children, future-proofing them against search and popularity.

That is a really interesting idea, isn't it? If a parent calls their child Jane Smith, say, or Priyanka Patel, they are almost guaranteeing them relative search engine anonymity. There are so many other human beings on the planet with the same name that most individuals would get drowned out in the sea of a Google search. That can be a problem: if you want to get your name out there to publicise your business you might have to consider changing it; however, for others, the relative anonymity might be considered hugely desirable. But regardless of our names (for most of us that is already fixed and out of our control), managing our online reputations is going to become more and more important.

1   M. Fullan, *Stratosphere: Integrating Technology, Pedagogy, and Change Knowledge* (Toronto: Pearson, 2012), ch. 2.
2   E. Schmidt and J. Cohen, *The New Digital Age: Transforming Nations, Businesses, and Our Lives* (New York: Vintage, 2014).

It is already becoming the preserve of the rich, with reputation management companies charging a fortune to use a variety of technological dark arts to shift and represent the online profiles of their clients. But mostly people are having to pay for this service because they have previously created profiles or footprints that they now want to change. Institutional and personal reputations stand and fall by online actions. It is now that we start shaping our reputations, treading softly and creating a powerful legacy.

It really isn't my intention to scare you, but it is always worth considering the growing number of legal cases of people who have been fired for posting things on Facebook about their fellow workers or their company that they – mistakenly – thought were private. One of the things you have probably heard is that universities will look at your Facebook profile. Will they? Probably not, to be honest. But if someone did look at it, would you be happy with the face you are turning to the outside world?

The grandma test is a good one: would you be happy for your grandmother to see what you have posted? If not, you might want to ask: is that something I really want to put up for possible public viewing? Another good test is to think about Shakespeare's Sonnet 105 where he writes, 'Fair, kind, and true, is all my argument'. Is it fair? Is it kind? Is it true? If not, probably better not post it. One helpful strategy is to think that anything you post online could be potentially public. The landscape for privacy is changing dramatically and my hunch is that it will be one of the most interesting areas of legal development over the next few years – and perhaps a field for the aspiring lawyers amongst you to grapple with.

The recent European legislation on the 'right to be forgotten' has seen thousands of applications to Google to have links to information deleted, and is beginning to shape a new set of attitudes towards privacy and the law. Regardless of the law, however, our well-being is shaped powerfully by our interactions with technology, so helping to develop that relationship as a positive, flourishing one is key. 'We live in the flicker,' says Marlow in Joseph Conrad's *Heart of Darkness*,[3] and it seems a good metaphor for the transient digital world. The threats to attention and concentration seem ubiquitous: they are always there.

That said, some of them are probably not as dangerous as some people would like us to believe; however, others are likely to be a real threat and we

3   Conrad, *Heart of Darkness*, ch. 1.

need to have the intellectual reserves and the wherewithal to counter these dangers if we encounter them.

Being mindful about the decisions we make and the reputations we shape will make us personally and institutionally more robust and better ready to make the most of the future whilst cherishing the best things from the past. 'So we beat on, boats against the current, borne back ceaselessly into the past,' says Nick Carraway at the end of *The Great Gatsby*.[4] We think in the present about the past to shape our futures.

I said at the top of this assembly that there would be poetry. One of my very favourite poems is by Thomas Hardy, that great nineteenth century novelist and twentieth century poet and, of course, another resident, in Poets' Corner, of Westminster Abbey. His poem 'Afterwards' is about how we are remembered and how we shape how we are remembered by what we do in life. It is often read at funerals, which always seems to me a little sad because it is being recited about someone who no longer has the opportunity to shape their legacy and, anyway, the poem – whilst sombre – is, in one reading at least, rather life affirming. In the poem, Hardy imagines what other people will say about him after he has died:

> *When the Present has latched its postern behind my tremulous stay,*
> *And the May month flaps its glad green leaves like wings,*
> *Delicate-filmed as new-spun silk, will the neighbours say,*
> *'He was a man who used to notice such things'?*
>
> *If it be in the dusk when, like an eyelid's soundless blink,*
> *The dewfall-hawk comes crossing the shades to alight*
> *Upon the wind-warped upland thorn, a gazer may think,*
> *'To him this must have been a familiar sight.'*
>
> *If I pass during some nocturnal blackness, mothy and warm,*
> *When the hedgehog travels furtively over the lawn,*
> *One may say, 'He strove that such innocent creatures should come to no harm,*
> *But he could do little for them; and now he is gone.'*

---

4 F. S. Fitzgerald, *The Great Gatsby* (London: Penguin, 2000 [1926]), p. 172.

If, when hearing that I have been stilled at last, they stand at the door,

Watching the full-starred heavens that winter sees,

Will this thought rise on those who will meet my face no more,

'He was one who had an eye for such mysteries'?

And will any say when my bell of quittance is heard in the gloom,

And a crossing breeze cuts a pause in its outrollings,

Till they rise again, as they were a new bell's boom,

'He hears it not now, but used to notice such things'?

Do you notice things? Do you strive to help the innocent creatures? Do you have an eye for such mysteries? It is in the present that we shape what in the future will be the past and our legacy. It is now that we mould our reputations. It is in every footstep we take that we make for ourselves the legacy of our own choosing.

'Tread softly', said William Butler Yeats, 'because you tread on my dreams.'

The message there is a warning to the students to be careful about what they post online, to have an eye to what a future employer might think, as well as to the way they want to, or should, present themselves. It was a message made necessary by a bit of WhatsApp nastiness between some of the students and was, to some extent, aimed at their habit of typing things that they would never write in an email or say face to face. Only at Harris Westminster could such a straightforward and clinical warning wear such literary clothes, dressed up in Yeats, Hardy, Achebe, Fitzgerald and Conrad: it is an example of us living the high expectations that we claim that we trust the students to pay enough attention to both enjoy the literary backdrop and internalise the behavioural instructions.

The WhatsApp nastiness was an infringement of our behaviour policy, which despite being in places vague, precludes all kinds of nastiness. A purely mechanical (in Harris Westminster Sixth Form terms) behaviour policy would not be right for a school that aims to lead its students into the adult world and give them a head start in engaging with it. A transactional behaviour policy, where transgression

X leads to punishment Y, is an infantilising device suitable only for major crimes: in the adult world when you make a bad decision there are complex negative consequences that you have to work your way out of. At the beginning of Year 12, of course, many students are little more than children (what might, rather cruelly, be described as Year 11s in suits and with eight weeks of summer behind them), but we want them to leave at the end of Year 13 ready to be young adults. Our policy, then, is that students should be free to make their own decisions – as long as they make good decisions. And our responsibility as teachers is to educate them in making good decisions, to remove their right to decide when they make bad ones and, as far as possible, to protect them from the worst consequences of their mistakes.

One of the core responsibilities of a school in terms of citizenship education is to deliver what are called 'British values': despite the vagueness of the name, these are four defined and enumerated values determined by the government as being central to being a good citizen. Our idiom would naturally be to develop and express these values tacitly without ever drawing attention to what we are doing, but this is not enough and we are expected to be sufficiently explicit that students are aware of the phrase and able to associate it with the required behaviours as well as exhibiting them.

We have had several goes at delivering these ideas – and, as will be seen in the next chapter, we have not always got it right (and one of the disadvantages of having an intelligent and alert student body is that they object quite vehemently if you stand up in front of them and express your message badly – they have high standards). By the fourth time round, however, in 2017, I think I gave it a good shot.

A Quadrichotomy of Values – 18 September 2017

This morning I will be talking about values. I shall be using as my lenses a piece of popular culture, some government guidance and a poem that I consider particularly resonant. As we talk generally I would like you to be thinking about your personal values and our shared values as a school.

I will start this morning with *Harry Potter*, a body of work with which I am assuming you have at least a passing degree of familiarity – my household is currently obsessed with it. My younger daughter is in Year 6 and thus eagerly anticipating her Hogwarts letter. I, meanwhile, listening to Stephen Fry's dulcet tones washing over me throughout the summer, have been musing on Hogwarts and the values it espouses. One Twitter wag decried the values of any school where students are sorted on entry into 'brave, smart, evil and miscellaneous', which is a funny but, I think, unfair interpretation of the Hogwarts house system.[5] I think that truer to the books is a model in which the sorting hat identifies your primary motivation from ambition, courage, intellect and loyalty and places you in a house accordingly. Truer or not, this is what I intend to take as my starting point this morning. This quadrichotomy is an interesting way of thinking about personality types, and the *Harry Potter* books can be thought of as an extended thought experiment in the consequences of using it to shape young minds.

My first observation is that ambition doesn't seem to come out of the exercise very well — it is difficult to find any defenders of Slytherin House even amongst those who embrace a drive for greatness. This should be a concern to us all — is not ambition the central plank of our ethos? Is this a school full of Slytherins? I have two responses to that accusation: no and no. On the one hand, legacy is, for us, of equal importance with ambition, and the followers of Salazar rarely consider the importance of leaving the world a better place than they found it. Let that, by the way, be a warning to us all — J. K. Rowling has painted a very clear picture of what we will become if we embrace the first of the Harris Westminster words but neglect the last: make sure that your ambitions benefit those around you rather than coming at their expense. On the other, I would say that we share the values of all four houses: ambition makes it onto our red wall but they are all woven into our ethos. I have, in the past, spoken about Westminster School's stone-balancing act — loyal dissent — and how being quite firmly on each other's side enables us to argue and challenge. Perhaps it is worth spending a moment with Toby Ziegler, my favourite character from my favourite drama. He is the director of communications in *The West Wing* and he says: 'We're a group. We're a team … We win together, we lose together. We celebrate and we mourn together. And defeats are softened and victories sweeter because we did them together. You're my guys and I'm yours and there's nothing I wouldn't do for you.'[6]

---

5   See https://twitter.com/tvscarlkinsella/status/762038953721597953.
6   'War Crimes', *The West Wing* (Warner Bros., 2001), season 3, episode 6.

Sometimes quoting allows you to say exactly what you mean but couldn't carry off in your own voice. You're my guys and loyalty is important. Also in assemblies past I have quoted C. S. Lewis' observation that courage is not just a virtue but the essence of all virtues at their sticking point.[7] Ambition (or loyalty or scholarship) that gives up when things get hard is no virtue at all – no, we should all, also, be Gryffindors. Finally, I hope that none of you would say that we hold intellect, learning or scholarship lightly at Harris Westminster. Rowena Ravenclaw would have been all over Harris Westminster were she still alive and not fictional.

My second thought on the subject of the Hogwarts house values is that nobody is driven by a single one. Almost every character has at least a second strand to their character. Take, for instance, the three central students. It is well-known that Harry was almost a Slytherin and it would be foolish to think that Hermione, the brightest witch of her generation, wasn't at least considered for Ravenclaw. Meanwhile, in the last book we find that Ron's destiny was shaped by his loyalty: when Dumbledore left him his Deluminator he knew both that Ron's courage would fail and also that his loyalty to his friends would bring him back.[8] It is worth noting at this point that the most cowardly of all characters, Wormtail, was placed in Gryffindor. There is a depth to the sorting that is not immediately apparent. I speculate that Peter Pettigrew's life was shaped by his desire to be brave and that his failure to share this virtue with his friends ate away at his heart and drove him to be the abject creature he became. Nobody, even minor fictional characters, holds only one value and it is clear that none of us can consider our values to be ours alone.

These thoughts returned to my mind last week when I attended a meeting of local head teachers and heard a senior police officer talk about the Contest strategy. The name might be unfamiliar to you but I think you will be aware of the strategy, at least in general terms. It has four strands – Pursue, Prevent, Protect and Prepare – and it is the government's approach to the threats of international terrorism. It is actually quite clever or remarkably simple, depending how you look at it: they plan to catch terrorists, to stop people becoming terrorists, to protect us from acts of terrorism and to be ready

7   C. S. Lewis, *The Screwtape Letters* (Quebec: Samizdat University Press, 2016 [1942]), p. 63. Available at: http://www.samizdat.qc.ca/arts/lit/PDFs/ScrewtapeLetters_CSL.pdf.
8   J. K. Rowling, *Harry Potter and the Deathly Hallows* (London: Bloomsbury Children's Books, 2007).

to deal with them when they happen. It is difficult to argue with any of that. I have responsibilities under the Prevent strategy, as do all your teachers. We are, broadly, expected to do what we can to convince you that blowing people up is neither good manners nor an effective way of making a better world. I hope we are doing OK at that, but if you are not sure and would like to talk to me about whether, maybe, it might be better to spend your time building bombs than doing maths homework, please knock on my door and we will try to thrash it out.

One of my other responsibilities is to teach you British values. These, like the Hogwarts values, come in a set of four (I tend to prefer things in threes but sometimes, like the amplifier in *This Is Spinal Tap*, you need one more). The four are democracy, the rule of law, individual liberty, and mutual respect and tolerance for those of different faiths and beliefs. Like the Hogwarts values, saying these are British is not to say that no other nation shares them – that would be arrogant nonsense of the first order. It is, however, to recognise that not everybody does. There are people and countries who would say that government of the people, by the people, for the people is undesirable; that laws should be bent to the needs of great men or women; that the individual's rights should be subsumed to the collective; or that those who disagree on matters theological should be persecuted. I have to confess that there are times when I think the only remedy for the country is to put me in charge and give me a free hand to sort things out – cut through some of the red tape, throw some perps into the pit of despair, that kind of thing – but then I reflect that this has never worked in the past. The myth of the benign dictator is a prevalent one, but the problem is that the world is too complex for a single person to sort it out, even me, and that an excess of power would corrupt anyone who wielded it, even, I fear, me.

We live within a structure that is grossly imperfect – we would all agree on that – but I don't think we would agree on which bits of it were wrong. Even if we, in the church this morning, agreed, we, the people who live in this country, wouldn't. It may be a terrible system, actually, but it is better than all the others, and what keeps it that way are those fundamental British values.

I return to the values of Harris Westminster and that poem I promised you. It is a poem I have quoted several times in assembly. It is by Rudyard Kipling, it is made up of four stanzas, all of which are worth reading, and it exists in an extended hypothetical – if. 'If—', goes the last stanza:

If you can talk with crowds and keep your virtue,

Or walk with Kings – nor lose the common touch,

If neither foes nor loving friends can hurt you,

If all men count with you, but none too much;

If you can fill the unforgiving minute

With sixty seconds' worth of distance run,

Yours is the Earth and everything that's in it …

I am not going to quote the last line – perfection is not to be found, even in poetry. My unforgiving minute is up, my musings on shared values are at an end, and the time has come to return to potions in the basement, astronomy in the tower or even mathematics on the first floor.

Perhaps unsurprisingly, Hogwarts references always get a greater response from the audience than poetry, and this piece received a rather charming rejoinder. One of the Year 13s listening to it and reflecting, a student called Josh, sent me an email in which he wondered if Harris Westminster attracted Hermione Graingers and developed Luna Lovegoods. The central distinction between these two characters, he argued, apart from the fact that Hermione is a Gryffindor and Luna is in Ravenclaw, is that Hermione's intelligence is primarily in regurgitating knowledge ('Books! And Cleverness' is how Hermione herself puts it[9]), whereas Luna is a free thinker, a creative who rejects the boundaries of 'normal'. This, I was told, was what being a Ravenclaw was really about, and it was this step, from successfully regurgitating facts for an exam to thinking for yourself, that some students found so challenging about joining our school. It was a wonderfully reasoned piece of writing which I think gets to the heart of some of our counter-culturality and which raises the question of how we present ourselves to the outside world.

One of the challenges that faces students, and which was so beautifully answered by Josh in his Hogwarts email, is how to take the assembly, 2,000 words or so crammed full of cultural allusion and advice, and make sense of it. How do you build the bridge between the esoteric

9   Rowling, *Harry Potter and the Philosopher's Stone*, p. 308.

and the mundane? How do you make the step from an ordinary background to something extraordinary? The last phrasing is, of course, the fundamental challenge of the Harris Westminster vision, rather than anything specific to assemblies.

Sometimes what gets in the way is practicalities – you can't take all the opportunities offered to you if you have childcare responsibilities at home or need to hold down a job to support the family finances. Sometimes it is that what is being presented is not a prescription but a choice – you can't read all the books or learn all the poetry mentioned in an assembly, but you are not meant to; and sometimes it is just difficult to believe that we (Harris Westminster) disagree with other authorities to the extent that we do – that we mean exactly what we say. The question of sleep falls into the final category: students hear what is said, they understand the meaning of the words, they are, by and large, capable of arranging a decent night's sleep before getting up in time to get to school for 9am, and yet many of them make poor decisions, lured either by the delights of social media or by the will-o'-the-wisp charms of a late-night cramming session. We have attempted, with limited success, to correct this in an assembly (at the very least this piece provides a formal policy on sleep habits).

Peace – 13 March 2017

This morning I will be talking to you about peace. I shall consider its merits, give you some advice on sleep hygiene, and emphasise the importance of discussion and communication, but first I will tell you about a book. It is a book I read in the sixth form and I will not tell you what it is because, firstly, it is not in the library and, secondly, it is not worth your time. It is a moderately engaging story, moderately well written and one of the heroes of the piece – and the reason I mention it now – is an Irish chat show host who, when drunk, has a habit of declaiming the poetry of William Butler Yeats.[10] This is portrayed, in the novel, as a very attractive attribute (the poetry rather than the drunkenness, let me be clear), and so Yeats and his poetry have, since then, had a special place in my heart. I am still not able to declaim yards of the stuff but there are four poems of his I know well: one you will already be familiar with from assemblies past – 'Aedh Wishes for the Cloths of Heaven'

---

10   In case you were wondering, the book is Jilly Cooper's *Rivals* (London: Corgi, 1988).

is one I have used when I have urged you to tread softly for you tread on my dreams; one will make an appearance in next week's assembly – it is a strangely prophetic piece called 'The Second Coming' that you might want to look up before I speak to you again; the third, 'Down by the Salley Gardens', is lying in abeyance waiting for the right moment; and the last, 'The Lake Isle of Inisfree', goes like this:

> *I will arise and go now, and go to Innisfree,*
> *And a small cabin build there, of clay and wattles made;*
> *Nine bean-rows will I have there, a hive for the honey-bee,*
> *And live alone in the bee-loud glade.*
>
> *And I shall have some peace there, for peace comes dropping slow,*
> *Dropping from the veils of the morning to where the cricket sings;*
> *There midnight's all a glimmer, and noon a purple glow,*
> *And evening full of the linnet's wings.*
>
> *I will arise and go now, for always night and day*
> *I hear lake water lapping with low sounds by the shore;*
> *While I stand on the roadway, or on the pavements grey,*
> *I hear it in the deep heart's core.*

The key words come in the second quatrain, 'And I shall have some peace there, for peace comes dropping slow, / Dropping from the veils of morning to where the cricket sings', and I am always struck by the evocation of peace in those lines: they just seem to make me feel calm. The gentle rhythm, the repetition of the words 'peace' and 'dropping' and the length of the vowels, 'peace', 'slow' and 'veils', seem to rock the reader like a lullaby.

What is peace, then? There is another book, also not in the library, called *Five Minutes' Peace* by Jill Murphy in which the mother of an elephant family, Mrs Large, decides she would like to just sit down and have a quiet cup of tea, but first the baby, then the primary school children and finally the teenager all want her attention.[11] The peace Mrs Large is looking for is calm, quiet solitude. Freedom from the need to achieve; the absence of stress and worry.

11   J. Murphy, *Five Minutes' Peace* (Harmondsworth: Penguin, 1986).

Eventually she finds it in the bath – for just five minutes before the children come in to join her. Yeats imagines this same peace and hopes that he will find it in Innisfree.

So, what is the place of peace in our lives, we who have ambitions, who are aware of the 168-hour limit to each week and who begrudge each tick of the clock – is peace something for our futures, something to find on the veranda when the work is done? I don't think so. I think that peace is an important part of our lives. Peace is a chance to reflect on our actions and think about whether they are in line with our aims. It is a chance to review our aims and decide whether they are in line with our ambition and our ethos. It is an opportunity to process the information we have absorbed, to internalise it so that we can use it in our work and studies. Peace, though, as Mrs Large found, can be difficult to obtain when you live with your family: there is always something going on and getting time alone can be tough. I urge you, then, to find peace at bedtime. The end of the day should be a time of quiet, but I know that some of you find it difficult to get to sleep. I know that sometimes I find it difficult to get to sleep and I will lie there with worries and stresses going round and round in my head. The peace I should find in the darkness and quiet eludes me. Rest is important – if you don't get a good night's sleep the next day will be harder. We must value our sleep and recognise how delicate it is and how easily disturbed. There is no magic wand, no spell for sleepiness, but there are things you can do to maximise your chances of getting a good night's sleep, even if your daytime mind is filled with stress.

If you listen to just two minutes of the assembly, make it the next two because here come my top tips for good sleeping:

1.   Have a routine. Go to bed at the same time each night and be reluctant to change the rhythm – my bedtime is 10pm and it is very rare that my eyes aren't shut by 10.30.

2.   Take some exercise. It is easy for those of us whose work is cerebral to feel that we are tired but to be unable to sleep because our muscles have been relatively unused. I have a series of exercises I do in the evening in the living room, but going for a run is also a straightforward, quick and free way of using up some energy, working your muscles and generating some endorphins.

3.   Turn your screens off. There is something about the interactivity of computers that is inimical to a peaceful brain. Turn them off and put

them away an hour before bed. We have a line of chargers in the living room, each with its phone or tablet, and they get tucked in at 9pm so our brains have a chance to unwind.

4. Read a little. In comparison with tapping and clicking, the exercise of reading is curiously soporific – as well as being useful scholastically. Take advantage of that last hour to catch up with a book and you will find that you drop off.

Back to peace – which is, of course, not just about solitude but is also a sign of good relationships with others. The opposite of peace is not just noise but war. My current bedtime reading is a book entitled *Why Switzerland?* which considers the peculiar nature of that peculiar country.[12] One of the peculiar things it highlights is the fact that it is a confederation of microstates that has survived from the Middle Ages in a way that other confederations haven't. Switzerland is small but it is far from uniform. The microstates are called cantons, and there are French cantons and German cantons; mountain cantons and urban cantons; Protestant cantons and Catholic cantons; original cantons and new cantons; rich cantons and poor cantons; and there has often been disagreement between the groups. The book suggests that the reason for their survival is that they have had a framework for disagreement – a forum where the representatives of the cantons can meet and discuss and come to a conclusion without there being a need to agree.

This framework for disagreement is one that I worry is missing from some other institutions. I read an article last week which said that the number of marginal communities in the United States was dropping rapidly, places where neighbours disagree politically are becoming rare and so the impression is that all right-thinking people agree: the country is becoming more polarised.[13] In this country there is a body of opinion which holds that since the EU referendum it is undemocratic to put forward a disagreeing view, and within the Church there has been some significant unpleasantness regarding the appointment of a bishop who disagrees with the position of the Church on the ordination of women. I went to the Afro-Caribbean Society a couple of weeks ago and one of the things I was most impressed with was the way in which you were able to express your views, to disagree with each other on an issue that is

12 J. Steinberg, *Why Switzerland?*, 3rd edn (Cambridge: Cambridge University Press, 2015).
13 D. Wasserman, 'Purple America Has All But Disappeared', *FiveThirtyEight* (8 March 2017). Available at: https://fivethirtyeight.com/features/purple-america-has-all-but-disappeared.

both emotive and, to many of you, fundamental and to leave on good terms. I know you are having an even more controversial discussion this week and I hope to see the same spirit. Being able to respect people you disagree with is vital to maintaining peace and having the opportunity to disagree is part of building this respect.

I will leave this idea here and pick it up again next week. In the meantime, let us hear the lake waters lapping with low sounds around the shore, and therefore arise and go now.

When writing the assembly on peace I was mulling over the Yeats poem and shared it with Ella, our librarian. The analysis of the second quatrain was taken almost verbatim from her musings on the subject. This is just one example of one of the joys of working at Harris Westminster, which has been spending time with an amazingly intelligent and erudite staff. In my previous existence as an eccentric maths teacher, my experience was typically of finding a new problem or puzzle and leaping into the staffroom to share it with my colleagues. If I was lucky I would find a spirit sufficiently kindred to engage with the idea, to work on it with me or, at least, to admire the solution; in fact, my working definition of a good maths department is one in which a teacher can leap into the staffroom with a new problem and not get confused looks from absolutely everybody.

At Harris Westminster I had two new experiences: firstly, it wasn't only (or even mostly) me who was doing the leaping in – there was a busy trade in wonderful problems, enthusiasms, poems and books from every corner of the curriculum; and secondly, I could no longer rely on being the quickest to find the solution.

On one occasion I picked up a rather beautiful problem from the MEI website (www.mei.org.uk): given three parallel lines, construct an equilateral triangle with one vertex on each line. After puzzling over it for five minutes or so without success, I left my office to do my lunchtime duty. When the first maths teacher came by I told him of my wonderful puzzle. 'Oh yes,' he said, 'that is a nice, easy problem.' I was a little dispirited, but I had chosen to put my geometry problem to a genius of Hungarian extraction and Euclidean disposition, and so I waited eagerly for the next victim to come by. It wasn't long before

Tom came along in search of a sandwich, and so I explained both my problem and the previous reaction. A moment's pause and then, 'Yes, that is nice and easy.' Five minutes later he returned with lunch in hand and a troubled look on his face. 'Actually, I don't think that's easy at all.' He set his further mathematicians to work on the problem, and meanwhile Andras, the Hungarian, wrote a short paper detailing six different approaches to the question. I retired to my office and applied brute force techniques to find the most disgusting solution of the lot.

The Afro-Caribbean Society was an innovation of the second cohort of Harris Westminster students. It was a response to the challenge of how to make sense of the liberal, scholarly environment of the school in the context of a student body from very different cultural and ethnic backgrounds. The society put on discussions, debates and events aimed at resolving the issues that come out of the melting pot that is twenty-first century London (it was later renamed Tirah to avoid appearing specific to one ethnic group when these are issues that affect every student). Other student-founded and student-led societies approaching this question from different directions include the GSA (which has been short for Gay/Straight Alliance and Gender and Sexuality Alliance at different points in its existence), Intelligent Believing (which attempts to take a scholarly look at different faiths despite its members failing to agree on exactly, or even approximately, what documents comprise inspired scripture) and Intersectional Feminism (which considers how gender affects experience as one aspect of the self).

It was always intended that there would be clubs and societies driven by the students' interests. and the expectation from the beginning was that they would found and run the groups they wanted to have in the school. I had expected things along the lines of the short-lived but rather wonderful British Comedy Society, but the groups that have had the biggest impact and have lasted the longest have been these discussion societies, grappling with the big issues and trying to make sense of what it means to live in an incorrigibly plural world. These societies have, I am sure, a far greater impact on students' understanding of respect and tolerance than any number of assemblies on British values.

Final Thoughts

▨ If something is important then it is important enough to appear in an assembly and important enough for the head to say it publicly – we shouldn't shy away from the nitty-gritty of students' lives.

▨ Students have only been alive for seventeen years or so – it shouldn't be surprising that there are 'obvious' things they don't know. Being a teacher is about teaching the obvious as well as the obscure.

▨ A culture that is dense enough in interest and open enough to communication will spark the minds of all members of the team. If you have conversations about Yeats with the librarian or receive emails from students like Josh, then you know you are doing something right.

▨ Even the most amazing students (or teachers or leaders) don't get it right all the time. It is important to be grounded enough to recognise when an authoritarian tone is required.

Chapter 6

Building the Community

In 2014, our 138 students and 23 staff fitted comfortably into the first three floors of Steel House and rattled around in the pews of St Margaret's: teachers on duty would encourage students into the front rows because spread evenly throughout the church we appeared very sparse. Making our way back from assembly was a straightforward exercise with a pleasing sense of togetherness – a community moving as one. In the first year we didn't need to do much to emphasise the communal aspect of our venture. I gave an assembly on cherishing our building (provoked by some graffiti in the toilets), but in general there were so few of us and we were so much living in each other's pockets that a culture of community grew naturally.

Students formed clusters around the teachers they most admired, or defined by the subjects in which they excelled, or in their extra-curricular interests, or formed by friendships or romantic liaisons (on the latter, I have always adopted an approach of noticing as little as possible and appearing entirely perplexed and somewhat embarrassed when evidence of such a relationship was thrust upon me). There was also a sense of everyone being on the same team (most of the time), with idiosyncrasies passed over or relished. Many of the students went from being defined by cleverness to finding that cleverness was assumed and they had an opportunity to develop other aspects to their characters.

By Celebration term 2015, the school was a tightly bound community with a few exceptions: some students had realised that the hard work, high expectations and long days were not for them, and a few of the staff had come to the decision that they would be more comfortable somewhere less idiosyncratic (a euphemism that covers many bases). Meanwhile, we had recruited another 250 students to join us in September – our numbers would almost triple – and were looking for a proportionate increase in staff. This was a daunting prospect, both for the students – a significant proportion of whom favoured shutting the place rather than allowing newcomers into what they considered to be their school – and for the staff. 'What happened to our little school?' bemoaned one teacher standing on duty and watching hordes of new Harris Westminsters cross Victoria Street after assembly.

Perhaps the biggest challenge, though, came to the new staff who joined us in Remembrance 2015. It was still a school finding its way, doing a lot of things for the first time (the whole of Year 13, for example) and not having made a plan for them all; it was a school that was used to being small and used to management instructions being communicated quickly to fifteen members of staff; and it was a school that operated well because everyone understood the ethos and had been steeped in it. Unfortunately, as of Remembrance 2015, it was a school where none of those assumptions held any more. New staff found that there were assumptions they had no way of guessing and which were not properly explained; they found that messages were delivered late and rushed; they had the sense (quite rightly) that traditions were being made up as we went along; and that there was a club of special staff and students and that they would always be on the outside.

The academic year of 2015–2016 was the hardest that Harris Westminster has been through so far (well, up to February 2020 – see later). New staff and students were expecting to be joining an established school, not a fly-by-night affair where we were managing by the skin of our teeth; existing students resented those immature Year 12s disturbing their scholarly oasis (and conveniently forgot what hoodlums they had been just twelve months earlier); and original staff found that their timetables were fuller and their classes larger – the inefficient overstaffing of a start-up that had enabled a lot of fun and freedom was over. Meanwhile, the senior leadership team (now up to four: Nic, Paul and I had been joined by a new assistant principal, Claire Scott) were struggling: I hadn't done enough to convey the ethos of Harris Westminster to the new recruits or to think about how it would transfer to a much larger institution (to be fair, we had, at the time, been recruiting to triple the size of the school whilst still going through all the events and milestones for the first time; having said that, I should have seen the problems coming); Nic and Paul both took on unmanageably large workloads as we tried to scale things up by a factor of three; and Claire found herself trying to share with staff an ethos she was figuring out at about the same rate as we were altering it to fit.

We have always described the school as having two sides, a 'Harris' side and a 'Westminster' one; walking a tightrope between being a state school, many of whose students added the challenges of poverty to those inherent in being a teenager, and aspiring to compete on an equal footing with the very best private schools in the country. Sometimes the tightrope has appeared vanishingly thin as the two sides have pulled us in opposite directions and we have had to decide which way to lean: whether to be too 'Westminster' (looking to long-term learning with a lot of freedom for exploration and expecting that the individual students will address their own needs and make good decisions) or too 'Harris' (a strong pastoral structure with a clear set of rules and uncompromising support for those who don't meet expectations). I should say here that the quote marks are quite important: neither of these caricatures are at all fair to our two partners. They are competing tendencies rather than descriptions!

In 2014, we erred considerably on the 'Westminster' side. This was a deliberate decision – we knew that we would have to do things quite differently from the state school norm and that it would be easier to rein in this liberalism later than it would be to create it in an already functioning school. In 2015, then, we needed a correction: we needed more systems, we needed to tolerate less idiosyncrasy and we needed more focus on getting the right answers to syllabus questions. To help us we had appointed four heads of faculty – new middle leaders with responsibility for curriculum and subjects (freeing the heads of house from their general factotum role to focus on pastoral and holistic issues). John took on mathematics de jure (having been de facto head of subject and keeping Tom and I in line since the beginning); Charlotte widened her jurisdiction from English to arts and literature (a catch-all faculty named for one of the Trivial Pursuit categories and including MFL, classics and art as well as English literature); in science we appointed an excellent physicist called Jon; and Fiona (who I have mentioned before) joined us as head of humanities (a rather sprawling collection consisting of history, politics, philosophy, geography and economics).

The question now was how, within this larger and more systematic school, we could maintain our culture, our ethos – and the biggest challenge for us was how to keep hold of that sense of community that had been so palpable in the first year. The answer, inevitably, was through assemblies, now down from two a week to five a month because of the huge investment of time required to travel to and from the church as a much larger body, but now including a monthly assembly in Westminster Abbey (a marvellous setting that we played up to, with a procession of students through the quire and with everybody standing to start and finish).

Being Kind – 4 April 2016

Today's assembly is about being kind, about being self-aware and about being self-confident. It is also a bit about sex but I will come to that later. The starting point is the news that Wimbledon High School has hired a consultant to teach its students how to cope in the feverish atmosphere of a private girls' school. They are to be taught the social skills required to navigate toxic friendship cliques with the idea that these will stand them in good stead when it comes to navigating future relationships with toxic bosses. Janice Turner, in *The Times*, responded by writing a piece suggesting that instead of teaching their students to handle mean girls, Wimbledon High should be teaching them how not to be one.[1] I have talked to you about both of these ideas before – I have warned you that there are jerks in the world and I have told you that to avoid being one you should be kind – and of those two ideas I agree with Janice Turner that the most important thing is to be kind. It is an easy thing to say but is it so clear what it means? Do we know what it means to be kind or even why it is important to make that effort? As an illustration, I would like to draw your attention to *The Big Bang Theory* – a comedy that has a deplorable habit of propagating lazy sexual and racial stereotypes but which possibly has the finest depiction of kindness in popular culture. I offer you the relationship between Penny and Sheldon. Much is made of the fact that Sheldon is a scientist and Penny isn't, that Sheldon considers himself a genius and Penny doesn't, but for me the key difference between their characters is that in almost every interaction between them Penny is kind and Sheldon is not. Penny is understanding, thoughtful and generous with her time, whilst

1   J. Turner, 'Girls Can't Escape From This Relentless Bullying', *The Times* (2 April 2016).

Sheldon is rude, self-centred and mean. And in that short sentence I think you have a guide to kindness and also, those of you who are aware of the work, an incentive to be kind should you need one: pause for just a second and think about which character you would most like to be compared to.

Being kind isn't always easy – there is always a temptation to put others down, to take advantage of them and to look out for our own interests – but it is always right; if you are kind you will find others are willing to be kind to you and that you live in a community of kind people. Occasionally others will take advantage – there are, as I have mentioned, jerks in this world – but your relationships will be stronger, healthier and longer lasting if they are built on kindness than otherwise, and that goes for sexual relationships as much as friendships. Other people, even beautiful ones, can be annoying, rude and hurtful, and the instinctive reflex is to want to hurt them back. But don't – be kind, and reflect for a moment that you are, in your turn, annoying, rude and hurtful yourself. No doubt you are those things by accident, no doubt there are excuses, but you will have been them nonetheless – being kind means forgiving in others what you are able to excuse in yourself.

This brings me to the second point of the importance of being self-aware, of seeing the impact you have on those around you, of realising when you are being annoying or rude or hurtful, and therefore being able to change your ways. This is particularly important for our community here. A community of scholars is a wonderful thing when it works well: whatever you are excited about there are others who will share your enthusiasm, or at least others who have enthusiasms themselves and understand your joy of discovering something new – it is a real privilege to be able to proclaim that learning is amazing and get agreement from your audience. The danger is that we take this community for granted, that we get too absorbed in our own studies to take joy in the successes of others, that we allow the stresses of our busy lives to make us intolerant of the stresses of others. A sharp word here, a snide comment there and instead of getting energy and support from each other, we find our strength sapped and our inspiration swept away.

A key part of kindness in any community is celebrating each other's successes, and the house drama was a wonderful example of that: each little company of players watching intently and applauding enthusiastically at the performances that each one of you put on. This is Celebration term, the time of year when you really get to show how clever you are and how much you have learned. That is what exams are for – exams are not something to be dreaded but anticipated with nervous energy: they are the day of the performance, the World Cup Final, your chance to be brilliant on a bigger stage. Each one of you has crucial exams to take this term and each one of you wants to do your best. Please remember that – please be kind to each other, please be aware that those around you might be on edge and please be aware that if you are not studying then your actions might be distracting to others who are. Being kind in Celebration term is doing your best to make sure that your friends will have something to celebrate.

And let me make it clear that each of you should have something to celebrate. You are all magnificently clever, and you have before you, and before your exams, a significant chunk of time which can be used to improve skills, hone techniques and use facts that will enable you to perform at your very best. The Year 13s will recall how much was achieved after the Easter holidays last year – it averaged something like two grades per subject per student: getting your heads down and focused is enormously powerful. Unless you are very lucky – and I hope you are – there will be days this term when it feels impossible, days when you feel a bit low, days when your stupid brain can't get itself round whatever it is you are struggling with, but don't let it get you down. You are amazing – whenever we have someone in to meet you, to see you in class or to talk to you, they comment on what an impressive group of people you are. Each one of you is brilliant and each one of you is brilliant at taking exams – we have GCSEs to prove this. Being confident in your future and believing in yourself is important because it enables you to make positive decisions – to study rather than going out, to read rather than pootling about on the internet – because you know it will be worth it. You know it is worth making long-term decisions rather than short-term ones. It is important to remember that, not just as you study for your exams but in your friendships and sexual relationships too. Each one of you is a wonderful, brilliant, interesting person who deserves friends and partners who recognise that, who treat you with respect, who are kind to you, and not one of you should compromise on that.

Clearly, I am far too old for my views on this to carry much weight, but I will tell you what my youth group leader said to me when I was 16 – he is now the Bishop of Basingstoke, so he has gone up in the world. 'Look at me,' he said, and you can google him if you would like to look him up, 'and look at my wife – if I can find someone as witty, intelligent and beautiful as that then none of you have anything to worry about.' Just as there is a temptation to give up on study because it can't make any difference, there is a temptation to give up on romance and to believe that you have to settle for someone who treats you badly. Resist both temptations.

I will close with a fragment of misremembered verse. One of the joys of living in a house in which Radio 4 plays constantly is that you can wander into the kitchen and hear Sir Ian McKellen reading a poem called 'Advice to a Baby'. One of the drawbacks is that if you don't immediately make notes you can forget the words of the poem, the title of the piece and, possibly, the particular Sir Ian who was reading them. Anyway, the last couple of lines – as I remember them – go like this:

> *Baby, the world lies before you – enjoy it, explore it, relish it and revel in it.*
>
> *Be fearless and intrepid, be joyful and wise.*
>
> *But baby, most of all, if you forget my other words remember these: baby, be kind.*

So there is my advice to you this morning – be kind and insist on the same from anyone to whom you give your heart.

I have already explained that we didn't attempt to deliver sex education through assemblies (this was the closest I came – and it felt very transgressive even to allude to it from the abbey pulpit). It turns out (something I didn't discover until 2019, this being something surprisingly hard to google) that my misremembered verse was originally written by Kurt Vonnegut and that my misremembering had altered it considerably. What I had heard Sir Ian McKellen (probably) read was this, from *God Bless You, Mr Rosewater*:

> *Hello, babies. Welcome to Earth. It's hot in the summer and cold in the winter. It's round and wet and crowded. At the outside, babies, you've got about a hundred years here. There's only one rule that I know of, babies – 'God damn it, you've got to be kind.'*[2]

I am glad, now, to be able to issue a correction.

It may seem strange to issue a correction to a misquote in an assembly via a book, but it would be no less weird to issue it in assembly with a completely different group of students present. This is a minor aspect

2   K. Vonnegut, *God Bless You, Mr Rosewater* (London: Vintage, 1992 [1965]), p. 79.

of a major challenge – that we are using assemblies to cover core ethos content (there are messages that we want or need everybody to hear) and this develops over time as assemblies build on and refer to each other. But any given student hears assemblies only for five and a half terms and, moreover, they don't hear the assemblies in the same order (the assemblies given in Remembrance 2015 were listened to both by Year 13s who had been through all the assemblies of 2014–2015 and by Year 12s who were new to the school and less in tune with the jargon and style).

Eventually, this problem was solved by an assembly calendar that specifies messages for certain dates during the year (for example, everyone gets mechanics, purpose and response explained to them and everyone has an assembly on the meaning of scholarship) and by a small number of additional Year 12 assemblies that we can aim quite deliberately, knowing that they won't have heard it before. In 2015–2016, however, we were still feeling our way – careful not to repeat ourselves (a temptation that we have only very occasionally indulged: there are themes that get echoed from year to year and favourite sources of inspiration – Taylor Swift, Yeats and Tolkien, for example – but we don't tend to give the same piece) but not careful enough to make sure that we were herding the new students gently into our ethos.

In the previous chapter we had the assembly 'Peace' in which I laid two trails to be followed up and developed at a future occasion: the first was the question of managing disagreements and the second was the poetry of Yeats. That occasion came a week later with an assembly in Westminster Abbey.

Three Stone-Balancers – 22 March 2017

A few years ago, I went on holiday to Lyme Regis which I enjoyed for several reasons: I like holidays; I like Dorset because it balances my desire to head to the seaside against my reluctance to travel too far from my house; I like dinosaurs and Lyme Regis is at the heart of the Jurassic Coast; I like tongue-twisters and she who sells sea shells on the seashore was Mary Anning, a palaeontologist from Lyme Regis; I like Jane Austen and Lyme Regis is the setting of her finest novel; and I like breakfast and in Lyme Regis there is a bakery where they have a fine morning repast. Particularly pertinent to today's assembly, however, is the fact that I like mad art and Lyme Regis has an artist-in-residence who makes the town the kind of place where interesting and beautiful things are created.

For example, there is a professional stone-balancer in Lyme Regis, who is encouraged by the artist-in-residence. He gets large stones and balances them on end on the seashore and then takes photographs of them which he sells. We stopped to speak to him as he was creating his work on the promenade, and he explained that the trick is not getting stones to balance – any stone will balance if you can find the sweet spot where the centre of mass is over the contact point with the ground; the trick is getting stones to balance in a way that it looks like they shouldn't be able to. The stone-balancer came to mind when I was giving my lab lecture last week and I was talking about the impossibility of a society being both equal and free, and it struck me that running a country must be much like balancing a stone – finding the sweet spot between those two contradictory ideas.

This morning I would like to tell you about two other stone-balancing acts, two other examples of cognitive dissonance, two examples of searching for the sweet spot between apparently contradictory ideas. The first comes from Westminster School: it is embedded in their ethos and runs deep in their DNA and it is encapsulated in the phrase 'loyal dissent'. Loyal dissent is the idea that one can question and challenge and still respect; that, in fact, the greatest respect that can be shown a scholar is to have her ideas, reasoning and axioms challenged and found sound. Loyal dissent is a stone-balancing act because it is working for the team without being a yes-man, it is being highly critical of sources and then spending time learning from the best scholars that have gone before. Loyal dissent is crucial to the peaceful communication that I spoke to you about last week – communities become insular and intolerant if the choice is between loyalty or dissent. The only way the centre can hold is if there is a forum for respectful disagreement. I commend the practice of loyal dissent most strongly to you and urge you to have in your mind that stone-balancing act: is the centre of gravity held over the point of contact or are you going to tip over into unquestioning loyalty or, possibly worse, into disloyal and destructive quarrelsomeness?

I think loyal dissent is a useful form of cognitive dissonance that will carry you far in life, but I want, inevitably, to rest for a little while and reflect on what it means for scholarship and our studies at Harris Westminster. I have often asked you to be more critical and I have also often asked you to spend more time memorising the wisdom of others, and whilst you may have noticed the potential conflict or, indeed, paradox of these instructions, I have never before admitted the contradiction and attempted to resolve it. It is a balancing act. You should be critical – when you are presented with information you should ask 'Why?' and 'How do you know?' and 'Isn't that a simplification?' But what you must not do is to allow this habit of critical scrutiny to become one of lazy rejection of authority. Please try to formulate arguments against orthodoxy, please test every dogma against the white-hot intensity of your intellect, but when it passes the test, when your arguments come up short, as they will do, more often than not, please accept the strength of what you have been taught and learn it. One of the reasons I urge you to be critical is so that you thoroughly understand what you are being taught. I suggest you ask hard questions not because I think that what you are being taught is weak but because I think it is strong and can take it, and that having argued against it you will be able to be more convincing when you reason in favour. Loyal dissent – keep the dissonance in mind.

The second dissonance follows on from last week from another Yeats poem. This one was written in 1919, in the aftermath of the First World War, and it strikes a different tone from 'The Lake Isle of Innisfree' and seems particularly fresh and relevant in 2016–2017. It is called 'The Second Coming' and it goes like this:

Turning and turning in the widening gyre
The falcon cannot hear the falconer;
Things fall apart; the centre cannot hold;
Mere anarchy is loosed upon the world,
The blood-dimmed tide is loosed, and everywhere
The ceremony of innocence is drowned;
The best lack all conviction, while the worst
Are full of passionate intensity.

Surely some revelation is at hand;
Surely the Second Coming is at hand.
The Second Coming! Hardly are those words out

When a vast image out of Spiritus Mundi

Troubles my sight: somewhere in sands of the desert

A shape with lion body and the head of a man,

A gaze blank and pitiless as the sun,

Is moving its slow thighs, while all about it

Reel shadows of the indignant desert birds.

The darkness drops again; but now I know

That twenty centuries of stony sleep

Were vexed to nightmare by a rocking cradle,

And what rough beast, its hour come round at last,

Slouches towards Bethlehem to be born?

There is a lot to love in that poem but the words that haunt me are at the end of the first stanza: 'The best lack all conviction, while the worst / Are full of passionate intensity'. Is this a statement of fact or a definition? Is it a withering criticism of our political leaders or a paean to the power of doubt? I don't know what Yeats thought but I think that passionate intensity can be a good thing. I think that one of the dangers that politicians, especially centrist politicians, face is a tendency to boring pragmatism, to dispassionate realism, and that they therefore lose out to the loud voices of extremism when, in fact, making the world a better place is something that we can all be passionate about, even if we disagree on how it should be done. And there, maybe, is the danger that the worst in Yeats' poem fall into: those full of passionate intensity have in many cases lost the ability to disagree, or at least to respect those with whom they disagree. They are so convinced of their own passions that they can't accept they might be wrong, so identified with their own viewpoint that any criticism is personal.

I would like to suggest a stone-balancing act – a cognitive dissonance. Can we be full of passionate doubt?

Passionate doubt might sound like a contradiction – that, of course, is why it fits into today's assembly. How can you be passionate about something you doubt? Well, I think that we can and, moreover, if we are to improve the world and maintain peace then I think we must. We should stand up for our beliefs, we should express them passionately and enthusiastically, we should bang our fists on the table as we argue our point, and we should do those things not because we believe but because we doubt, not to browbeat our audience but to provoke discussion, argument, dissent. The more passionate we are about something, the more we believe the truth of what we say, then the more we should welcome challenge and criticism, because either we are right and our cause can take it or we are wrong and really need to change our cause.

I am not sure passionate doubt links nicely into scholarship – loyal dissent is a more useful idea day-to-day in the school – but as you look out into the wider world, as you think about what causes you will put time and energy into, as you consider what career paths are worthy of your talents, I urge you to develop passionate doubt. If we don't want things to fall apart, if we want to build a better society, then we need a centre that holds and we need to find a way for the best to be filled with passionate intensity without becoming the worst. I am not saying it is easy – we watched the Lyme Regis stone-balancer working for an hour holding a single, sea-worn rock on its end, gently shifting the centre of gravity until he felt it directly over the rock below and was able to remove his hand. In fact, whenever I have tried to replicate his work I have found that the point of balance is one I can only find with conscious readjustment – I can't remove my hand but instead need to keep it there to give constant nudges. Stone-balancing, like cognitive dissonance, loyal dissent and passionate doubt, is clearly something that takes practice.

We have never been a community of agreement – debate and discussion are at the heart of what we do. Students are encouraged to ask hard questions of their teachers (a proposition that can be challenging as the person in front of the class – no matter how broad and deep your own knowledge, you need to be ready to put your hands up, accept that you don't know and offer to find out for next lesson), and I hold termly meetings where staff are encouraged to come and question my decisions – or suggest better ones. However, this was a time of growing partisanship in politics and, as well as addressing a misconception that some of our students had acquired (that questioning was all that was required for scholarship and that learning was, therefore, irrelevant), I wanted to create a framework for students to respect views with which they disagreed.

Loyal dissent (a venerable tenet of Westminster School) and passionate doubt (I think an original coinage) are useful ideas that have gained a toehold in our lexicon, but I think the first time I really felt that these messages had made their way through to the student body, and had overcome the chasm between assembly rhetoric and quotidian practice, was in January 2020 (with our sixth cohort). I had assembled the leaders of the big student societies (debaters of issues to do with race, sexuality, gender, religion and social action) for a morning's conference entitled 'Kindness and Scholarship', kindly compered by a vicar I had sat next to at one of the abbey dinners. The most striking thing (in a morning of rather wonderful students talking about how they could make the community stronger and kinder) was when the two leaders of Intelligent Believing spoke. By 2020, Intelligent Believing had developed a fairly large membership from three main groups: Christians, Muslims and atheists (other religious views are held by smaller proportions of the school community), and the leadership was therefore split between one Christian student and one Muslim. They explained that Year 12 students were often excited by the prospect of attending this society, thinking that they would soon set the other side to rights, but found that this approach didn't work. It couldn't work, would never work. What new students eventually realised was that the discussions weren't debates where the idea was to convince the other side that you were right and they were wrong, but real discussions in which you asked questions to understand their thinking more clearly. A mathematician might say that they were working from different sets of axioms but could still appreciate each other's logical deductions.

Back in Remembrance 2016 we didn't have this insight, loyal dissent was a concept still locked away at Westminster School, and passionate doubt still a glimmer in the corner of my eye. We were, however, faced with three problems. Firstly, our original students, our link to 2014, had left us in the summer. They had gone through a unique experience of being part of setting up the school and they left deep imprints in the ethos, but they were now on their way. Some of them had done very well, overachieving on what might have been expected of them based on previous performance; and a few had underachieved (some of these I have caught up with later – quite often I am told that they now understand what I was getting at and that they had learned from Harris Westminster, it had just taken them a bit longer than we might have hoped). The second problem was that, inevitably, we had another new year group to bring into the school, to develop, to whom to explain the ethos (hopefully doing so more clearly and logically than we had two years previously so that a higher proportion would pick it up within the twenty-two months of sixth-form) – a year group that brought our student number to over 500 (a big increase from the 138 we started with!). The third problem was that Ofsted were on their way.

Ofsted have the remarkable privilege and remarkable challenge of inspecting schools: of spending a few days on site, visiting lessons, speaking to teachers and students, reading documents, and trying to come up with an intelligent, incisive and objective view of the quality of education provided. Their words and judgements carry great weight and so an impending visit is inevitably the cause for stress. We did our best to concentrate that stress in my office: that I would take their judgements personally and be deeply concerned to make as good an impression as possible was inevitable; that the senior team would need to do a great deal of the preparation was unavoidable; but we aimed to keep the list of things that classroom teachers were 'doing for Ofsted' to a minimum and hoped to make the experience all but invisible to students. How successful we were in this I am not in a position to judge, except to say that we got through it without a mutiny.

Our greatest concern was that the tacit and implicit content of our curriculum, where we taught students what to do by example and action rather than slogan, would not necessarily be visible to an inspector and that our jargon, useful as it was to us for communication within the school, would require a significant glossary if it weren't to be confusing and distracting to the inspectors. We therefore prepared, in Remembrance term 2016 (our seventh term of existence and thus the time laid down in the laws of the Medes and Persians for inspection of a new school), for the inspection by tightening up our paperwork, checking classes for consistency and being a bit more explicit in our messaging, particularly on British values – the catchphrase of the moment. In preparation for this we received a great deal of support from the Harris Federation (who had been through it all a million times before, although possibly not with such an idiosyncratic and high profile school) and a welcome understanding from Westminster School (who understood the importance of the exercise and were impressively tolerant of our requests/demands).

Ofsted came and went, as they were bound to do, and they made their judgement, which was briefly gratifying but ultimately of far less concern than the qualifications gained by the students (which, as we often tell them, are of far less import than the learning they have actually acquired). It is, of course, easy to be blasé when you get the results you want (a fact that I should probably make more of – an assembly for the future, maybe). We then had the job of getting back to our ethos and smoothing over the bumps that had come up whilst we were looking forward to the inspection.

Nuance (A Dinosaur Joke Disguised as an Assembly) – 12 October 2016

Before I start today, I would like to share with those of you who share my appreciation of all things dinosaurial a joke; those of you who find giant reptilians offensive or boring will, I am afraid, have to tolerate my amusement. The question I would like to put to you is: why do you never hear a pterodactyl in the toilet? The answer I will come back to later.

Last week, as you will recall, we had a visit from Ofsted. During that inspection I felt enormously privileged to be part of Harris Westminster. It was a wonderful feeling to know that everyone in the building was working together, doing their bit to show off the school in the best possible light, and when the inspectors were leaving they asked specifically for me to thank all the students they'd spoken to and all the staff they'd had meetings with or whose lessons they'd seen, so thank you. Actually, the impressive thing for me was what was going on when the inspectors weren't there, and I would like to say thank you to everyone who was working hard last week but who barely came across the inspectors, because another thing they said when they left was that Harris Westminster was notable for being a community of scholars – and a community is something that you feel rather than see and taste rather than hear. It is in all the little interactions, in the confidence we have in each other, in the way we look after each other. It is something that every single one of us contributes to, so thank you all.

I love the phrase 'community of scholars', and I think it describes perfectly Harris Westminster at its best. It is a privilege for me to be part of such a community. It is a privilege to be amongst people who read widely – to be able to drop literary allusions and fragments of poetry into conversation and to see by the glint in someone's eye that they have caught and enjoyed it. It is a privilege to be able to sit down to lunch in the canteen and to have a rollicking good argument as to whether politics or philosophy or English are worth studying, for each of the diners to have views and to be able to defend them fiercely. Of course, the answer is that all three are – or we wouldn't be teaching them at Harris Westminster Sixth Form. It is a privilege to be able to teach a maths lesson or deliver an assembly sprinkled with dinosaurs and to find students who are amused without being distracted – who can extract the important facts from the entertaining ideas.

Some of you will be writing personal investigations as part of your Pre-U studies, and I am told on the highest authority that the best personal investigations are niche, nuanced and nerdy. Ideally, they should be enquiries into something small so that you are able to go deep; they should be painstakingly precise and show an utter fascination with the topic that appears to consume the author to the exclusion of all else; and they should be clever – and they should assume that the reader is also clever. Rather than appealing to simplistic tastes and black-and-white arguments, they should trust the reader to have a well-developed scholarly palate that enables them to distinguish between a palette of many greys.

I think that at our best Harris Westminster is also niche, nuanced and nerdy. And if our nuance has failed us over the last weeks, I would like to assure you that it was not your palate that we were questioning but that of any putative inspector. I fear that some of you think that we may have been heavy handed in our handling of the anti-radicalisation agenda and our teaching about female genital mutilation (FGM), forced marriage and other such dangers. I think that some of you have also come to suspect that we have only taught you such things because we are obliged to by the government and that they have no place in the curriculum of a truly scholarly institution.

The time has come for me to be frank – not in the way that most of the characters in the rather marvellous children's book, *Augie and the Green Knight*,[3] are Frank, nor in the manner of Charlemagne's forces, but simply I feel that I should explain myself. There are two goals here and I don't want the less important one to get in the way of the more important. The important thing is to educate you about these things that are going on in the world. We want to keep you safe from radical ideas, to give you the tools to think through your

---

3   Z. Weinersmith, *Augie and the Green Knight* (Brooklyn: Breadpig, 2015).

beliefs and to challenge assertions made by others. We want to let you know about the awful things that jerks are doing to people, partly so that you can be warned about them yourself but more so that you can help to keep others safe. And here, I think, some of you are approaching these messages wrong-headedly.

FGM, for example, is a terrible thing and one that I would like to think is far from the experience of any of you, but if I actually let myself believe that I would be wrong. It is estimated that there are 137,000 FGM survivors in the UK and many of those will be in London, that over 1,000 girls each year are born to mothers who had FGM, which is a terrible risk factor for those babies being likely to face the same thing, and that over 100 incidents of FGM take place each year on UK soil.[4] This may be barbaric, it may be unpleasant, but it is not irrelevant: it is taking place right here, right now, and if you think it must be happening in some other part of London, stop and think. It is about a kilometre from HWSF Towers to Charing Cross station. I walk there and back each day – it takes about twelve minutes. Imagine a circle with a radius of a kilometre around your house: how many homes are there? How many neighbourhoods do you cross? How many communities are there that are very different from yours? London is an amazingly vibrant and multicultural city – don't kid yourself that these things are taking place far away: they could easily be going on within a twelve-minute walk of your house.

That is the important thing: that as a community of scholars we don't become so obsessed with each other's arguments that we forget the physical needs and dangers that surround us and those we meet. In the Simon and Garfunkel song 'I Am a Rock', Paul claims to be shielded in the armour of books and poetry, safe from the hurt others can cause, but the I in that verse is no scholar – better are John Donne's words:

> *No man is an island, entire of itself; every man is a piece of the continent, a part of the main. If a clod be washed away by the sea, Europe is the less, as well as if a promontory were, as well as if a manor of thy friend's or thine own were: any man's death diminishes me, because I am involved in mankind, and therefore never send to know for whom the bell tolls; it tolls for thee.[5]*

4   A. J. Macfarlane and E. Dorkenoo, *Prevalence of Female Genital Mutilation in England and Wales: National and Local Estimates* (London: City University London in association with Equality Now, 2015). Available at: http://www.trustforlondon.org.uk/publications/prevalence-female-genital-mutilation-england-and-wales-national-and-local-estimates.

5   J. Donne, *Devotions Upon Emergent Occasions; Together with Death's Duel* (Ann Arbor, MI: University of Michigan Press, 1959 [1623]), sec. XVII: Meditation. Available at: http://www.gutenberg.org/ebooks/23772.

The less important thing is that I didn't want our amazing school to get marked down because you didn't answer correctly in response to Ofsted's questions, and so we have used the government's language. British values is one that particularly sticks because although those I have spoken about before are values that are held within Britain, they are not especially British rather than Swiss or Canadian or Australian, and nor are they the only tenets to which we would hold, but that is the rather clumsy, un-nuanced term that the government uses and so the term that you need to use when talking to their representatives. I would have liked to think that I could have nuanced those two needs rather more cleverly, but it turns out that I would once more be wrong. I shall apologise and try to be more clever in the future. By the way, did you like the use of palate and palette earlier in the piece? I had to rewrite that sentence three times before I was happy with it.

Finally, for those of you who have been clinging on in the hope of a punchline, I must remind you of the one fact that everyone knows about pterodactyls: they have a silent p.

This assembly is an addition to the collection of slightly rude things I have said in Westminster Abbey (I don't know if anyone else has such a collection – I am certainly interested in claiming the world record). One of the reasons I am circumspect is that I am aware that the audience is not restricted to the school community (whom I would trust not to be offended by such things whether or not they were sufficiently childish to giggle at my jokes): the abbey is a very large building and as we have our assemblies in the lantern and quire, there is a vast acreage out of sight where the abbey employees are preparing for the day's events and visitors. I don't imagine they are listening carefully to my words, but they can definitely hear them – the amplification and acoustics are excellent.

That assembly came about as a result of the effective working of the community of scholars to which I paid heartfelt tribute. The reason that I felt I had to unpick some of what we had said, to explain some of our decisions, was that students had told me that they had felt rather patronised by our approach in the weeks before Ofsted came. That the students had high expectations of our communication and that they felt able to tell me when we fell below the required standard are both examples of a community that is working effectively, that is both critical (in that it demands much) and scrupulous (in that it is careful to work for improvement).

Final Thoughts

- When you have a position of authority you can get a lot of mileage from being ever so slightly naughty – it is good to be able to laugh at yourself.

- Communities don't happen automatically – they are built brick by brick. If you want a kind school, you have to both be kind and exhort others to follow your example.

- Culture isn't permanent – it is eroded as personnel change (as is inevitable in a school). Induction for new staff and students is probably more important than you think it is (certainly more important than I did).

- Finding the sweet spot for a school is a process of continual correction, unless you happen to be a genius for stone-balancing.

Chapter 7

Hard Times

As we built our community of kind and scrupulous scholars, we lived through a time in which the wider world seemed increasingly unkind and unscholarly. Politics appeared to fracture, with moderate views getting polarised and immoderate views gaining credence; terrorism troubled the streets of London; and Islamophobia made things difficult for young women in headscarves and anyone with a Middle Eastern appearance. The challenge for us was how to face this world and how to prepare students to go out into it without compromising our ideals. How could we, as scholars, hold firm to our goals of kindness and equality, whilst accepting that not everyone shared our vision and guarding ourselves from those who might take advantage of us?

This wasn't a challenge that was long in arriving: before our first week was out, there was an incident after school in which one of the unpleasant consequences of our pavement being a busy London street became clear. Two female students were chatting in the September sunshine as a group of tourists went by. One of them felt a tap and asked, 'Did you just pat my bottom?' 'No!' replied the other, shocked, 'Of course not.'

They came back into school, we called the police who arrived swiftly (one of the advantages of our location is the proximity of large numbers of police) and before long had picked up the offender before he had made it out of Parliament Square. The incident passed off fairly quickly (and the two students became firm friends), but it made us think about the challenges of safeguarding students. Inside the building we have ID cards and different coloured lanyards (crimson for the school community, teachers and staff, except for the senate who wear gold; green for Disclosure and Barring Service checked volunteers; blue for visitors who need to be accompanied; red for students who forget their own; nobody should be in school without one – a quick and easy way to identify strangers in a large group of people who don't know each other well and have no uniform). Outside, however, to and from school and at lunchtime, there is no such protection.

It was November before this issue crystallised into something I wanted to say in assembly. Another incident with a student, this time on the way to school, was the catalyst: a student of Turkish heritage had been wearing a white poppy (a symbol adopted by several of the school community as an affirmation of pacifism) and had been verbally abused by a commuter on the Tube for not wearing a red one. He mistook her for a Muslim and roundly berated her for all the failings that he attributed to the religion, as well as for a lack of respect and patriotism by not supporting what he considered to be the core message of the season. Meanwhile, we had a domestic issue to address.

Symbols and Jerks – 10 November 2014

In today's assembly I am going to talk about symbols and jerks, which is quite a surprise to me as I was planning something rather different. Still, we work with what we have, so here goes.

Symbols come in many shapes and sizes: there are religious symbols, like the crosses that adorn this church; there are national symbols, like the Union Jack that flies over the Victoria Tower over there; there are symbols you can wear, like the uniform of the Horse Guards I saw on my way in this morning; symbols you perform, for example the haka; and symbols like the coats of arms in Dean's Yard that are carved in stone to last hundreds of years.

Some symbols have straightforward meanings, like the picture of a bald person standing somewhat splay-leggedly that has represented blessed relief when I have found myself in a strange building after over-indulging in lemonade – talking of which I do need a word about the school toilets … Later. Most symbols, however, are less clearly defined. I am always interested in the symbolism of chinking glasses and saying 'Cheers!' before a meal. What do people mean when they do that? What do I mean when I do that? Well, you will not, I think, be surprised to learn that I have thought about this a bit and that I do know what *I* mean, even if I am a bit confused about everyone else. For reference, should it ever come up, when I chink glasses with someone at a social gathering I mean 'I'm glad you're here'. Actually, it doesn't much matter with glass chinking what everyone else means; we can all have slightly different understandings of what the symbol means and still enjoy our time together. This is not the case with all symbols: the haka is said by the New Zealanders to be a symbolic dance of cultural respect and team bonding. To me – and, I think, to the teams playing against them – it is a symbol of dominance and threat. The haka, being a sporting symbol, is rather harmless, if annoying, but it is similar in many ways to the symbolic Orange marches in Northern Ireland, where one group of people marches through the city symbolising their cultural heritage and history but are seen by another group of people to be a threat and an attempt to display dominance. The marches have frequently spilled over into violence because of this clash of symbols (that is not my joke, I purloined it).

The only way to avoid this problem is to use the symbol as a personal display – to perform the haka in your dressing room, to march around the kitchen, to put your cross on a chain around your neck and wear it beneath your thermal vest, to fly the flag in a cupboard. Once you bring a symbol out into the world it has at least two meanings – one to the displayer and one to the observer. Most of the time this will be fine, but it is much less likely to be fine if one (or more) of those people are jerks. Now, there are two things you should know about jerks. One – there are jerks in this world. It is a sad fact but it is true, and neither you nor I nor David Cameron can do anything to change that. Out there, there are people whose aim in life is to get their own way and to please themselves at the expense of others. Some of them cut you up when you are navigating roundabouts; some avoid taxes; some hurl abuse at those weaker, poorer and less well-connected than themselves; and some start fights, steal, rape or murder. The second thing you should know is that the problem with jerks is that they are jerks: there is no point in saying, 'Well, they shouldn't do that' or 'I shouldn't have to change what I do because of them.' You are right, but they are jerks and you can't change that. Actually, I have been unfair. Individual jerks can change – in fact, I think we are all capable of behaving like jerks, realising our mistake and trying to avoid doing it again. At least, I hope it is all of us because it is certainly me. Individual jerks can change, they can even stop being jerks, but what you can't change is the existence of jerks. No matter how good your argument, no matter how reasonable your position, there will be some jerks out there wanting to take advantage of you for their own amusement.

Jerks and symbols came together last week when one of our students got verbally abused for wearing a poppy. Wearing the poppy was a perfectly reasonable thing to do, but sadly the person looking at it was a jerk. The poppy is an interesting symbol. It wasn't until I lived in the United States that I realised that it is primarily a British symbol, and it wasn't until the England football team wanted to wear them on their shirts a couple of years ago that I realised it could be considered a political symbol. Until then, I always thought that it was an international, neutral remembrance of the dead and that the closest it could come to a political statement was that it said, 'It's probably not a great thing when millions of people kill each other.'

Of course, the poppy is more complicated than that. Even our idea of remembrance is complicated: last week I spoke about remembering the sacrifice made for us and being inspired by their lost lives to make the most of the ones we have. That is quite a big idea to be summed up by one flower – and not everyone has the same idea. Some people see poppies as glorifying war, or supporting the politicians who choose to go to war, or celebrating the victory of the Allied powers in the First or Second World War, or in some way supporting soldiers who are currently serving. There are white poppies that send a different message: I think that the official message is that they commemorate all deaths in wartime rather than just servicemen and women, but I am not sure that is always how they will be understood by people seeing them. To wear something other than a red poppy is quite a political statement, which is interesting because normally it is the wearing of a symbol that is the political statement, but if someone goes on television at the beginning of November they are expected to wear a poppy and anyone who doesn't (for example, Jon Snow) is inviting criticism. There are people who think that wearing a poppy should be compulsory, although what kind of symbol that would be I don't like to think – certainly not a symbol of freedom.

So, what do I want you to take away with you today? Firstly, I want you to think about the symbols you display: I want you to think about what they mean to you and also what they might mean to others. I would also like you to consider that displaying a symbol is not a very sensible act of courage: I want you to be brave, to be bold, to take on the world and change it, but I would like to remind you of my Granny's tea tray – we need the courage to change the things we can, the serenity to accept the things we cannot change and the wisdom to know the difference. Symbols of whatever kind have never changed anything, at least not for the better – they are definitely able to make things worse, upset people and start fights. Save your courage for those situations where you can make a difference, although the poppy reminds us that it is not always easy to identify. Should Britain have gone to war in 1914? Did those deaths make a difference? Did those battles need to be fought? Maybe another thing the poppy symbolises is that it is difficult to be sure, that the only thing we know is that those deaths were a terrible waste.

Finally, and this is really important, please, please, please don't be a jerk. Stand up for the rights of others, by all means, but don't start fights to defend your own. Think about how other people see things – what they need, want and deserve. And whatever you do, whatever the provocation, no matter what the circumstances, don't put paper towels down the toilets – use the bins.

This assembly introduced a new word to the Harris Westminster jargon: jerk; it was one that would prove useful as the years went by (as you will have seen in 'Being Kind'). I find it a useful word, and its status as the worst insult that I can (officially) think of means that within it I can express all the contempt I have for certain actions without saying anything that could be misconstrued were it heard by those who aren't part of the community. The tourist who assaulted a young woman on her way out of school, the commuter who harangued another on her way in, the student who put paper towels down the toilet, they were all jerks, and the trouble with jerks is that, until they change their ways, they are jerks.

By saying jerks, we also cover up the fact that some of the people whose aim in life is to get their own way are actually terrorist murderers and that there are worse things that might happen to us than being shouted at on a train (worse even than having to mop a flooded toilet). Between the opening of the school in September 2014 and the writing of this book in the summer of 2020, there have been a number of terrorist incidents: London Bridge has been the location of two (both tragic, one with a hint of comedy as the assailant was overcome with a narwhal tusk), the Bataclan in Paris, and the Manchester Arena. Each time someone thought their cause was more important than the lives of strangers, and each time we as a community have had to stand up and say that they were wrong, whilst registering that our peace was fragile and our security illusory. There have been days when I have felt that to run a school in central Westminster was to walk around with a target painted on your back, just waiting for someone to notice.

That feeling too, though, is an illusion. We are, as we found out that evening in September 2014, in the most densely policed patch of the country; our building fronts on to the open street but our doors are secure. We are, as we should be, alert and aware, but not afraid.

The closest we have come to an incident was on 22 March 2017 when my PA came into my office to tell me that the news said shots had been fired on Westminster Bridge – 400 metres from the school on the far side of Parliament Square. The news websites were unclear about what had happened – the full story of an attacker driving his car into pedestrians, killing four, before breaking into the Palace of Westminster and fatally stabbing PC Keith Palmer came out later. At the time we went into lockdown, with the front doors and rear entrance closed, a register taken and contact made with trips that had gone out that day. Before long we were fielding phone calls from parents who had also seen the news and were worried. Once we had made contact and were sure that none of our groups had got caught up in it, we asked students to text their parents to reassure them. It was a good drill: we wrote up what we did, along with a series of improvements, and have practised it at regular intervals (sometimes adding in the refinement of asking students to hide within their classrooms). But, in fact, we worked out that by the time the shots had been fired it was all over: the dangerous period was the eighty-two seconds before.

Westminster Bridge was the geographically closest that terrorism has come, but the attack that concerned me most wasn't even in the UK – it was the shooting that took place on 7 January 2015 in Paris – and, although it took place on the streets we had walked down with our Paris trip three weeks earlier, it wasn't our adjacency that worried me but the response. Lots of people responded by saying 'Je suis Charlie' and I didn't want our impressionable, principled students to feel that they were expected or morally obliged to follow suit. I felt that I should say something in assembly (where else), but quite what to say and how to frame it was a more complex question.

Charlie Hebdo – 12 January 2015

I often start my assemblies with a piece of whimsy – a story that I hope will entertain you before I link seamlessly, or not so seamlessly, into my main point which I hope you will take away with you. Today, though, I am going to start with a story which is neither whimsical nor entertaining because I am going to tell you what happened in Paris on Wednesday 7 January 2015. At 11.30am a black car stopped on a street in central Paris, north of the Seine and about 400 metres from the Place des Vosges – one of the places we visited on our trip to Paris last month. Two masked men, dressed in black and carrying Kalashnikov assault rifles, got out of the car and burst into one of the office buildings. In a moment of farce in an otherwise bleak story, they then realised they had chosen the wrong building and burst out again, moved down the road and burst into another building. This time they were in the right place and had found the offices of *Charlie Hebdo* – a French satirical magazine (*Private Eye* is the closest British equivalent). They shot the caretaker and made their way to the editorial offices where the main meeting of the week was taking place. Once there, they shouted 'God is greatest' and called out the names of the journalists they wanted to kill. After achieving their goals they left the building. By the time the black car left that street eleven people were dead – eight journalists, the policeman guarding one of them, the caretaker and a visitor – but the violence wasn't over. On their escape journey they came across another policeman, a Muslim, whom they shot and wounded. As he lay on the ground, one of the gunmen got out of the car and shot him again, taking the death toll to twelve.

An event like this raises two questions: why did it happen, and how should we respond? Before I begin I should admit that I don't have the answers. I am not in the position of being able to talk you through it like a mathematical theorem and come up with a conclusion clear and inviolable. Instead, I am going to tell you what I think and you can accept it or challenge it depending on your own thoughts and beliefs. Challenges and beliefs will come up again in what I have to say – both are powerful ideas, and the combination can be dangerous.

How should we respond? Do we join the Parisian crowds in their cries of 'Je suis Charlie', identifying ourselves with the cartoonists? Do we seize on the religious aspect of the attack, noting that the gunmen shouted 'God is greatest' and seemed to be motivated by anger at depictions of the Prophet Muhammad in the cartoons? Do we remind ourselves that the problem with jerks is that they are jerks and try to avoid being jerks ourselves, meanwhile hoping that it was an isolated event, a one-off? Do we say that the cartoonists brought it on themselves – that making fun of religion was the wrong thing to do and that to some extent they deserved it? Let me start off by saying that murder is a crime, it is wrong, it is never the right answer and nobody deserves it. This is the 'they're jerks' response which is, I think, right but inadequate in this situation. Behind the dreadful actions there is anger, and if we don't understand the anger we can't be sure it is a one-off event and we can't make sure we avoid behaving badly when angered ourselves.

The anger does seem to come from religion. The magazine published some cartoons that the murderers felt were making fun of something that was sacred to them. What do we think about making fun of people? How do we react when people make fun of us? Mocking people, making fun of them or something important to them isn't a nice thing to do – put like that it sounds awfully like bullying. And yet, that was, is, the trade of *Charlie Hebdo*, so why are so many people identifying with them? Why is it so clear to the people of France that the journalists' right to mock and make fun should be protected? Why don't we just make a law against it like we do in school: no bullying?

There are a lot of questions there. Let us start with freedom of speech, particularly with what happens if you don't have it. Without freedom of speech the government is in the position of telling people that there are some things they can't criticise. However that starts, whatever first appears on the list, eventually some government will put itself on the list, and when the government can't be criticised then you can't have an effective opposition – a real alternative choice – and so you no longer have a democracy. We can't pass a law to stop people being criticised or mocked, but that doesn't mean it is the right thing to do: something can be legal but doing it can still make you a jerk.

I don't read *Charlie Hebdo* and so I am not in a position to judge whether or not the magazine is a jerk: it may be, but I think there are times when making fun of other people is the right thing to do. People in power, prime ministers, kings, archbishops, principals are all capable of letting the power go to their head, of thinking that they are more important than they really are, of thinking that they are right because of who they are rather than because of the quality of their argument. They are also in danger of only listening to people who agree with them, of employing yes-men, of disregarding the opposition as ideologically wrong. They need someone to point out their mistakes, to bring them back to earth, to poke fun of them. Traditionally this was the role of the court fool: to say something wise and apposite and then to bonk themselves on the head with a pig's bladder and trip over their own feet. Everyone laughs, the fool is clearly no threat to the king, but the point has been made. That role has now been taken by satirists, cartoonists and journalists; it is an important role but it is not a safe one. If the king feels too threatened, the fool loses his head.

One of the cartoonists killed on Wednesday, Stéphane Charbonnier, had been living under police protection for some time because of death threats made against him. He knew the risks and yet he carried on mocking those more powerful than himself, the pen against the sword. He is quoted as saying, 'I'd rather die standing than live on my knees'[1] – as a result of which a Shania Twain song has been running round my head for the past week. 'Black Eyes, Blue Tears', a fairly ordinary song from her 1997 album *Come On Over*, had lain dormant in my brain for over a decade, but you can't listen to a CD for six months on continuous loop without suffering long-term effects, and I wondered why this Parisian cartoonist was quoting a Canadian country singer, but it turns out that, unsurprisingly, they were both quoting a Mexican revolutionary, Emiliano Zapata: 'I'd rather die on my feet than live on my knees.'[2] It is a brave choice and one that Charbonnier knew he was making. I am not sure that all those who say 'Je suis Charlie' are ready to make the same sacrifice.

It is not just kings who are powerful – secular power. Religions and those who lead them are also powerful and need challenging, but the difficulty is that religions are important to ordinary people. If you make fun of David Cameron you might upset him, or his mum, which may be unkind but you know who you are attacking – you can predict the response. If you make fun of Jesus, Buddha or Muhammad, you are in danger of upsetting or angering millions of people – too many to keep an eye on, too many to predict. Is religion, then, the problem? Richard Dawkins says it is and would ban it completely if he could. I agree that it is a problem but not that banning it is the solution.

The story of what happened in Paris is familiar to me, although on a different scale. I have often been asked to pick up the pieces when someone has been verbally bullied and has lashed out physically because they have felt powerless to engage with words, where they have had no answers. Violence is never acceptable but in this situation it is not that unusual. The solution is for us to

1   X. Ternisien, 'A "Charlie Hebdo", on n'a "pas l'impression d'égorger quelqu'un avec un feutre"', *Le Monde* (20 September 2012). Available at: https://www.lemonde.fr/actualite-medias/article/2012/09/20/je-n-ai-pas-l-impression-d-egorger-quelqu-un-avec-un-feutre_1762748_3236.html.

2   Quoted in L. D. Nieto, 'Toward a Chicano Liberation Theology'. In G. H. Anderson and T. F. Stransky (eds), *Liberation Theologies in North America and Europe*. Mission Trends, no. 4 (New York: Paulist Press, 1979), pp. 277–282 at p. 281.

challenge ourselves. Challenge your own beliefs, your own words, your own actions: do they make sense or are they ridiculous? Do you know why you do what you do? Do the reasons satisfy you? If you have challenged yourself enough then nobody else's words can hurt you: they can raise questions but you will have the answers. Individually this is tough – we all have areas of ourselves where we think and behave irrationally, often out of habit. Institutionally it is even harder but it is equally important: if we sign up to a nation, a religion or a group then we need to be prepared to challenge it, to ask hard questions about those shared beliefs so that when the challenge comes from the outside we can answer it with calm words rather than angry violence.

The events of last week were dreadful. The murderers were cowards and criminals. Hopefully this kind of event will remain a rarity but my advice to you – which, of course, you should feel free to challenge – is to challenge yourself unmercifully, but to be careful when you challenge or, worse, mock others. Sometimes it is safe and sometimes it is the right thing to do but it is never both: mocking the powerless is bullying; mocking the powerful is dangerous.

I think we got the response to *Charlie Hebdo* right – the mixture of specific and immediate messages with more nuanced long-term issues worked well. We were able to apply our ethos to get through the difficulties whilst reinforcing and building that same ethos. Two and a half years later we didn't do so well. On 14 June 2017, a fire broke out in the Grenfell Tower in North Kensington, four and a half miles from the school. The fire spread quickly through the flats and, despite the work of the London Fire Brigade, there were seventy-two fatalities, making it the most devastating domestic fire in the UK since the Second World War. As a school community we were not immediately affected – none of the seventy-two fatalities was a student, teacher, parent or sibling of the school. The most immediate concern for us was the A level physics exam that took place the next day: some of our students who lived nearby had been up all night working to help as best they could or worrying about friends or family and were now faced with one of the most challenging trials of their academic life. We supported them as well as we could, gave them all the flexibility that regulations allow and applied to the exam boards for special consideration. We also joined in with local schools to raise money for the immediate support of those made homeless with a 'Green for Grenfell' day, but what we didn't do was pause to reflect. We didn't do an assembly on Grenfell, we didn't allow it to percolate into our ethos, and so our ethos supported us less than it should or could have done.

The summer exams period is a manic one at Harris Westminster, because the Year 13 is half the student body and because each student is taking three or four A levels, each with at least two papers: there are a lot of exam students. They are obviously quite focused on the trials and tribulations of assessment and the senior team are rushed off their feet trying to ensure that everything goes smoothly (a task rendered significantly more tricky by the small number of students who misread their timetable, oversleep or otherwise need to be reminded by phone call that they have an exam that started five minutes ago and if they are not in the building sharpish they won't be getting a grade). The Year 12s, meanwhile, are looking forward to university applications and their teachers are juggling Year 13 exam preparation with UCAS mentoring and their ongoing teaching load. In the midst of all this business we didn't give Grenfell the time and reflection it should have had. I hope we would do better now.

The most difficult assembly I have given is one I don't have a script for: you can't read it because I don't know exactly what I said. In April 2015, we returned from the Easter break to find an answerphone message telling us that Yurij, our physics teacher, had died. He had been spending the vacation back in Canada and the message was from his father letting us know. We told the students in an assembly: it wasn't the moment for flights of oratory or clever allusions and so I just went to the front and talked a little bit, trusting in our shared vocabulary and view of the world to give me the words I needed to say. The only line I can remember is that I said Mr Petlura would always be one of us, always be a member of the Harris Westminster community, a truth that we recall every year with the awarding of a prize in his name for music in the community. Yurij's main love other than physics was music, and his playing of the bandura – a Ukrainian stringed instrument – at the staff Christmas party was a highlight of his time with us.

In happy times we imagine that the friends and opportunities we have will always be there; in tough times we think of our past waiting for us to return. Ambition drives us ever onwards to new challenges. When we think about legacy our focus is on that moment of leaving, as if what we leave will remain as it was, frozen in aspic, improved by our genius but changing no more. This is, of course, an illusion (as I am reminded whenever I meet alumni – they have inevitably grown and matured and become even more impressive than they were when I knew them); just as we change with the passing seasons so do those we knew. People change, things change, time moves on.

Tempus Fugit – 19 September 2016

This morning I will be musing on a music festival, summing up the summer and thinking wistfully about wisdom. What is more, as a break from twentieth century English poets, my quotations come from a genius of 1960s folk-pop and from a rather special tea tray.

Firstly, I would like to talk about the Last Night of the Proms – not, as you will recall, one of the fundamental British values but an annual event that invariably causes me to reflect upon them. The Proms, or Promenade Concerts, are a music festival that takes place each summer in the Albert Hall. They are the brainchild of Sir Henry Wood, who feared that classical music was becoming elitist and wanted to bring it to the masses with amazing concerts priced so that everyone could go. Every summer, a series of top-flight orchestras and choirs perform new pieces and great stalwarts of the musical canon to two halves of an audience: the first, the great and good, sit comfortably in the posh seats and the second, standing in what in a rock concert would be called the mosh pit – the real audience who paid just £6 to hear the music and aren't bothered by the lack of seats – they are the prommers.

At the end of this amazing summer of concerts comes the last night. The first half of the last night is a concert in line with all the others, but the second half follows a strict routine of patriotic songs and flag waving: a fantasia of British sea songs, 'Rule, Britannia!', 'Land of Hope and Glory' and 'Jerusalem'. At first sight it looks like a most un-British exhibition of xenophobic nationalism, but when you look more closely you see that, unlike most patriotic flag-waving events, everyone is welcome and, crucially, they can bring their own flag. It is not just Union Jacks but crosses of St George and St Andrew, Welsh dragons,

Irish tricolours, Canadian maple leaves, French, Italian, German and Jamaican flags, banners from the EU and the US, from Australia and Argentina. This amazing outburst of patriotism comes not at some nationalist celebration of being the best but to mark the end of the largest classical music festival in the world.

If you haven't watched it in the past, well, you have missed this year's, but I commend to you watching next year's celebration on the telly (and, since the Albert Hall is just three stops on the Underground, you might like to take in one of the earlier proms for real – £6 is a bit of a bargain). I watch the last night every year and sing along with gusto, if not tune, and then, at the end, a lump comes to my throat because, when the trumpets fall silent, the prommers lead the audience in a rendition of 'Auld Lang Syne' – a song of farewell – and the festival comes to a close. It is rather poignant – the end of something special, the sense of people saying goodbye for another year and, after all that patriotic nonsense, I feel my mind travelling to the end of summer 1939 and the people who said goodbye to each other then, knowing that they might not meet again in 1940 because the Second World War had just broken out and the world had changed.

The Last Night of the Proms, for me, marks the official end of summer, and the fact that it is always a week after term starts gives the sense that I have managed to stretch the holidays out a little, but that I really have to face the fact that those glorious long days of reading, resting and revising are over and it is time to knuckle down to work. This brings me to the first of the quotations I promised: from the pen of Paul Simon, a memory of his time in England. Inspired by the summer of 1964 he wrote a short and simple song about a love affair starting with 'April, come she will,' and slipping through the months inexorably to its conclusion in September when the romance grows old and fades away.

Time hurries on and we now find ourselves in the third week of term, well into the swing of things. You should, by now, have your files organised and filling up: if you are still living on scraps of paper and folders then you are soon going to get lost in a drift of mixed up pages. You should, by now, have worked out your study timetable: if you are just snatching what minutes you need to meet deadlines then you are about to fall behind. You should, by now, have worked out how to use the library and have got a book to read on your commute: if you are still saying to yourself that you don't like reading or that the *Metro* is good enough then your cultural capital will soon be deficient.

Time hurries on, and at the end of this week we find we have earned our first exeat. An exeat is a thing of wonder, a time of glory, a treasure to be celebrated. On these golden occasions we find ourselves on a Saturday morning without school. How will you take advantage of this circumstance? An exeat is too rare an occasion to allow to slip by unmarked – it demands festivity. My exeats are marked by a lie-in until about 9.30am and then breakfast of black coffee and eggs with the paper. It may seem like a simple ritual to you, but it is a delightful comparison with the usual Saturday morning of 5.50am alarm, a mug of tea and a slice of toast.

Use your exeat wisely – make good decisions about your time. And this is when I peer in a headmasterly fashion over the top of my glasses: do not indulge too freely in the joys of lemonade. Using time wisely is an important skill whether your time is the inexorable tick of the school week, marked out by lesson changes and the chimes of Big Ben, or the unexpected (or long awaited) arrival of a half holiday – wisdom is a valuable attribute.

When I tell people I am from Sheffield they almost invariably remark that they wouldn't have guessed from my accent. This is because I don't have a Sheffield accent and that is because I am not really from Sheffield. I was born in Rochdale in Greater Manchester but my family moved south before I could walk and I went to nursery school in Surrey before we moved again, this time to Bolton. It was only when I started secondary school that we moved to Sheffield, since when I have lived in Oxford, Massachusetts, Swansea, Sydney, briefly in a basement in Paddington, Blackheath and now Sidcup.

I don't really come from anywhere, but as I grew up the one constant was my grandparents' house in North Wales. It was a large guest house on the edge of Snowdonia called Glasfryn, with three acres of land and an impressive collection of sheds – a vast kingdom for a small boy and one that seemed forever fixed and unchanging. I can recall the drive there from the nearest town, the turn in the lane, the shape of the gardens, the steepness of the stairs and the make of the camp beds in which we would sleep. We would go to Glasfryn twice a year with the whole family, and occasionally, as we grew up, we would leave the parental units at home and go alone. There was one time that my sister and I went to stay and at the end of the visit we wanted to buy a present for Granny to say thank you (for some reason this kind of affection always attached itself to Granny rather than Granpapy but I think, and hope, that they thought, as we did, that a present given to one was shared by the other). Fortunately, the nearby town was Conwy, a veritable tourist trap of cheap tat, and so we were able to find a tea tray with a suitable message. The tray became a fixture of Granny's kitchen and the words are fixed in my mind: 'Grant me the serenity to accept the things I cannot change, the courage to change the things I can and the wisdom to know the difference.' Despite an unscholarly lack of attribution this is not the original thought of the tea tray – in fact, these are the words of an American theologian called Reinhold Niebuhr. But that desire to commit courageously to the changes you can make, to accept peacefully that there are some that you can't, and to develop the understanding needed to direct your time and energy accurately is, for me, the wisdom of the tea tray.

The story comes with a sting. I thought Glasfryn would be there forever, that wherever my travels took me I would be able to return to Granny's kitchen and Granpapy's sheds, but I was wrong. Granny died when I was 17 and eventually Granpapy grew too old to look after himself and a large house, and so Glasfryn was sold. It is now more than a decade since I have visited Snowdonia. I hope another small boy has the opportunity to explore the fields and the sheds, but for me time has moved on, as it always does. Summers pass, new loves grow old, friends part not knowing whether they will meet again. We can't change that and must accept it serenely, but what we can do is direct the time we have, the now that lies before us, to make the changes we want to make, to take care of those we love and to fill with joy the times of celebration. That is wisdom.

To be able to share something real and close to your own heart is to make yourself vulnerable, and so it is not a privilege I take advantage of very often, but every time I have done so I have been rewarded with a positive response: students and staff coming up to me and saying that they liked what I said. Perhaps this is an indication that I should be personal more often, but I am not sure – I think there is a self-indulgence and a suggestion that my life is inherently interesting (rather than merely a story from which to draw lessons) that I shy away from. I think the rarity of the vulnerability makes it more special.

However, I think it is right to share a little bit, sometimes. Young people are inherently vulnerable; as a teacher, and especially as a principal, you are in a position of unequal power and if you stay shielded in your armour you put up a barrier where there should be a human connection. The trick, if you are really clever, of course, is to give enough of an impression of sharing to create the bond without ever making your real self the centre of attention. I have not mastered that one.

Final Thoughts

- However much we focus on good times, schools are communities in the real world and both national and personal tragedies will hit.

- Having a culture, a relationship between leaders, staff and students that can cope with tragedy is therefore an important goal.

- Reacting to news stories is an art: ignoring things that feel important to the community makes you feel distant; dwelling on the negatives is draining of time and energy.

- It is important to reflect on the times you make mistakes – leadership is hard and nobody gets it right all the time.

Parenthesis (2020)

It would be perverse to write this book in 2020 and not to mention how Harris Westminster coped with the coronavirus, even though we won't really know the outcomes for a long time yet as the economic and educational impact of lockdown and the emotional impact of bereavement becomes clear over months and years.

On 20 March 2020, schools in the UK were locked down, with students and teachers having to adapt to online learning and teaching. During the week before we had been forced by the depredations of sickness, vulnerability, shielding and isolation to reduce the school to one year group – sending the Year 12s home to be provided for online by those staff who were well but unable to come into school, whilst those of us in Steel House did our best to prepare the Year 13s for what looked inevitable.

Day by day over the previous few weeks we had watched death tolls increase and listened to convoluted advice on handwashing and shaking. With Spain and Italy on the same course and a few weeks ahead, we were able to predict what was coming and get ourselves ready. The two vice principals, Claire (promoted from assistant principal) and Al (who had joined the school on Nic's departure in 2016), had worked hard to prepare for online teaching: making sure that students and staff had the right equipment and access to the internet at home, and checking through the myriad details of Microsoft Teams – the vehicle that the federation IT team had chosen. (That team performed heroic feats of organisation and set up everything so that online school for almost fifty academies went smoothly.) I, meanwhile, found myself back in a 2014 world of new challenges each morning, new adaptations and new decisions to be made.

By the time lockdown was announced and my attention was turned from the immediate difficulty of running an evaporating school to the next stage, a virtual one, Claire and Al were able to produce (apparently from their back pockets) a thorough plan to ensure that our lessons could continue according to the existing timetable. We sent everyone home early on the Friday, and once I had finished my chores I found myself alone in the school, locking up with a tear in my eye, patting the building I had come to love and promising it, 'We'll be back.'

I caught the (almost deserted) train home in a turmoil of emotion and found myself troubled, not by the organisational challenges (which had been sorted for me) but the emotional ones. If I (who am generally a logical and stoic mathematician with a stable home and years of experience) was feeling this discombobulated, how were the 650 students and teachers scattered across London feeling? What could I do from Sidcup to keep the spirit of the school going as well as the activity? How do you stoke an ethos in a community that never meets?

By Monday morning I had the glimmerings of an answer and sent this email to staff and students.

The commute this morning is a small step for each of us but a giant leap for the Harris Westminster community. This morning we step into a new world where the old certainties of a 9am start, lessons in classrooms and endless stairs are replaced with virtual opportunities, the danger of loneliness and an almost infinite set of possible distractions. Unlike Neil Armstrong, the new world we have found is not an airless wilderness where reaching it is far more interesting than what is done there; we have to stay here a while, make a new normal, find a way to thrive. It is clear to me that across the country there will be two groups of students drifting away from each other, slowly but inevitably: the first group will impose some structure on their new lives and resist the temptations of daydreaming, *Diagnosis Murder* and social media; the second will relish the chance of an extended holiday and will take the opportunity to get idling down to a fine art. The first group will find new interests and sharpen existing ones; they will improve their study skills and become more intellectually independent; and they will find that even though they are trapped indoors their world grows as they learn more about it. The second group will enjoy the first week off, find the second week drags a little and by the beginning of the third will be going stir-crazy; they will complain incessantly on social media and take their frustrations out on those with whom they interact; and as they troll total strangers, their brains, once living and flexible, will turn slowly to stone and they will find themselves unable to catch up with those who were once their peers.

Or something like that – I may have got too caught up with the troll analogy (there is, by the way, a rather enchanting short story by C. S. Lewis which combines moon exploration, petrification and, going one up on my piece this morning, a Shakespeare reference[3]).

I hope that you will all do what you can to join the first group. It will not be easy and your teachers will be doing all they can to help you make that decision. For my part, missing assemblies and the opportunity to beset you on the door or in the canteen with questions about what you have learned, I shall send you a message at eight minutes to nine each weekday morning. This is the first one – I don't know what future ones will be like: it may be that they will be longer and more fanciful, it may be that they shrink to the point where I am saying nothing more than 'Good morning!' or 'Learning is amazing!' (I suspect it will depend on what feedback I get. If you are interested in what I say, please feel free to say, please feel free to disagree, please feel free to follow up on one of my allusions and inspire me.) But, technology and health permitting, I shall be here at 8.52 – I hope you will join me.

The response was everything I had hoped for – a scattering of emails of encouragement, picking up on words or ideas I had shared; and so I continued with the 8.52 emails sending one every morning for the rest of the school year. These took the place of assemblies and let me share poetry, popular culture and advice on scholarship, and the emailed responses often sparked new ideas and new topics for future emails (which I credited to an anonymous tweeter from the north of Scotland: @Jock1772).

They also provided a vehicle for encouraging community activities. We started a tradition of a Friday sing-along in which one teacher played DJ, taking suggestions from the school body and emailing out YouTube links to songs – the conceit being that we took one recommendation from each floor of the school, each sub-community sharing its favourite songs with everyone else. We had an art club, with a new subject each week and students and teachers encouraged to send in their offerings for a gallery that occupied the 8.52 slot on Sunday. By June, one of the heads of house, Rohit (of house Somerville), had worked out a way for us to play a version of Radio 4's *The Unbelievable Truth* with 'Unbelievable Saturdays' taking up the other weekend slot.

---

3   C. S. Lewis, 'Forms of Things Unknown' (1966), in *The Dark Tower and Other Stories* (New York: HarperCollins, 2017), pp. 165–178.

Meanwhile, the clubs and societies were meeting online and we even had concerts (recorded separately, spliced together and then sent out at a given moment for everyone to listen to at the same time, if not in the same place).

An additional challenge to the community was provided when, on 25 May 2020 George Floyd was killed by a policeman in Minneapolis. Responding sensitively to this horrible event when separated from the community I was responding for was not something I was equipped to do well. Fortunately, I was rescued from attempting to say something, or nothing, or from dithering whilst trying to work out a response, by two Year 13 students, Maram and Ella, who provided me with a ready written 8.52 (in Maram's words) and an amazing document of resources and sources (Ella's work) to share with the students.

As time went by the 8.52s became more sophisticated: Monday to Thursday would come as a podcast version attached to the email, Friday would be a video (for which I created a YouTube channel and thus learned something from the lockdown experience), Saturday was the 'Unbelievable' audio and Sunday the art gallery. We had definitely created a new kind of normal as lockdown unravelled and, as I promised in March, we returned piecemeal to Tothill Street.

By the end of term, in July, it was possible to record a video version of our Celebration Evening (the student president Stephanie and I speaking from the abbey pulpit) and even a sort of videoed assembly (beamed to the community from the reception desk). On 10 July I sent what I hoped would be the last 8.52 message.

Welcome to the final 8.52 of this academic year. Thank you for coming with me on the journey from that first, short commute via the coffee pot. Thank you for being kind when they have come out a few minutes late (or a few hours, or one Saturday, due to a technological foul-up, a few days late). Thank you to @Jock1772 and his unfailingly useful suggestions, and thank you to all of you who have, on one occasion or another, provided the anonymous tweet from the north of Scotland. The infectious times have been hard and they are not completely over, but the strangeness and fear of March and April have passed and we should all be back together come September.

Looking back at that first email, the one I sent out into the void hoping that some of you would read it, I see that I spoke of trolls but more about two groups of students drifting away from each other: one group in lazy loneliness and the other part of a constructive community. I am delighted to be able to report that you have definitely formed the second group – studying hard in your subjects, taking part in competitions, quizzes, art galleries and sing-alongs. My only lingering regret is that we never managed to get 'These Infectious Times' written as a rock anthem – my stadium tour will have to remain on hold. And so, farewell, dear friends, as I fall into Gandalf mode, as is my wont in times of trial: stay safe this summer, take your equal measure approach to the vacation's tasks seriously and remember, above all, whatever comes, to be kind, and that learning is amazing.

Final Thoughts

- Deputies who can not only run the school but anticipate problems so that you have the brain space for big thinking are invaluable.

- School is meant to be safe, reliable and predictable; when the real world becomes unsafe you have to work doubly hard to make it so.

- Schools should be places where people have ideas – recognise, celebrate and nurture other people's ideas and there may be times when they ride to your rescue.

Chapter 8

Resilience for a Better Tomorrow

In the first year, the community of Harris Westminster was quite internally focused: we had a lot to do in terms of developing our own ethos and relationships, and a student body that was entirely Year 12 and therefore adapting to their new environment rather than looking towards the next one. By the end of 2015, however, the students were beginning to look outwards and were wondering what legacy would mean for them: it was time to think about changing the world (two years after I had abandoned it as a tagline).

As well as some volunteering, a greater interest in political debate (assisted by the introduction of politics to our curriculum as an examinable subject) and an onward gaze to university, this change in mood was manifested in a desire to look deeper at and think harder about some of the world's injustices. Two of the first cohort of Year 13s came to us and asked if they could deliver an assembly on Black History Month in October. We were keen to support this engagement with difficult topics, but aware that sensitive subjects need to be handled sensitively and that the way we started would set the tone and paradigm for future student-led assemblies. We scheduled the slot and Nic worked hard with the students to put something together, but the timing wasn't right – Remembrance in Year 13 is an incredibly busy time combining a renewed focus on exams with the need to complete university choices and applications. Finally, with the students struggling to balance their work against the need to set an example, we felt we had to cancel the assembly – or, at least, postpone it significantly – and ended up doing nothing special that October, which left the students feeling disappointed and us wondering if an opportunity had been missed.

We still wanted to create a time for focus on the injustices of the world, to tell the stories of populations that are marginalised, oppressed or just forgotten, but we didn't want to make the same mistakes again – and nor did we want to have to wait for the next October, particularly facing the disquiet of students who felt that we had 'cancelled' Black History Month. Reflecting more deeply, we decided that we wanted to celebrate more than just black history (particularly important in a school as multiply ethnic as Harris Westminster), that a month was not enough time to tell all the stories we wanted to tell and that October was too early in the school year to do the preparation we needed (as well as having a two-week half-term in the middle of it). We therefore invented a new festival for Harris Westminster to celebrate: the first half-term of the calendar year would be dedicated to telling the histories of all the school's ethnic minorities and other marginalised groups under the banner of 'Resilience for a Better Tomorrow'. We would tell these stories through assemblies – and here I threw down the gauntlet of imagination – in whatever forums the students or teachers wanted to create.

Jerks and a Massive Hedge – 13 January 2016

I have an abiding fondness for the TV show *Only Connect* – if you were to listen to me rave about it you would be forgiven for thinking that this (and maybe *University Challenge,* about which I feel similarly) were all I watched. I must confess that this is not true because both shows suffer from the same crippling drawback – they are simply not on enough. Two half-hour quizzes is not enough to get me through the week. Fortunately, the world of catch-up TV is supplied with what seems to be an infinite quantity of *Pointless* – a marvellous twenty-minute quiz rendered almost unwatchable by being stretched to forty-five with a series of inanities best consumed on fast-forward whilst screaming 'Get on with it!' at the screen. One recent question asked for the authors of a series of children's books, the toughest of which was entitled *Captains Courageous.* This was a question to which none of the surveyed members of the public knew the answer – the holy grail of *Pointless* – and so I was delighted, having read it, to be able to firmly assert that it was Rudyard Kipling.

I enjoy much of Kipling's writing – *Stalky & Co., Kim* and *Captains Courageous* are all great books, and I am entranced by *Puck of Pook's Hill* and *Rewards and Fairies,* two children's books exploring the history of England. I am also fond of the poem 'If—' which appears in the latter – the line, 'If you can bear to hear the truth you've spoken / Twisted by knaves to make a trap for fools, / Or watch the things you gave your life to, broken, / And stoop and build 'em up with worn-out tools', is a heart-wrenching challenge and one I know I would struggle to face up to. The poem 'If—', if you will allow a brief diversion, is one of a collection of poems I intend one day to publish in an anthology entitled 'Poems That Would Be Improved By the Removal of the Last Line' – the collection currently stands at 'If—' and Shakespeare's Sonnet 116, but I shall keep you informed of any more that occur to me. Kipling's offending line is, of course, the second half of 'Yours is the Earth and everything that's in it, / And – which is more – you'll be a Man, my son!' – a piece of sexist doggerel without which the earth would be enormously improved.

Kipling has his detractors, not just for his male-centred view of the universe but also for alleged imperialist jingoism. No less an author than George Orwell said that he was morally insensitive and aesthetically disgusting and that every enlightened person has despised him, although he went on to explain that Kipling's identification with the ruling power gave him a certain grip on reality because the ruling power is always faced with the question, 'In such and such circumstances what would you do?'

Both aspects of Orwell's comment are reflected in the poem 'The White Man's Burden' which contains the lines, 'Take up the White Man's burden – / And reap his old reward, / The blame of those ye better, / The hate of those ye guard'. The generous reading of this is that it echoes the advice of Spider-Man's Uncle Ben, that with great power comes great responsibility (of course, the physicists amongst you will mentally correct this to say that with great power comes great current squared times resistance), and that rich countries should help poor ones without expecting thanks or praise. The more cynical response is to note that the poem doesn't say 'richer' but 'better' and that guarding is a rather fanciful term for military oppression. Which, though, is the right reading? What is the right way to interpret history or politics? I think this is an important question and one that comes up in different circumstances across the world and across time: the tale of humanity is littered with oppression, prejudice, abuse and stereotyping. As we ask ourselves why people behave in this way, as we remember those who fought for the freedoms we enjoy now and those who are still fighting against discrimination today, we must remember that it is not just the strong who use stereotypes and prejudices and not just the oppressed who fight for equality. My current reading is a detective novel set in Ireland amidst the tensions of the early 1900s when Protestants were a minority in a Catholic dominated country, but it was the Protestants who held the money and the power. There is violence, fear and anger on both sides but there are also people trying to do the right thing: trying to be fair and kind even when they are frightened and angry.

I tend to a view of humanity which says that most people are decent and that they broadly try to do the right thing – you will have heard me talk about those who don't as jerks and, if you have been listening carefully, you will have heard me acknowledge that even decent, good people get things wrong some of the time: we all have the capacity to be jerks. If the dean were here he would tell us that humanity is fallen, nobody is perfect, and that whilst we can admire some actions and appreciate the ideals that are held we must be careful not to worship our heroes.

I say this because I want to tell you about two situations where a group of people I broadly admire and respect have let me down: they have shown that they are jerks. The first is the British in India – something that Kipling writes about at length. I am a long way from thinking that they got everything right or even from being persuaded that the attitudes would be remotely acceptable today, but British India doesn't seem to have been noticeably worse than the regimes that followed it and in many ways was better than those that preceded it or, indeed, than the regimes in other places at the same time. It seems to me that most of the British in India were decent people broadly trying to do the right thing and yet, and yet …

Let me tell you about a hedge. It is a magnificent hedge and growing a decent hedge is such a British thing to do. This hedge stretched 4,000 kilometres across India and was up to 12 foot tall – that is about half the length of the Great Wall of China – and it was a customs line. It was patrolled by 7,000 customs officers and was as effective as you would expect a whopping great hedge to be at preventing smuggling. It is an amazing feat of engineering, horticulture and tax bureaucracy – a tribute to British ingenuity – but the problem comes when you find out what was being smuggled that required such enormous energy. Drugs, surely, or stolen goods? No, it was salt, and it was smuggled because the taxes on salt on one side of the hedge were much larger than those on the other. The British in India imposed such a high salt tax that it was both necessary and worthwhile to build this hedge to collect it. Salt is required for life – and deficiency can make you very sick, especially in a hot climate. I am left asking what kind of jerks can possibly have thought that placing heavy taxes on it was a reasonable thing to do? (To pay the tax for a family cost about 20% of a labourer's annual income.) The British in India were jerks … some of them, some of the time – we mustn't stereotype or generalise.

The other group is you. You will have seen an email from Mr Amy last week telling you that chewing gum is no longer allowed in school and may have thought that this was rather dictatorial. Hopefully it will have come as a shock – huh, I wonder why they have come over dictatorial all of a sudden, they are normally so reasonable? Well, the reason is that some of you have come to the end of enjoying your gum and have disposed of it by sticking it to the bottom of a table or dropping it on the floor. It is ridiculous. This isn't like your secondary schools where there were squillions of awful Year 9s who couldn't be trusted to behave in a civilised environment – this is us. We are decent, intelligent people, and yet some people, and not just one or two judging by the quantity of gum, several, lots, have behaved in a disgusting, disrespectful, damaging way. You guys are jerks … some of you, some of the time. Apologies to the rest of you – I had hoped not to have rules like this but it turns out that expecting people to be decent and to do the right thing doesn't always work.

This half of Resilience term contains a lot of anniversaries of people and events related to oppression, overcoming prejudice and fighting for equality. None of them are flawless – some of them, some of the time, were jerks – but over the next few months we have the anniversary of Mahatma Gandhi's assassination, Constance Markievicz's and Martin Luther King's birth, the liberation of Auschwitz, the signing of the Mahlabatini Declaration of Faith and the beginning of the Prague Spring. I would like, therefore, to dedicate this half-term to equality, to liberation, to treating people as individuals rather than as groups against which one can be prejudiced, to treating people with respect, to not being jerks. If you are interested in any of these issues – sexism, racism, homophobia, antisemitism, discrimination, prejudice, unfairness or inequality of any kind – then please take advantage of this half-term. Our assemblies will be circling around these issues, amongst others, and if you would like to lead an assembly on one of these subjects then please talk to your head of house in the first instance and we will do our best to help you put together a presentation that is interesting and scholarly enough to fit into our programme, either in a house assembly in the hall or in a whole school one at St Margaret's Church. If that sounds daunting but you would still like to do something, then please speak to your form tutor: I look forward to hearing about a whole range of class debates and discussions on these issues.

I wouldn't write the same assembly now – I would be less surprised by the misbehaviour of the colonists and keener to have an Indian viewpoint on the massive hedge as well as the British ones of Kipling and Orwell (and, of course, me). I think this change is part of a national or global shift in awareness and emphasis, but it has been heightened for me and for those of us who are part of the incredibly challenging, interesting and thoughtful community of Harris Westminster where the lazy recital of comforting stories is challenged by the full rigour of well-informed scholars.

The Resilience for a Better Tomorrow assemblies tend to be the ones that get me into most trouble with the students – when you are trying to bring fairness and nuance to controversial and emotionally charged topics any missteps are noticed and commented upon. I have often reflected that it would be easier to have an assembly on Martin Luther King and Rosa Parks in October and to let fitting in with the expected norms act as a cover for failing to address a wide range of real and important issues. Fortunately, so far, the feeling has passed and I remain convinced that it is better to try to do the right thing, even if it is sometimes clumsy, than to duck out of the difficult conversations. If I ever get to the point where this principle is no longer worth fighting for then I will know it is time to move on and let someone else take the lectern.

As the school has grown from those first years, so our ability to reflect the vast diversity of the student body has matured: the student discussion societies have become more confident and have built up their own traditions, with Tirah now taking responsibility for both Black History Month and, in theory, an Asian History Month in May (the 2020 version of this was limited due to the viral intervention); the Kindness and Scholarship conference in January is something that we hope will be a fixture on the calendar; and one of the houses has adopted a revolving hero model with a new figurehead taking the limelight every time a new leader takes the role of head of house. We will continue to make mistakes, I am sure, continue to be clumsy occasionally, and continue to say things that jerk ourselves out of a comfortable vision of the world and into troubling reality. But we are travelling in the right direction and our first efforts, springing out of our ethos, gave us a firm footing on which to build.

Resilience for a Better Tomorrow has provided a platform for student assemblies, many of which have been incredibly powerful and moving. A particular highlight was in 2019 when Jemima spoke to us of how in her reading she came across the Biafran War – a conflict that had never appeared in her education despite causing (via famine) over two million deaths in Nigeria, the country her parents had moved from to come to London. She told her father about it and asked if he had heard of the Biafran War. I remember clearly the next line, as Jemima quoted her father, 'Remember it, child? I was there.' To stand in front of 600 of your peers is a daunting experience; to present your words as something to be listened to is to measure yourself against a high standard; to share something personal in public is to make yourself vulnerable; but to watch as that whole crowd draws breath and stills themselves is a shiver of incredible oratorical power. Jemima had such a moment and it was a privilege to be there.

This half-term is also an opportunity for staff to put their hands up, to think about the stories that haven't been told, the injustices that are close to their hearts, or that they feel the students need to think more about, and I am sure that we made the right decision when we chose not to restrict ourselves to issues of race and ethnicity. The assembly slots in the first half of Resilience are invariably keenly fought over (even though we have frequently allowed the 'season' to spill over past the break and into the second half of term). As a result, we have heard a variety of different voices raising different issues and have had the opportunity as a school to pick up each other's causes and to think about injustices that don't affect us personally.

One of the joys of bringing together students from every background, heritage and belief system that London has to offer is that there are a huge number of causes to think about – sometimes for the first time. One of the difficulties then is the need to challenge each other, to bring our scholarship to bear on matters of human injustice and prejudice. It is important that we are able to challenge each other, and also important that we are sensitive to each other and accept that intolerance can come innocently from ignorance. Squaring this circle is a challenge that foxes many adult societies, but fortunately we have our guiding ethos (learning is amazing, learning about other people and the way they think is amazing, thinking hard about why we think in certain ways and learning to think better is amazing) and assemblies to help it along.

On What to Say – 13 January 2020

An assembly by Al Grant

How do you tell someone you love they are being racist? Or sexist? Or homophobic? Or antisemitic? What do you do when someone you respect and admire says something racist? I think we have all been there. I think we have all reacted, at different times and with different people, in different ways. One solution is to just walk away and never speak to them again. We see this often on Twitter and social media, where it is easier to do. You block that person or mute them. I can see that this might be the best response when your mental health may be under pressure. Your mental health and ability to manage life, at times for us all, can depend on just hearing positive things. When we are going through a rough patch, through the Slough of Despond, or the Difficulty Hill, or are being held up in Doubting Castle by the Giant Despair, as John Bunyan wrote about in *The Pilgrim's Progress*, we may need to mute the negative voices, both our own and others.[1]

But we should be aware that walking away from that person shuts down dialogue. It closes down possible ways forward for that person. It prevents them from learning. While it restricts the negative influences on you, it also limits your positive influences on them. The echo chamber it produces, for everyone, can further fragment communities. There is a really interesting podcast by This American Life called *Red State Blue State*,[2] which explores the increasing polarisation in the United States, which has come about by people on different sides walking away from dialogue, living in their own echo chamber and how that has created a political system where solutions are even harder to find.

1   J. Bunyan, *The Pilgrim's Progress From This World, To That Which Is To Come. Part 1: Delivered Under the Similitude of a Dream* (London: Printed for Nath. Ponder, 1678). Available at: http://www.gutenberg.org/ebooks/131.
2   This American Life, *Red State Blue State* [podcast] (2 November 2012). Available at: https://www.thisamericanlife.org/478/red-state-blue-state.

We make a better world by figuring out alliances, by reaching out to those on the opposite side, by finding common ground with them and building upwards from there. Instead of walking away should we call them a racist? Call them out for what they are? I was going to say 'call a spade a spade', but it was pointed out to me recently how this expression has picked up racist overtones. I only knew a spade as a piece of gardening equipment. There is the great line in the play *The Importance of Being Earnest* by Oscar Wilde, where Cecily and Gwendolen are having a right old ding-dong over whether Cecily has coerced Ernest into proposing marriage to her. Cecily says, 'Do you suggest, Miss Fairfax, that I entrapped Ernest into an engagement? How dare you? This is no time for wearing the shallow mask of manners. When I see a spade I call it a spade.' To which Gwendolen replies, with a degree of nonchalance and perhaps a bit of glee, 'I am glad to say that I have never seen a spade. It is obvious that our social spheres have been widely different.'[3] However, around the 1920s the word spade evolved to be a coded word for a black person. According to the Oxford English Dictionary, the first occasion when it was used in this way was in the 1928 novel *Home to Harlem* by Claude McKay, which gives a remarkable depiction of life in Harlem in the 1920s.[4]

The question is, does calling someone a racist move the conversation forward? We want to build a fairer world for ourselves and future generations, and calling someone a racist might make us feel better – that sense of outrage coursing through your body can be hugely comforting; but it does not win arguments, it does not win allies, it does not lead to dialogue and the construction of a pathway. It might be technically right to call a shovel a shovel, it may even be necessary, but we must ensure that it is not the end of the dialogue.

I have never advocated the position that you should not rock the boat. Rocking may be exactly what the boat needs, or at least telling everyone our boat has holes and is going to sink unless we recognise and do something about them. I think a far better way forward is to separate the person from their behaviour. To call their words racist but not them a racist. As William H. Whyte said in 1950, 'The great enemy of communication, we find, is the illusion of it. We have talked enough; but we have not listened. And by not listening we have failed to concede the immense complexity of our society – and thus the great gaps between ourselves and those with whom we seek understanding.'[5]

3   O. Wilde, *The Importance of Being Earnest: A Trivial Comedy for Serious People* (London: Methuen, 1915), Act II. Available at: http://www.gutenberg.org/ebooks/844.

4   See https://oed.com/view/Entry/185450.

5   W. H. Whyte, 'Is Anybody Listening?', *Fortune* (September 1950).

The only constructive way forward is to change people's perspectives through dialogue, to expand their moral universe. This requires that we also expand our moral universe. If we seek for someone else to understand us, we must also seek to understand them. In a letter to his 14-year-old nephew, James Baldwin wrote, 'There is no reason for you to try to become like a white person and there is no basis whatever for their impertinent assumption that they must accept you. The terrible thing, old buddy, is that you must accept them.'[6]

How do you create dialogue and change minds? The short answer might be through scholarship and kindness. The longer answer might be these four principles developed by Megan Phelps-Rogers who was raised in the notorious Westboro Baptist Church. She began to change her views when she started speaking to people who were willing to listen to her, to treat her as a human being, despite her views. From her own transformation, she has four suggestions for effectively talking to people you believe are wrong or immoral:

1. Don't assume bad intent on the other person's part. Assume good or at least neutral intent.

2. Ask questions. This shows the person that you want to listen, that you want to hear them and this in turn this makes them feel safe enough to ask you questions. No one is going to listen to someone who is not prepared to listen in turn.

3. Stay calm. Being right does not justify being rude. If you need to, step away for a time and come back to it later. Avoid name calling; avoid *ad hominem* attacks. Cleave to the specific argument.

4. Make the argument. Do not assume that the value of your argument will be obvious to others. If you want someone to change, you need to make the case for it. You need to make the case in a way which means they will hear what you are saying, not what they imagine you are saying.[7]

---

6   J. Baldwin, 'A Letter to My Nephew', *The Progressive* (December 1962). Available at: https://progressive.org/magazine/letter-nephew.
7   Adapted from M. Phelps-Rogers, 'I Grew Up in the Westboro Baptist Church. Here's Why I Left', *TED.com* (February 2017). Available at: https://www.ted.com/talks/megan_phelps_roper_i_grew_up_in_the_westboro_baptist_church_here_s_why_i_left?language=en.

The great obstacle to communication is the illusion that we have been understood by the other person. So, how do you tell someone they are being racist? Or homophobic? Or Islamophobic? Or antisemitic? If you want to change their minds and so their behaviour, the only way is through dialogue, which means listening to them and using empathy. To return to James Baldwin again, he wrote, 'I imagine one of the reasons people cling to their hates so stubbornly is because they sense, once hate is gone, they will be forced to deal with pain.'[8]

Al Grant joined the school as vice principal in September 2016, as Nic left, and brought with him a different hinterland of interests and inspirations. (He also brought with him the word 'hinterland' which we use to describe our cultural capital, the things we know and are interested in, not because we believe them to be directly applicable to the task in hand but for their own sake and because we know that a well-developed hinterland is a resource that can be drawn upon in all kinds of situation.)

Al's assembly is a call to us as a community to help each other become better – for Resilience for a Better Tomorrow's focus on the injustices and untold stories to mean something and not to be merely howling into the void or comfortably reinforcing our own sense of superiority. The third element of our ethos, legacy – the idea that any situation, organisation or even room should be better as a result of us having been there – is an active one; we do not say 'do no harm' but 'change the world'. We encourage students to be bold as well as wise, to have passion as well as nuance, to stand up for what they know to be right as well as to seek their own personal development, education and economic security.

Taking 300 16-year-olds from every background and neighbourhood across London who are united only by an affinity for academic learning and shaping them, in a confined space, into a community is going to be a challenge every year. We will always find that some of them come to us with stories and backgrounds that we know little about, that there are injustices and unkindnesses that we have managed to escape. We will also find that some of them bring with them illiberal views

8   J. Baldwin, 'Me and My House', *Harper's Magazine* (November 1955).

or partisan opinions on nuanced issues. Every year we need to ensure that all parts of the community are celebrated and that small groups are not squeezed out or marginalised by larger ones, and we need to work hard on our framework of scholarly discussion so that ideas can be debated and challenged without the individuals who suggest them feeling attacked.

Two areas where feelings run high are religious views on homosexuality and the Israeli–Palestinian conflict. Neither of these issues are, of course, specific to Harris Westminster, and it is not surprising that problems which have avoided resolution by adults for generations are thorny amongst our young people.

The religious works of the two largest religious groups in the school, Christian and Muslim, both contain teachings that condemn homosexuality, and it can be difficult for students whose upbringing is conservatively within these frameworks when they come to a liberal school where some members of the community are openly gay. It is even more challenging for teenagers who are exploring their own sexuality if they feel under attack from their peers as well as, potentially, members of their family or home community. The school position is quite definitely that individuals are free to make romantic relationships with whomever they choose (so long as it doesn't interfere with their scholarship) and that this is not an area for imposing your own moral code on others. The student-led society Intelligent Believing provides a forum for those who are interested to grapple with religious texts and to try to come to a thought-through and sound position. I suspect that this remains a difficult issue to resolve for most students, but I am delighted that they are thinking hard about it and challenging themselves rather than relying on others to do it for them. (See Chapter 5 for more on the discussion societies.)

We don't, institutionally, have a position on the Israeli–Palestinian conflict, at least not one that gets beyond the general principles of kindness and equality, and we find it a difficult issue to discuss because the student body tends to come down quite heavily on one side: we have many more Muslim students than Jewish ones, and inherited viewpoints tend to be similarly biased. We have, therefore, run cultural perspectives classes to provide a forum for examining the politics without entering an echo chamber in which right appears to be on one side only. For similar reasons, we have had teachers (a few of whom have Jewish heritage) giving assemblies on the Holocaust; the fact that Holocaust Memorial Day falls in January is a convenient hook on which to hang these addresses.

Assemblies during Resilience for a Better Tomorrow can be quite straightforwardly factual – telling stories that students may not have heard; letting them know about places and times that are missed out of the standard geography or history curriculum. Assemblies should always be a learning experience, but there is more scope in this season for them to be short lectures on a suitable topic. Claire Scott (who has been introduced as an assistant principal and was promoted to vice principal in 2017) has given several such non-fiction assemblies, from which I have reproduced excerpts to whet the reader's appetite and give a flavour of the topics covered.

The Underground Railroad – 1 February 2016

This morning I am going to talk to you about the Underground Railroad. This is not, as one of my Year 13s thought, a cryptic reference to the Tube; the Underground Railroad was, in fact, the term used to describe the network of meeting places, secret routes, passageways, safe houses and people that helped escaped slaves to travel from the southern US to freedom in the north during the 1800s.[9]

The Underground Railroad was neither underground nor a railroad. It got its name because its activities had to be carried out in secret, using darkness or disguise, and because railway terms were used by those involved with the system to describe how it worked. It consisted of figurative stations, depots and lines. There were 'stationmasters' and 'conductors' and stockholders who contributed money or goods. Fugitives would get 'on board' (remember that travel was by boat or on foot as often as by train) in the south and make their way northward. Many went on to Canada, where they could not be retrieved legally by their owners.

---

9   R. B. Mitchell, Underground Railroad: Information and Articles About Underground Railroad, One of the Causes of the Civil War, *HistoryNet* (n.d.). Available at: https://www.historynet.com/underground-railroad.

Sometimes a conductor, pretending to be a slave, would go to a plantation to guide the fugitives on their way. Among the best known conductors was Harriet Tubman, a former slave who returned to the slave states nineteen times and brought more than 300 slaves to freedom. It is said that she would restore courage to any whose hearts quailed with the aid of a shotgun.

Harriet Tubman and others like her have inspired generations of Americans struggling for civil rights with their bravery and bold actions. More famous names, which undoubtedly you have heard of, are the African-American civil rights leader Martin Luther King Jr and Rosa Parks, whose simple action of not giving up her seat to a white person on a bus led to civil disruption and a broadening of the civil rights movement.

Tubman, King and Parks did not set out in search of fame or fortune or to top the lists of influential African-Americans. They were simply ordinary people who had firm principles and a sense of justice that they would not allow to be bent. They had a strong moral code, so when they saw injustices happening or witnessed something that didn't seem fair to them, they spoke up, regardless of the impact on themselves. It is people like these who can make an impact in our lifetime, who can make changes that can improve the lives of the many who are still suffering injustices.

I wonder how many people in this room would speak up if they saw something they didn't agree with, perhaps if no one was giving up their seat to an elderly person on the Tube, or a fellow student leaving their rubbish for someone else to clean up in the canteen, or a group of disruptive students stopping others from studying. These may be small actions but they all have a positive impact on someone. And that is something that we all must strive to remember when we are choosing whether to make our voices heard.

From Sappho to Turing – 10 February 2017

Sappho was born sometime around 620 BCE on the island of Lesbos and is one of a few known female poets of ancient Greece. She was one of the first poets to write from the first person, describing love and loss as it affected her personally. What sets apart her poem, 'Immortal Aphrodite', though, is that it is written by a woman about her love for another woman. That Sappho's poetry was not condemned in her lifetime for its homoerotic content suggests that perhaps love between women was not persecuted then as it has been in more recent times. Especially in the last century, Sappho has become so synonymous with love between women that two of the most popular words to describe female homosexuality – lesbian and sapphic – have derived from her.

Perhaps the most familiar figure to us when it comes to twentieth century struggles with homosexuality is Alan Turing. As I am sure that all those in Turing house know, he was a computer scientist and mathematician who worked for the government during the Second World War, broke the Germans' Enigma code and, by some accounts, helped to shorten the war by up to two years. Turing was prosecuted in 1952 for homosexual acts, specifically 'gross indecency' which was still a criminal act in the UK. He accepted chemical castration treatment as an alternative to prison. Turing died in 1954 from cyanide poisoning. It wasn't until 2009, following an Internet campaign, that British Prime Minister Gordon Brown made an official public apology on behalf of the British government for 'the appalling way he was treated'.[10] The Queen then granted him a posthumous pardon in 2013. The 'Alan Turing law' is now an informal term for a 2017 law in the United Kingdom that retroactively pardons men cautioned or convicted under historical legislation that outlawed homosexual acts.

So where does this leave us now? We, as a school community, treat all people – regardless of their sexual orientation, race or religion – equally. Legally, no one should be treated differently as a result of any of these things, but we recognise that in practice this is not always the case. Last week, the captains of Wilberforce house spoke about anti-racism and I would like to extend the notion of anti-racism to being actively anti all things that mean people aren't treated equally. Whether it is a racist term, a homophobic slur, Islamophobia or general ignorance, I hope that everyone in this school community would have the courage to speak up against it.

Child Refugees – 12 February 2020

When Soo-Min was 14 years old, her family decided that it was too dangerous for her and her older sister, Bennu, to continue living at home. At that time, home for her was North-West Burma and her family were existing under

---

10   C. Davies, 'PM's Apology to Codebreaker Alan Turing: We Were Inhumane',
     The Guardian (11 September 2009). Available at: https://www.theguardian.com/
     world/2009/sep/11/pm-apology-to-alan-turing.

very strict state controls. The details are unclear, but their living conditions were so severe that the decision was made for Soo-Min and Bennu to flee the country, on foot, for Bangladesh. Before reaching safety Bennu was captured – her fate is unknown. Soo-Min was left to continue the journey alone. She had to hike for days on end through the dense vegetation and dangerous waterways of the river deltas, with no food or water and no belongings.

Eventually she arrived in the city of Chattogram. Here, she found herself living on the streets, before being approached by a charity worker who helped to look after her and find her a safe place to stay. Through this charity, Soo-Min was able to move from country to country, trying to find somewhere she could safely claim asylum. Eventually she found herself in the UK. There isn't a lot of information about this journey, but what is certain is that Soo-Min's experiences were physically and emotionally destructive – some of the people she met were supportive and helpful, some were not. She has never spoken in detail about this stage of her journey. Remember, she was 14 and on her own. When she finally arrived in the UK, Soo-Min was put in touch with a charity called Refugee Support, which in turn was able to place her in foster care and into a school. Despite knowing almost no English when she arrived, Soo-Min threw herself into her new British life, gaining GCSEs and A levels. Soo-Min is still living safely in the UK. She still doesn't know what happened to Bennu.

Soo-Min's story is almost unbelievable – that a teenage girl had the courage, perseverance and desperation to complete that journey – and I hope for her that her ending will be a happy one. But for so many child refugees, they don't have a happy ending.

Save the Children states that there are 25.4 million refugees worldwide, and 52% of them are children.[11] Four million refugee children around the world are currently out of school, leaving them vulnerable to discrimination and potential abuse, as well as exploitation by traffickers or the pressure of entering into early marriage.[12] More than half of these out-of-school refugee children are found in just seven countries: Chad, Democratic Republic of the Congo, Ethiopia, Kenya, Lebanon, Pakistan and Turkey. According to UNICEF,

11 Save the Children, *100 Years of Fighting for Children: Annual Report 2018*. Available at: https://www.savethechildren.org.uk/content/dam/gb/reports/annual-report-2018-save-the-children.pdf.
12 UNHCR, 'Four Million Refugee Children Go Without Schooling: UNHCR Report' (29 August 2018). Available at: https://www.unhcr.org/uk/news/latest/2018/8/5b86342b4/four-million-refugee-children-schooling-unhcr-report.html.

one third of the refugees and migrants who have arrived in Europe are children, some travelling with families, some alone.[13] They are fleeing their homelands to escape conflict, poverty or persecution, unsure as to whether or where they will find a new home, but the hope is that they might settle somewhere where their rights will be respected, they will have a chance to further their education and get ahead in life.

Currently, the largest refugee population in the world is found in Turkey and is made up of more than three million Syrians, almost half of them children. Their host communities are often poverty-stricken and hundreds of thousands of these refugee children are out of school. As a result of the EU–Turkey statement and Balkan border closures, if any of these refugees want to try to find a better life in Europe, they are now forced to make increasingly dangerous journeys. And what awaits them when they arrive at their new host countries? Aside from the difficulties that arise from the language barriers and cultural differences they will confront, they face immense psychological trauma, potentially tricky political situations and financial hardship.

For many of you, this talk of child refugees might feel quite abstract or separate from your real life. For others, it may be striking a chord. But the plight and journey of child refugees sits closer to home than you might think. I didn't quite finish Soo-Min's story. I do, in fact, know exactly what happened to her since she arrived in the UK. The school she was placed into, where she started to learn English and took some GCSEs, was in London. The sixth form where she took her A levels was this one. Moreover, she is not the only child refugee who has worked hard to make themselves a member of the Harris Westminster community.

Soo-Min isn't her real name, and I have changed some of the details of her story, but she is an ex-student of ours – one who epitomises ambition, perseverance and legacy. She is now studying engineering at university. Of all the amazing things about Soo-Min's story, perhaps the most amazing is that she is not unique – there are others who, as children, fled terrible regimes to make their way to safer countries in the hope of a better life. Sometimes, one of those millions of child refugees finds their way around the world to Harris Westminster and works hard to make themselves part of our community.

---

13 See https://www.unicef.org/eca/emergencies/refugee-and-migrant-children-europe.

You never know what the experiences are of the person sitting next to you or just how resilient they are.

It often strikes me how little we know of each other's lives, how little we see of the hurdles that our classmates and colleagues navigate each day, but sometimes we get a glimpse of someone else's life – a glimpse that gives us pause, makes us re-evaluate our own challenges and gives us cause to be thankful that we are not walking in their shoes. The stories we tell during Resilience for a Better Tomorrow are often not academic curiosities but the real experience of those we share a school with.

Resilience for a Better Tomorrow is a time for us to lift our eyes beyond our own concerns and to think about others, their challenges, their triumphs; but it is also an opportunity to apply those lessons to our own lives, our own struggles. By telling big stories about faraway injustice, we hope to allow students to think about their own difficulties in a new way. We hope they will be inspired to do better, to flourish rather than just endure. We hope they will be distracted, their attention focused outside of themselves so their own difficulties are obstacles to be overcome rather than fetters to hold them in place. We hope they will be reassured that there are others who are going through something similar to them. We also hope that they will reflect on those they spend time with and be more aware of their privileges and the way their actions can marginalise or welcome others.

My ambitions for the good the school will do are lofty rather than realistic, and I know we won't see the impact for generations (possibly not until the first Harris Westminster alumni are running their own schools), but one of the goals is that by sending these idealistic, intelligent young people out into the world with nuanced ideals and refined arguments, we really are helping to make a better tomorrow.

Final Thoughts

- Either you duck out of difficult issues or you accept that sometimes you will say things that offend some people. If you choose the latter, then you have to work hard to make amends.

- A school community is inevitably more diverse than any subgroup – it is important to have avenues for getting all voices heard.

- Sometimes teenagers make bad decisions; sometimes they let you down. We mustn't let that get in the way of trusting the next ones.

- Assemblies should be an opportunity to learn something new and to refine your own thoughts as well as to educate.

- The potential of young people is huge – we shouldn't limit our ambition to the grades they might get or jobs they might do.

Chapter 9

Esoterica

Writing an assembly is an art in which ideas are woven together. Typically, I start with a message that I want the students to hear which might be the importance of using time wisely or even an exhortation not to block the toilets with paper towels; quite often I have more than one such message. I then start to look for a story to tell, one whose moral could conceivably be the message. Sometimes the story will be a personal one, sometimes it will be a piece of news or literature, but often I will look for a personal hook – a place for me to stand as I talk to the school, a way to make the assembly human rather than functional. Finally (usually), I will go in search of some cultural illustrations: some poetry or pop music, film, art, history or mathematics that I can drop in along the way. These will always be things I think it is worth the students following up, sometimes for the cultural depth and heft it will give them, and sometimes because I want to share the joy I have found (and, of course, at my brightest moments, both).

Resilience for a Better Tomorrow assemblies are different – there the story comes first, the message second and the cultural references can be an afterthought. There is a third sort of assembly that comes up, serendipitously, from time to time when there is nothing pressing to be said and I have been free to share one of my enthusiasms ('We live in a querulous age', says Bernard Levin on the cover of his book *Enthusiasms*[1] – I have absorbed the message of this work and am keen to avoid this particular zeitgeist). Then I start with the culture, the enthusiasm, look for a moral of sorts and maybe, if there is time, dress it in an anecdote.

This chapter is dedicated to that sort of assembly, but before we get there, here is an assembly that illustrates the writing technique nicely – a piece that started off with a message but spiralled into something quite esoteric before I got to the end.

---

1   B. Levin, *Enthusiasms* (London: Sceptre, 1983), p. 1.

I Got Rhythm – 2 December 2019

Ira Gershwin wrote the lyrics to the jazz standard 'I Got Rhythm' in which he explained that because he had rhythm, music and his man (it is written for a character originally played by Ethel Merman, so technically it was her man) he was chipper, content and had no need to ask for anything more. I don't know about you, but I could do with being 'chipper all the day' and 'happy with my lot', so I thought I would explore his ideas. I am not sure I have got much to say to you about romance, and my musical skills are considerably less impressive than many of yours – as we saw in last week's carols. This leaves me with rhythm and the thesis that if you have rhythm then your lot will be inevitably happy. Actually, that claim is too bold – what I really want to say is that there is a natural rhythm to Harris Westminster life and if you get this right then your time will be smoother, happier, and more successful.

The rhythm is quite sophisticated, with a regularity to the weeks – I hope you have your 168 hours organised with slots for homework, prep and wider reading. Then there is the regular beat of term and vacation – we are having another one of those shortly, which I will speak about next week.

These are not the rhythms I want to talk to you about, though. What I want to explain today, with illustration from the world of music, is how there is a rhythm to the two years – how the experience of each term at Harris Westminster is, or should be, different to the last, how the beat of that drum carries you from the beginning of Remembrance Year 12 to the end of Celebration Year 13. Let us start with this term – I will tell you what you should have achieved and you can work out how you have got on. The main goal of Remembrance Year 12 is to get started, to get a rhythm going, to get organised, so let us think about a straightforward rhythm – 4/4 – common time. This is the rhythm that lies behind most pop songs and much classical music. 4/4 simply means that there are four beats in the bar (that is the first four) and that each beat is a quarter of the longest note – a semibreve (that is the second four and we don't really need to worry much about that – the most important thing is the number of beats in a bar). 4/4 is a versatile rhythm: you can foxtrot to it, quickstep and even tango. Your weekly rhythm will also have some fours in it with four subjects and four sets of homework. There is a strong beat on the 1 and a lesser one on the 3, and if you get that beat right you can do some very interesting things. 'I Got Rhythm' is in 4/4 and is a great exploration of what you can do by playing around with that time signature – I commend it to you.

To play well you have to listen to the music and pay careful attention to what the beat is doing, make sure that you can hear and respond to the 1, the first beat of the bar, the pulse of the music. And there is the link to scholarship – as well as getting your routine set up, you need to get the hang of response this term. If you didn't do too well last time, that is OK – you get another go when the second assessments come back this week. One more thing I want to tell you about, before we leave 4/4, is a video of Harry Connick Jr that you should definitely look up on YouTube.[2] He is playing the piano and singing and the audience are clapping on 1 and 3, which is rather square – cool kids clap on the 2 and 4. Harry is cool, the audience are not, and so to help them out, without them noticing, he slips an extra beat into one of the bars so they clap on 1, 3, 5 and then on the next one they are on 2 and 4. Suddenly his audience of squares are transformed. For some of you, this term, we have put in some extra beats, some nudges to get you into the proper rhythm – don't fight the nudges, they are there to help you.

That was this term – what about next? Well, if Remembrance Year 12 is the response term, Resilience term is purpose, and for my inspiration here I am turning to the film *Dirty Dancing* – if you have not seen it then you should. It is about a 1950s teenager who learns to dance to modern, Latin syncopated rhythms. One of the first challenges is not moving on the 1 – remember, that is square. The heroine, Baby, needs to learn to be cool and to move on the 2. One scene later, a new dance, and she has to try something even cooler: the dance starts after the 1 but before the 2. Johnny, the teacher, says, 'It's a feeling, a heartbeat, ba doom.' Really understanding the rhythm requires feeling, not just counting – something that has held back my dancing throughout the years: I have always been better at counting than feeling. Similarly, really understanding subjects requires purpose, not just mechanics, and for most of you this is a change of approach. Use next term to feel your subjects, to understand why, to let go of the routines that got you through GCSE and embrace the deeper rhythm of the subject, the feeling, the heartbeat.

And so, on to Celebration term. Here the temptation is to worry about your end-of-year exams and to revert to good old 4/4 time. This is an error – you do have to do well in your end-of-years, you should take them seriously,

---

2   See https://www.youtube.com/watch?v=UinRq_29jPk.

but this is not the time to close down. It is the last chance to really open up, to embrace new ideas. Time signatures may normally be 4/4, possibly 3/4 or 2/4, but many amazing and interesting songs come from experimenting with different rhythms. 'All You Need is Love' by The Beatles is in 7/4, as is 'Money' by Pink Floyd. 'Seven Days' by Sting and 'Mars, the Bringer of War', from Holst's *Planets* suite are in 5/4. The American rock band Tool took this further with their 2002 hit 'Schism' (which I hadn't come across before I started writing this assembly). Tool say that 'Schism' is in 6½ time which they achieve by alternating 6 and 7 beat bars. The world is big and full of interesting things – don't get focused on exams too early. Spend Celebration of Year 12 expanding the borders of your knowledge.

After that it gets complicated – you will have seen the Year 13s looking rather stressed this term. This is because they are trying to do two things at once: studying their subjects with lots still to learn and, at the same time, sorting out UCAS applications and coping with offers and rejections from universities. A time signature that does two things at once is called a compound time signature and the simplest one is 6/8. In 6/8 there is a strong 1, 2 but each beat is broken down into threes – a suitable example is Queen's 'We are the Champions'. Within it, sometimes the 3 dominates, particularly the lilting verses, and sometimes the drums hammer out the 2 and remind you who exactly are the champions of the world. Look at how the best of the Year 13s have been working this term – that is what you are aiming for.

Resilience, Year 13, is finally the time to focus on mechanics, to make sure that you have got all your knowledge spot on, to make sure that the wonderful ideas you explored in Celebration can be translated into clear and accurate answers. It is the time to return to 'I've Got Rhythm' and appreciate the way the 4/4 metronome holds the highly syncopated jazz classic together. It is time to listen to The Stranglers' 'Golden Brown' – not for the lyrics (which are disappointingly about heroin abuse) but for the way it is written in 3/4 except for one bar in four which is in 4/4. If you did enough exploration in Year 12 then you will consider the possibility that this is really a single long measure of 13/4. This might then get you to reflect that maybe 'Schism' is also in 13/4 and to wonder what other masquerades there are. Worry about the mechanics when you have already felt the purpose, listened, responded and explored widely, and then some truly wonderful things will come into focus.

Finally, Celebration Year 13, is the performance. Half a term of final rehearsal, careful focus, going over the tricky bits until they are easy and then the exams.

This is when you get to be Harry Connick Jr, where you get to toy with the examiners, to manipulate them into being cool kids, to take them out of their usual and rather square idiom.

That is the rhythm of Harris Westminster: response, purpose, look wider, two things at once, mechanics and performance. You should have your response sorted out – take this half-term's tasks really seriously: both subjects and cultural perspectives – and if you are feeling this is too much, look at the Year 13s and up your game. You should also have organised your weekly routine, your weekly rhythm. And if you've got rhythm, you don't need to mind old man trouble, you've got daisies in green pastures, you've got learning – and who could ask for anything more?

The opportunity for this assembly arose because the Year 13 students were taking their mock exams and were either in the hall or on study leave, which allowed me to speak directly to the Year 12s. For a long time I'd had the idea that there was a structure to how the best (most successful) Harris Westminster students progressed during their time, but I had never formulated it clearly, even for myself. This was the starting point: what are you meant to have learned so far (restricting this to one thing would hopefully come as good news for some students who were struggling to keep up with everything), and what will you need to move on to next term and the terms thereafter (emphasising the importance of having got this term's learning solidly under their belt and taking the opportunity of the Christmas vacation to achieve that goal if necessary)?

Having got the idea and what was a substantial message (there is a lot of content in this assembly), I also had a title and my first piece of culture: 'I Got Rhythm'. I was also freed from the need for a story (the six terms of a Harris Westminster career provided the necessary narrative structure), although we still started with the hook of what I can talk about when I know nothing about romance (officially) or music (actually). Finding songs in different time signatures required a little research (as did the information on Gershwin and Merman), and I was fortunate to have been reminded of *Dirty Dancing* by watching it at home the week before.

The biggest challenge was tying it together and getting through all six terms within 1,500 words (I just missed that challenge but nobody is actually counting), and the biggest reward was when one teacher and one student spoke to me on the way out of the hall to explain that they were huge fans of Tool, adored 'Schism' and wondered if I had come across any of their other mathematically experimental time signatures. Unfortunately, I had merely googled 'unusual time signatures' and picked out the most interesting, but they were delighted to have the mention and I was thrilled to find out what I should have guessed – that if any group of people is going to contain fans of a band that makes music in $6\frac{1}{2}/8$ (the fact that the beats in 'Schism' are quavers rather than crotchets was a complication that I had decided to skip over in the assembly) then Harris Westminster is that group.

This is not, however, my most bewilderingly obscure assembly, and nor does that title go to the time I regaled the students with my version of US history structured around the order in which the fifty states joined the union. My training is in mathematics and I still teach a few lessons each week of the subject, but I rarely manage to work it into assembly (there may be good reason for this – you will shortly be able to judge), and so, apart from the few who are in my class, students don't get to see me enthuse and expound my own area of true scholarship – merely on those myriad pieces of learning that I have, at one point or another (possibly precisely for the purposes of giving an assembly) deemed amazing. Once or twice, therefore, I have delivered a mathematical assembly in order to redress the balance.

Lub and Dub (Conjectures with Noodles) – 12 March 2018

Last time I spoke to you, I explained my long-term plan to retire – eventually – to a veranda and to shout theorems at passers-by. I thought, therefore, that this morning would be a good opportunity to indulge my particular academic passion. You would be forgiven, after listening carefully to months of assemblies, for thinking that this is the poetry of William Butler Yeats but, as I think is well publicised, poetry is a bit of a sideline – a lengthy exercise in academic promiscuity – and that I am, in fact, a mathematician. I delight in logic, I see patterns everywhere, I can't resist a carefully constructed diagram (geometric or statistical) and if you cut me I bleed numbers.

So, welcome to a few of my favourite things: proofs in white dresses with blue satin sashes, theorems and lemmas and conjectures with noodles. Actually that sounds quite good – I just need a tune to go with it.

That veranda, though – what theorems would I be shouting? Well, probably not Fermat's Last Theorem which states that if you have four positive integers a, b, c and n which obey the rule $a^n + b^n = c^n$ then $n < 3$. I have nothing against the theorem actually – it is quite pretty: easy to state and counter-intuitive (which I consider to be a bonus in a theorem). It is a strange thing to be true, right? There are infinitely many Pythagorean triples (solutions to $a^2 + b^2 = c^2$) and $a^1 + b^1 = c^1$ is even easier to solve, so why should there be no solutions whatsoever with higher powers? Very odd. No, the reason I wouldn't be yelling it is that I wouldn't want to hear the proof yelled back – it is a bit of a monster.

When I was a graduate student I had weekly meetings, supervisions, with Richard Taylor – one of the key players in the proof of Fermat's Last Theorem – and at my first meeting he handed me a sheaf of paper. 'Here,' he said, 'this might help.' When I took it back to the cubby hole I called an office and looked at my new treasure (a bit like Gollum, 'my precious'), I found that it was a sixty-seven page mathematical paper which explained how the two papers that proved Fermat's Last Theorem worked. I spent a week trying to understand the first page and then went back to my supervisor to explain what I had learned. Unfortunately, I had got it all wrong and had to start again. The proof of Fermat's Last Theorem is hard.

However, I am not one to turn down a challenge so I shall attempt to sketch it for you now. It involves a type of shape called an elliptic curve: it is like a special kind of doughnut shape that is defined by an equation with x, y and z in it. We also need to know about a type of function called a modular form which looks a bit like a crazy set of tiles on a plane. The key idea was that for a long time people had known that there was a way of matching elliptic curves to modular forms, but finding out quite how it worked and proving that it always worked was hard. In the 1980s, someone pointed out that the Fermat equation 'x to the n plus y to the $n = z$ to the n' gave you an elliptic curve which should match to a modular form, and that if there was an integer solution then it would be a special point on the doughnut which would match to a special bit of the tiling. Someone else then noticed that such a special bit of tiling was impossible if n

was bigger than 2, and so all they needed to do was to fix up the matching of elliptic curves to modular forms. That was what the two papers of proof did, and the reason that it takes sixty-seven pages to explain it is that both elliptic curves and modular forms are more complex and complicated than I have said and that the matching process is exceptionally devious. I spent three years working with the mathematicians whose favourite thing was figuring out exactly how the matching process works – and I still don't really understand it.

Fermat, by the way, claimed that he had a marvellous proof that didn't involve elliptic curves or modular forms and was only slightly too long for a margin, but Fermat claimed a lot of things, including a rather marvellous theorem that all numbers of the form 2 to the power 2 to the power n + 1 are prime. He did a bit of checking – if $n = 0$ you get 3 which is prime, if $n = 1$ you get 5, if $n = 2$ you get 17, if $n = 3$ you get 257 and if $n = 4$ you get 65,537 which he showed was prime. If $n = 5$ you get 4,294,967,297 which is probably prime, and that is as far as Fermat's checking got. It was a decent guess but unfortunately for Fermat 4,294,967,297 is not prime and nor are any of the numbers that come afterwards, as far as have been checked so far. So I won't be shouting that theorem either.

When I say none of the numbers that come after, I mean numbers of the form 2 to the power 2 to the power n + 1. There are, of course, primes bigger than 4,294,967,297. I say of course, but Dr Hrasko will tell you that maths is always obvious when it has been proved (except for Fermat's Last Theorem which I still hold to be entirely not obvious), and so mathematicians only know obvious things. How do we know this? Well, there is a great theorem which says there are infinitely many primes, and that is a good one to shout because the proof is completely shoutable back. Suppose there was a biggest prime – let us call it 4,294,967,297 for the sake of argument. Now think about what you get if you multiply all the numbers up to 4,294,967,297 together – well you get a pretty stupidly large number, that's what – but the key thing is that you do get a number. In theory, you could write it down and add 1 to it, and the answer you get when you have written it down and added 1 to it can't be divisible by 4,294,967,297 – we know for a fact you would get remainder 1. Similarly, it can't be divisible by 2, 3, 4 or 5 or any of the numbers less than 4,294,967,297, and so there are two possibilities: either nothing divides into it except itself and 1 and so it is a prime, or something else does divide into it but all of its proper factors must be bigger than 4,294,967,297 and so, since every non-prime has a prime factor (there is another theorem I could shout if

I had time) there must be a prime number bigger than 4,294,967,297, although we don't know what it is and so there can never be a largest prime number.

I love that 'we don't know what it is' in the proof. Some mathematicians look down their noses at this kind of non-constructive proof – they like a proof where if you are showing that something exists, you at least go to the trouble of finding it – but I like the uncertainty. Another of my favourite theorems to shout from the veranda has a nice bit of uncertainty to it. The first thing to say is that some numbers are rational – this does not mean that they are perfect logicians and philosophers but simply that they can be written as fractions: p over q where p and q are integers without a common factor. Some numbers, meanwhile, are irrational: the square root of 2, for example (and that fact has a lovely proof which is certainly veranda-worthy). Now, when we do one number to the power of another sometimes we get rational numbers: like if we do 2 to the power of 3, and sometimes we get irrational numbers: like if we do 2 to the power of a half (hopefully you all remember that would give you the square root of 2). Both of those examples were a rational number to the power of another rational number, but we can use irrational numbers too, and my question, my theorem, regards what happens when you do an irrational number to the power of another irrational number. That is a pretty irrational way to behave, and sure enough most of the time you get an irrational answer, but can you ever get a rational answer? The theorem is that you can and the proof is so deliciously clever that if it were a poem it would be by W. H. Auden.

Firstly, let us think about the number root 2 to the power root 2. Don't – unless it really amuses you – try to work that out, just let it sit there floating in space. Now, there are two possibilities: either it is a rational number or it isn't. If it is then we are done – we have found the rational answer and we can go home – so let us suppose that it isn't. And now for the clever bit – the part of the proof that is as cunning as a fox that has just been made professor of cunning at Oxford University: take this answer, which we are supposing is irrational, and raise it to the power of root 2. Whoa – mind blown, right? Well, maybe not, but look at your answer and remember GCSE power rules. We have root 2 to the root 2 in brackets to the root 2 and when you have a power to a power you multiply the powers, which means we have root 2 to the power (in brackets) root 2 times root 2, but root 2 times root 2 is 2 and root 2 to the power of 2 is just 2. So, that answer we supposed was irrational to the power root 2 is the completely rational and well-behaved number

2. We know one of these paths leads to a rational answer to our hideously irrational question, but we don't know which one.

Other theorems high on my veranda list are Pythagoras' theorem which has a collection of entertaining proofs; the generalisation of Pythagoras you know as the cosine rule (for which I only know the one). Leading on from root 2 to the root 2 to the root 2 we have the countability of the rationals – which means that there aren't very many of them even though it seems like there are – and the uncountability of the irrationals – there really are a lot of those which makes it even more amazing that you might end up with a rational number when you take one irrational to the power of another. It is like firing a rifle at a haystack and hitting a needle, except the haystack is infinitely far away and the needle is infinitely small.

Theorem and proof; the echo of mathematics, the lub-dub, the heartbeat; the idea that we don't really know something until we know why. In the Harris Westminster lexicon we might call this critical thought, and the same idea appears in other subjects. Without the question, 'How do we know this?', history is just the study of fairy stories; without it, science is just alchemy. In language, the question leads you from how French is taught in the classroom to how it is spoken on the streets of Paris or Kinshasa. In literature, one expects a degree of internal consistency, which is why I am still wondering about the philosophical status of orcs. One expects, I say, but maybe one has no reason to expect and maybe as, with art, the role of literature is to challenge and subvert our expectations, but, I would say, we should be aware of those expectations and know when they are being subverted or the point of the piece will sail blithely over our heads.

Theorem and proof. Lub and dub. What are we told and how do we know it to be true?

When giving this assembly I was aware that about two-thirds of the audience was lost – whether it was when I started talking about doughnut-shaped curves or when I said 4,294,967,297 for the third time. I worried that I had taken it too far, but on the way out a fair proportion of the remaining third were the most animated I had ever seen after an assembly, talking enthusiastically about numbers and shapes and proofs. 'Best assembly ever!' said one. I am happy to be able to indulge them occasionally, but it is definitely easier to tell a story in poetry or history than in mathematics.

Another assembly in which the content clearly drove the moral (such as it was) involved a detailed dissection of Paul Simon's album *Graceland*. I talked the students through the tracks on the album and the stories that lay behind it – particularly the ethical question of breaking the United Nations' cultural boycott on apartheid South Africa. It was a real joy to put together even though I didn't, this time, manage to get to the end of the album before running out of time. There wasn't even a closing paragraph on the heartbeat of scholarship – just an extended musing on art and collaboration and the complexity of ethics.

In the last assembly I mentioned my passion for 'academic promiscuity', and it is an approach that we encourage in students: we don't want them to get pigeonholed, to think that they should be learning only about the subjects they are studying for qualification. This is partly because I think learning is amazing (of course) and that if you turn your back on any branch then you are missing out, and partly because I think that the interesting places in the world are the gaps between subjects, that interesting careers lie in places where expertise overlaps, and that students who have unusual collections of skills will find it easier to stand out in a competitive job market.

In ten chapters of this book (there is still one to come) there are thirty-two assemblies (plus a reflection that looks a lot like one in the Coda) – rather less than a year's worth – and in this collection we have gone from the discovery of Neptune, through at least three Shakespeare plays and poems by Donne, Yeats, Larkin, Shelley and Hardy to Africa and the problem with statues (an issue that is as current in 2020 as it was when Nic delivered his assembly on Rhodes four years earlier). We have taken inspiration from Laurie Lee and Samuel Beckett, J. K. Rowling and J. R. R. Tolkien (more than once), Taylor Swift, Calvin and Hobbes, and Arundhati Roy; and we have found wisdom on tea trays, in bike races, built into the Swiss constitution and balanced on a pebble in Lyme Regis.

Students, particularly when new to the school, don't always know what to make of our assemblies: they don't fit into the framework they are used to and so they are not sure how to refer to them. 'That was a nice speech this morning, sir,' they will say, or 'I enjoyed your lecture in the church yesterday.' I don't think that assemblies are speeches, though, or lectures. A speech can attempt to convince or amuse (as assemblies also often do), but it is not a vehicle for education (and assemblies definitely are – if students come out having listened carefully and not learned anything new then I feel I have let them down). A lecture, meanwhile, is closely argued and focused, often with visual aids to assist the audience in concentration, whereas an assembly is more playful: a good assembly flits and teases in a way that a good lecture really doesn't.

Some of my favourite assemblies are the ones I am listening to rather than giving, when I learn something new, something niche and obscure that I would have been unlikely to stumble across on my own but have presented to me in an easily digestible package at 9am on a Monday morning. You might have thought it was difficult to make punctuation interesting for long enough to fill an assembly – but you would have been wrong.

On the Question Mark – 3 February 2016

An assembly by Nic Amy

My theme today is a humble piece of punctuation. My second favourite piece of punctuation, no less; after, of course, the semicolon – that sly forger of loose allegiances. My theme today is the question mark.

But let me start with a story. Every assembly needs a story and every story needs a setting. Our setting today is Deptford, in South-East London. Deptford is a lovely place if you are from there; if you are not then ... well, let us just say it is a salubrious suburb which is fighting a surprisingly successful battle against the forces of gentrification. But I want to take an imaginative journey to a different Deptford: the same geographical Deptford but a different temporal one. I want to go back in time, back some 420 years. Let us travel to Deptford in 1593. Queen Elizabeth I is on the throne and Deptford is a village on the banks of the Thames two or three miles outside of the City of London. I want you to imagine a room in a house; a house owned by a widow: one Eleanor Bull. It is the end of May. It is a balmy early summer's day. And four men have spent all day in the house – eating, chatting, playing games, passing time together.

Let us meet the four men. Nicholas Skeres is a con artist, a confidence trickster, a grifter. He has a history of drawing young men into the clutches of people in the money-lending racket and he is – at this very point, at the end of May 1593 – engaged in just such a swindle with the second of our cast of four: Ingram Frizer. Frizer is described as 'a property speculator, a commodity broker, a fixer for gentlemen of good worship' and a confidence trickster gulling 'young fools' out of their money.[3] Robert Poley, the third member of our May gang-of-four, is a government spy, a sometime Catholic sympathiser and a slippery maverick.

They are all three professional and consummate liars; all are deeply embroiled in the murky, dirty world of Elizabethan espionage and diplomatic subterfuge. And so was, regrettably for many, the fourth man in that room in Deptford on that warm late May afternoon. The fourth man is the playwright Christopher Marlowe.

Kit Marlowe was born in Canterbury, the son of a shoemaker, in 1564. He won a scholarship to Cambridge, wrote several astonishing plays and then found himself, at the age of 29, in Deptford. On that sultry May day in 1593 Christopher Marlowe was killed; he was stabbed in the eye by Ingram Frizer in that room in Deptford.

There was an official inquest, and although it might have been politically manipulated, it seems pretty incontrovertible that Marlowe died that day. The witnesses testified that Frizer and Marlowe had argued over payment of the bill (now famously known as the 'Reckoning'), exchanging 'divers malicious words'[4] while Frizer was sitting at a table between the other two and Marlowe was lying behind him on a couch. Marlowe snatched Frizer's dagger and wounded him on the head. In the ensuing struggle, according to the coroner's report, Marlowe was stabbed above the right eye, killing him instantly. The jury concluded that Frizer acted in self-defence and within a month he was pardoned.

---

3   C. Nicholl, *The Reckoning: The Murder of Christopher Marlowe* (London: Picador, 1993), p. 25.

4   J. T. Rowling, The death of Christopher Marlowe, *Journal of the Royal Society of Medicine* 92 (1999): 44–46 at 44.

Marlowe was buried in an unmarked grave in the churchyard of St Nicholas, Deptford, immediately after the inquest, on 1 June 1593. Kit Marlowe is the great precursor to Shakespeare; he is the poet who wrote the line, of Helen of Troy, 'Was this the face that launch'd a thousand ships?'[5] He is the author of the uncannily good *Edward II*, which some of you know. But he was also inveigled in the mire of intelligence and counter-intelligence that spun out the days at Elizabeth's court.

He is suspected of having started spying whilst at Corpus Christi, Cambridge – some tradition there, one might note, of spying, stretching forward all the way to the twentieth century – and had been arrested for coining, for forging money, in the Low Countries on the continent a year or so before his death.

In the weeks leading up to his murder, a scandalous verse, posted on the door of the Dutch Church, amongst other rumours and notes, had contributed to the speculation that Marlowe was both a diabolical atheist, consorter with Sir Walter Raleigh and guilty of both treason and sodomy. And suddenly, even though he seems to have had some powerful protectors, Marlowe became a target of the state's covert intelligence networks, a web spun and controlled at the centre by Elizabeth's spymaster Sir Francis Walsingham and enforced by shady characters like Richard Topcliffe, the Queen's 'rackmaster' – a man who balanced the unlikely dual careers of member of parliament and torturer.

A few weeks earlier, the playwright Thomas Kyd had been on the rack (a particularly gruesome instrument of torture) in the Tower of London. His testimony concerning Marlowe, exacted under torture, argued that an atheistic text discovered in the apartment they had once shared belonged to his erstwhile flatmate. The world suddenly closed in around Kit Marlowe. Sir Francis Walsingham – the spymaster, remember – controlled a powerful nexus of informers and agents, and Frizer, Skeres and Poley (Marlowe's three companions on that fateful day in Deptford) had all been employed by Walsingham or one of his allies. Marlowe's fate was written. And he died a violent death, stymying his career as an author at the age of just 29. Perhaps he would have gone on to produce as powerful a body of work as Shakespeare, but that is just a 'what if'.

About 20 metres to my left as I talk to you today is a section of the south transept of the abbey traditionally called Poets' Corner because of the number

---

5   C. Marlowe, *The Tragical History of Doctor Faustus* (1604). Available at: http://www. gutenberg.org/ebooks/779.

of poets, playwrights and writers buried and commemorated there. The first poet interred in Poets' Corner was Chaucer in 1400. And there are also monuments to such writers as Dickens, Hardy, Spencer, Tennyson, Auden, Austen, Brontë, Blake, Byron, Coleridge, Keats and … Christopher Marlowe.

Yes, there is our friend Kit Marlowe. Killed in Deptford in 1593, aged just 29. But if you look at the memorial – which is part of one of the windows in Poets' Corner – just over there, you notice something rather odd. The window gives the dates of Marlowe's life as 1564–?1593, but, rather weirdly, there is a question mark before the date 1593.

Despite the overwhelming weight of historical evidence, you see, some people doubt that Marlowe did, in fact, die then. They think that the whole room-in-Deptford-May-afternoon thing was faked. And, given the dubious records of the four men in the room, it is not so much of a stretch. That question mark worries away at what we believe. It posits an alternative narrative: that Christopher Marlowe, the author of those amazing plays – *Doctor Faustus*, *Edward II*, *The Jew of Malta* – did not, in fact, die on that warm day in late May 1593 in a room in the house of the widow Eleanor Bull, stabbed in the eye by Ingram Frizer. You see, some people think Marlowe wrote the works of William Shakespeare.

After all, Shakespeare, also 29 in 1593, and yet to write any of his masterpieces, was only the son of a glover from rural Stratford. Surely, the plays of 'William Shakespeare' could only have been written by a man from one of the universities – and Marlowe was, of course, a Cambridge man. So, some people think that Marlowe's death was faked, that he was whisked away to a Catholic seminary in France from where he wrote all those wonderful plays. The argument holds little truck with me. But many have argued differently that someone else – the Earl of Southampton, our friend Christopher Marlowe, the Earl of Oxford, Sir Francis Bacon, even Queen Elizabeth herself – were, in fact, the true authors of 'The Works of William Shakespeare'. Figures as eminent as Sigmund Freud and Mark Twain are counted amongst the conspiracy theorists. Even contemporary actors such as the former director of the Globe theatre, Mark Rylance, have questioned whether Shakespeare really wrote the plays. Perhaps they were actually written by Kit Marlowe 1564–?1593.

The two extant bodies of work certainly display some uncanny similarities. Both writers engaged sympathetically with characters who suffered from racial and religious intolerance; albeit not without significant complexity and problem: Marlowe's Barabas, the eponymous Jew of Malta, at the start of the play at least, presents a paradigm of empathetic otherness. Barabas, like Shylock in Shakespeare's *The Merchant of Venice*, is a deeply ambivalent yet nonetheless and in some ways sympathetic figure.

This term we are thinking about victims of discrimination and prejudice – victims who, as we have seen, are given key, if not unproblematic, dramatic expression in the plays of both Marlowe and Shakespeare. However, as many of you will feel all too keenly, religious and racial intolerance are an ongoing matter of daily life. Both Shakespeare and Marlowe engage with that; it is another of the very many compelling reasons to turn again to their amazing bodies of work. And who knows (insert question mark here) they may both have been Catholic adherents of that old faith, keeping it hidden in the brutally policed Elizabethan Protestant state, wearing their recusant masks against the world. But whether they were or not, and – unlike the date of Marlowe's death – we will almost certainly never know, their plays invite us to hang a sagacious question mark over every judgement, value and prejudice we encounter.

So, let us finish by returning to the idea of the question mark. As I have argued, we ought to embrace the question mark – with its hint at plurality, different levels of meaning and multiple possible answers. And most of us, most of the time, would probably be better off – as we outline our latest viewpoint, as we explain our latest thesis, as we confidently tear down someone else's assertion – if we prefaced that exhortation with a silent question mark. That we acknowledged to ourselves the evanescent fragility of our every utterance. That we partake in a show of humble recognition that the views we so confidently espouse are, at the very least, open to challenge.

But, equally, we also need to pay due attention to the weight of evidence, to the scholarly research of others, to our own faith and values, and step out of the shadow of the question mark. I believe it but I can't ever *really* know whether Christopher Marlowe *really* died in Deptford on 30 May 1593. But we can read his plays and recognise in them a world refracted by doubt, uncertainty, counterfeit and cunning; a world of masks and subterfuge where it is rarely very easy to be yourself. In our intellectual lives we ought to live in the embrace of the question mark: it is a marker that another version of events (someone else's version of events) might also, or alternatively, be right.

But know also when it is time to remove the mask. Sometimes it is better to accept things for what they are and remove the question mark. Period.

This assembly of Nic's is an example of the weird and wonderful – it is, admittedly, not really about punctuation (there is the joy of playing with ideas and leaping blithely from one to another) but about Christopher Marlowe and the dispute over Shakespeare's authorship. Inspired, I think, by the reading of James Shapiro's book *Contested Will*,[6] and indulging all the intellectual passion and curiosity that great teachers have for their subjects, it raises questions rather than presenting a moral. There is also a delicious turn of phrase – I really like 'that sly forger of loose allegiances' as a description of the semicolon – Nic excelling at what we all aimed to do in our assemblies: combine interesting ideas with relevant stories into a piece of really great writing.

The goal of Harris Westminster is to develop students into scholars, to move them from memorising facts to developing their own reasoning and creating their own arguments. We want them to sponge up knowledge as fast as they can through the two years and then to process it and squeeze it out as something polished and beautiful. Mostly their education takes place in classrooms – it is in the capable and reliable hands of their subject teachers – but assemblies are my chance to chip in, to model learning, to model thinking and to model good writing, as well as I can, and to point them towards those who do it better.

Final Thoughts

- We should be enthusiastic about learning and about sharing what we have learned – there is no need to be apologetic about being geeky.

- Both academic promiscuity and niche subject specialism have their place.

....

6   J. Shapiro, *Contested Will: Who Wrote Shakespeare?* (London: Faber and Faber, 2011).

- There is a craft to writing assemblies – like with everything else, you get better with practice.

- The same is true of delivering them.

- Assemblies are not lessons or lectures or speeches; they are an opportunity to educate, inform and amuse, to share and to enjoy the sharing of both humanity and intellectual treasure.

Chapter 10

Saying Goodbye

Too soon, the twenty-two months of Harris Westminster passes by. Too soon, the opportunities for learning and scholarship evaporate. Too soon, the longed-for freedom of adulthood is just a few examinations away. There comes a time towards the end of most students' schooling when they are ready to move on, when the rules they have been protected by for so long feel less like a shelter and more like a cage. That this moment leads to a struggle that is traumatic for both student and school might lead you to believe that both parties would invest in avoiding it, but in reality, for all its sadness, this is a moment that both have worked towards as a desired goal as well as an unavoidable reality.

School is not just a question of instilling knowledge (although that is an important and enjoyable part of the process), it is about getting students ready for the next step – your biggest job as an educator is enabling your charges to do without you. If they were still hanging on your every word, still dependent on your advice, still content with the protective environment that has supported their development, then they wouldn't be ready to move on – and move on they must. If there aren't at least some who have, quite frankly, had it with your tinpot dictatorship and authoritarian rule-making then you have been forming automatons, not adults.

I imagine that this is not a surprising revelation to many people, but I had not properly grasped it until the summer of 2016 when the first cohort of Harris Westminster students came up to their study leave. For more than two years, my life's work had been building a school for these young people: I'd sold them a dream and promised them a school in which their ambitions would be realised; I'd chosen them by hand, designed the building for them, created a curriculum; I'd had late nights and early mornings, sat through interminable train delays and written a hundred assemblies; I'd done my best to knit together a school that would provide them with everything they needed for their sixth-form education; and now it was no longer enough – now they were ready for the wider world (or, at least, they had better be).

I overstated my role, of course: they had friends and teachers and family to whom they were closer and more dependent than me; and even in the development of the school I had been supported and guided by Harris and Westminster whose vision for the school predated my own. But this is how it felt in May 2016.

The only thing to be done was to send them off with due ceremony, create a space for them to share their memories and to cement relationships with the school and each other. Obviously there would have to be an assembly, so we booked our slot in the abbey and worked out the choreography that would allow the Year 13s to leave whilst being applauded by the Year 12s. Then there was the simple question of what to say, of what words could sum up the roller-coaster of our time together.

The Time Has Come – 11 May 2016

'The time has come,' the Walrus said,

'To talk of many things:

Of shoes – and ships – and sealing wax –

Of cabbages – and kings –

Of why the sea is boiling hot –

And whether pigs have wings.'[1]

It was with these words, according to family legend, that I was brought into the world: an extended and overdue labour having reduced my mother to the point where, on prompting with the first four words, she felt impelled to complete the poem before deigning to give birth. I find myself similarly sidetracked – let me begin again.

The time has come, the principal said, to talk of legacy. Of our Harris Westminster words I think this gets the least airtime. I have spoken to you in the past of ambition – indeed, six months ago in this abbey you chose a

---

1   L. Carroll, 'The Walrus and the Carpenter'. In *Through the Looking-Glass and What Alice Found There* (London: Macmillan and Co., 1871).

180

piece of masonry into which to insert yours. Perseverance and resilience have gone hand in hand throughout the depths of winter and early spring, but it never quite seems the right time to talk about legacy with its overtones of departure, of leaving something behind. Well, today – our first annual leavers' assembly – seems like the right time to talk about it. What do you, who leave us today, leave behind? What do you who have another year to make your mark wish to leave to those who follow you? What will I look back on when I leave this place to sit on my veranda and shout theorems at passers-by? What will your – what will our – legacy be?

It will come as no surprise to you to learn that, in my opinion, one of the nicest (in the sense of precise and accurate as well as pleasing, should the adjective police be listening) illustrations of legacy comes from Radio 4. Every Saturday morning, in the middle of an hour and a half of amiable but meaningless burble from a retired Communard, there is a seven-minute interlude called 'Inheritance Tracks' in which some sort of celebrity tells you about a piece of music they inherited from their parents and a second piece they would like to pass on to their children. It is a charming vehicle for a very short autobiography and a lovely way to think about a person – receiving something wonderful from the previous generation, experiencing the world in some way and then passing something different, but also wonderful, on to the next.

Listening to it, I inevitably consider the tracks I would include were I to be invited on to the show (our guest today is James Handscombe who was once principal of Harris Westminster Sixth Form but is now best known as the lunatic who shouts theorems from his veranda). I spent my childhood completely uninterested in music: disco, punk, new romantic and synth-pop all passed me by until the autumn of my Year 12 when I discovered my parents' record collection (it was in the front room – *quelle surprise*). Over the next two years I raided it for inspiration, and my father put together carefully curated collections of songs recorded from vinyl onto audiotape. Any track I inherited would therefore come from one of those tapes and any track from those tapes would be a candidate.

If I am honest I vacillate: it is fortunate that the veranda, and thus the inevitable call from the Reverend Richard Coles, lies far in the future for I don't know what I would choose. One possibility is the charming nonsense that starts Carly Simon's wonderful album, *Hotcakes*. Rather more relevant is another possibility that I plan to discuss with you today: it is by Kate Bush, from her first album, *The Kick Inside*, and it is called 'Them Heavy People'. It turns out, having done a spot of research for this assembly, that Kate Bush thinks that the heavy people of this song are religious teachers. I am not in a position to say she is wrong exactly, but for me it has always been about teachers more generally – people I can learn from, people who are trying to help me – and a realisation that rebelling against this help was ungrateful and unwise. Reflecting back, it is just possible that my father is an emotional genius who selected this song in order to communicate exactly this message, although it might just be that he liked the tune. To be honest, knowing him well, it could be either.

Inheritance tracks represent a picture of humanity as a chain, each one of us a link in the chain, receiving from those who went before and passing on, hopefully improved by our experience, something to those who come after.

When, though, does legacy take place? When should I be passing on my songs to my daughters? Do I have to wait until I die? The Venerable Bede, who predates even vinyl, described a human life as a single sparrow flying through a lighted hall filled with food and merriment. Out of the darkness the sparrow comes, speeding between the burning torches, feeling briefly the light, warmth and joy of the hall before, too soon, it flies out of the window at the far end and back into darkness.[2] It is a rather cold view of life and not one I recognise. Inheritance tracks remind us that, at the very least, we are one of a flock of sparrows flying through the hall, each one following the sparrow in front and leading the way for those behind.

What I think is more interesting is the story of how I first heard that story. In one of the schools I once taught in, it was told by the head teacher every year during the leavers' assembly and he compared their time in the school with the flight of the sparrow. He, of course, thought of himself as one of the feasters in the hall, a fixed point watching an endless succession of sparrows fly in and out of the windows, but after twenty-five years in the job, twenty-five leavers' assemblies (I didn't hear them all), he retired and left the hall himself. Part of his legacy was that story which stuck in my mind and which I am telling you today: we are not sparrows flying through a feasting hall, because we leave the world behind us changed – for better or worse. We have a legacy but, like the sparrows, we do inevitably leave.

The Year 13s are leaving today, although we will see them visiting for exams and, often I hope, for revision and help from some heavy people as they

---

2   St Bede, *Bede's Ecclesiastical History of England*, tr. A. M. Sellar (London: George Bell and Sons, 1907), ch. XIII. Available at https://www.gutenberg.org/ebooks/38326.

prepare. The Year 12s will leave next year, and every year some of the teachers will move on to new schools and new challenges – one day even I will head for my veranda. Whilst you are living it, each phase of your life feels like it lasts forever, but things change, opportunities come and you move on to the next feasting hall leaving your mark on the last one. So, that is your legacy: each time you move on you leave a mark behind you, and I encourage, exhort, instruct you to make your mark a positive one; a mural rather than a piece of graffiti, litter picked up rather than chewing-gum left on the floor, a song started rather than a harsh word halting someone else's ballad. The marks of the Year 13s can be seen in all we do as a school: the rules we have are those that were needed to keep them scholarly; the societies that exist are those they wanted to go to or run; the enthusiasm of the teachers is the result of students who wanted to learn; my grey hair and wrinkled brow the impact of those who haven't.

Kipling encourages us to fill every 'unforgiving minute / With sixty seconds' worth of distance run', and although I don't think you can live like this the whole time, I think it is a wonderful challenge. Our legacy is the result of each minute we live, each conversation we have, the words we write, our kindnesses and cruelties. There is no way to stop that clock, no way for the sparrow to slow down its flight, and so the answer to my question of when legacy takes place is that it takes place now. Now is when I should be giving songs to my daughters and thinking about the ones they need to hear, the words that will give them tools to make sense of the world. Now is when we leave our mark on those around us – even if we don't realise it, like that head teacher and his story: he had no idea I would still be thinking about it fifteen years later. Now is when we build our characters in response to hard times – our actions leave a mark on ourselves as well as on those around us. Now is the time when we move towards our ambitions – the sixty seconds of distance run is sixty seconds closer to our destination – so look up into the vaults of the abbey and find, if you can, the particular spot into which you wedged your ambition in September and remember the promise you made in Remembrance term. Now is the time to act upon that promise.

That rallying cry was the cue for the Year 13s to file into the aisle and, led by their house captains, to process out of the abbey whilst the rest of the school rose to their feet and applauded their departure. (There is a double-edged aspect to this symbolism that I have often contemplated: is it a compliment to cheer when someone leaves? I remain in two minds, but it doesn't seem to have bothered anyone else so far.)

Thus ended stage one of our farewells. Stage three would see us return to school for snacks in the hall and student-led festivities: there were silly awards (student most likely to become prime minister, student most likely to make a million pounds, student most likely to appear on *Strictly* …) and a collection of photographs from the past two years. There was hugging and crying and signing of autographs. Stories were told, memories shared, shirts were signed and then, when the moment came, they were chased out of the building – free to return to study if they so chose (and many of them did, some of them performing a perfunctory U-turn on Tothill Street before beetling back to their place in the library), but only after they had ceremonially left and officially completed their course of study.

In-between these two stages was a second assembly, just for Year 13s, held in the slightly more homely setting of St Margaret's Church. As the students came in we gave them a pin badge – Harris Westminster Sixth Form 2014 (the date of joining the school – we are resolutely holding out against the American approach of naming the year of graduation). Then they settled down to hear the heads of house regale them with tales of the past two years – often recalling the first time they had addressed the group, from the same spot on the day of the treasure hunt in the summer of 2014 (the May 2016 audience was much less bedraggled). These addresses were funny, personal, fond remembrances of the time we spent together. After all four had spoken I took my turn, trying to do something similar – perhaps a little more formal (as befits my office). Most of this is of little interest to anyone who wasn't part of that group, but one passage (which I have echoed in every subsequent farewell) is, I think, worth reproducing.

A Private Farewell – 11 May 2016

Our ambitions for you don't stop at university and I would like to look forward a little to when you go into the world of work. I hope that the drive and confidence you have gained whilst being here will stand you in good stead when you start out on your career. I hope that the interests and specialisms you have developed will make you stand out from the crowd. I hope that the resilience you have learned will carry you through the difficult times. I hope that the time you have spent in the shadow of Big Ben will call some of you back to Westminster, and that as you walk up to the Treasury for your interview, I hope you will remember that you used to have lunch in St James's Park. I hope you will drop in to see us.

I do hope that some of you will go to work in one of the great institutions of state that surround us here, and that you will use your intelligence and talents to make the country stronger and the world better. I hope that some of you will become lawyers and doctors and work to improve the lives of individuals. I hope that some of you will become bankers and stockbrokers and will earn enormous piles of cash, and I hope you will remember Harris Westminster when you do – it is nice to think of your generation one day supporting the future of Harris Westminster in the way our benefactors have supported the present. I hope that some of you will stay in academia and think and experiment and write and continue to learn, because fourteen years of school and four as a student barely scratches the surface of all that is wonderful about the world. I hope that some of you will be creative – artists, journalists, film-makers, photographers and poets – some of you finding success in popular acclaim and some in crafting something truly beautiful but thoroughly uncommercial. However, I hope the brightest and best of you will become teachers and that you will pass your scholarship and love of learning on to the next generation.

This passage encapsulates our ambition for the future of Harris Westminster students. All through their time with us we have been aiming not at success at A levels as an end goal (although they are important), but at the world beyond the end of their degree. We have wanted to give them ambition and desire and study habits and employability skills that will enable them to ply their trade (whatever that might be) on the stage of their choosing. There is no 'ideal Harris Westminster alumnus' – they are all different, rightly so, desirably so – and in shaping them we have sought to give them the tools with which to shape their own futures. Obviously, possibly inevitably, though, it is important to emphasise that teaching is the pinnacle of ambition and we will be proudest of those students who make the decision to devote their future to the future of subsequent generations (we really are an enterprise that looks to the long term).

We said our goodbyes to the 125 students who made it through the two years (out of 138 who began with us – sadly we lost some along the way, mostly those who wanted the future we offered in theory but weren't prepared to do the work that went along with it, who had forgotten that it is not ambition or perseverance: Harris Westminster comes as a package). The school then returned to the quotidian business of teaching and learning, but I couldn't. Their departure left me unsettled – we had come into this together and now they were moving on and I was not. I felt abandoned.

A swift march around St James's and up to Green Park was called for: some fresh air, a sight of the sky, a bit of exercise for the muscles and a reminder of the glories of London. I don't do this often enough but whenever I do, I feel invigorated and ready to face the next challenge.

In the assembly above, I mentioned the need to say goodbye to staff. This is an inevitable part of running a school and, sadly, when you choose to employ interesting and energetic people they quite often decide to move on to the next interesting and energetic challenge before you really feel you have got everything you can out of them. Some move on to promotion, some move out to interesting challenges outside education and some move around the world and find the commute to Westminster has become unmanageable.

We say goodbye to departing staff in two stages: the first is at the Celebration Evening (our version of Speech Day), an evening of prize-giving and esteemed guest speakers, in which I deliver a review of the last year interspersed with thanks to all those who have supported us through the year. A special section is devoted to staff who are moving on (and another, since 2019, to those who have stuck with us for five years). The second stage is at the end of the last day of Celebration term when the staff get together for speeches and farewells.

Saying goodbye well is important, and it has been interesting as the years go by to see how things have changed and evolved whilst still staying the same. Some ideas have survived and become traditions, some have slipped away and some new traditions have been added, as can be seen by the fourth leavers' assembly in 2019.

Moving On – 8 May 2019

This morning is a momentous occasion and so I begin with a story from George Mikes, a momentous Hungarian. In his book *How to Be an Alien*, highly recommended, he considers the difficulties of a European immigrant to England and tells how his friend, a Russian, once exclaimed at a dinner party, 'Oh, I have such a nostalgia.' His host, all attentive, replied, 'Oh dear, are you missing Nizhny Novgorod?' 'No,' he answered, 'I simply have terrible pain in my lower back.'[3]

This joke, of course, works better if you know the meanings of both the word nostalgia and neuralgia, although even then it is not very good. Perhaps better is his observation that continentals think life is a game whilst the English think cricket is a game, but that would have worked less well as an introduction to an assembly on nostalgia. I have three wordsmiths for you today – in order of increasing antiquity.

From June 1992, Madonna's song 'This Used to Be My Playground' in which she remembers the safe places of childhood as a refuge, somewhere to run to, and rues the ending of such simple times.

From 1896, Alfred Edward Housman:

Into my heart an air that kills
From yon far country blows:
What are those blue remembered hills,
What spires, what farms are those?

That is the land of lost content,
I see it shining plain,
The happy highways where I went
And cannot come again.[4]

---

3   G. Mikes, *How To Be An Alien: A Handbook for Beginners and Advanced Pupils* (Harmondsworth: Penguin, 1973), p. 34.

4   A. E. Housman, *A Shropshire Lad* (Boston, MA: Four Seas, 1919), XL. Available at: http://www.gutenberg.org/ebooks/5720.

From 731, the Venerable Bede:

The present life of man upon earth, O king, seems to me, in comparison with that time which is unknown to us, like to the swift flight of a sparrow through the house wherein you sit at supper in winter, with your ealdormen and thegns, while the fire blazes in the midst, and the hall is warmed, but the wintry storms of rain or snow are raging abroad. The sparrow, flying in at one door and immediately out at another, whilst he is within, is safe from the wintry tempest; but after a short space of fair weather, he immediately vanishes out of your sight, passing from winter into winter again.[5]

Today is the day when we ceremonially say goodbye to the Year 13s although, like the queen and her birthdays, there are multiple goodbyes: we don't actually say goodbye for another week and even then they will be back for revision, and then for exams, and then for Celebration Evening, and then, we hope, to say hello and tell us of their adventures out in the wintry world of which we have so little knowledge.

In fact, perhaps we should start by thinking about in what way we are saying goodbye at all: is Harris Westminster a happy highway that once you have left you can never come back to again, or is it a place you can forever run to whenever you are in need of a friend? Like Madonna's playground, like Housman's blue remembered hills, it is a bit of both – unlike being a king or queen in Narnia we can't say, 'Once a Harris Westminster student always a Harris Westminster student', and once you have left you will find that you neither want to, nor can, spend your days in the classrooms working for your A levels and Pre-U's. The school stays the same, rehearsing the same ground – each new group of students facing the same challenges you have faced and finding their own solutions. The Year 12s will take your place, they will become Year 13s for a short while and then, in twelve months' time, we will gather here once more and they, like you, will move on.

That step of moving on is a big one. We have prepared you for the academic leaps – lectures, problem sets, essays and libraries will come as no surprise – but I suspect you are more worried about the social leap into the dark. There will be new people, new places, new independence and new responsibilities, and alumni have chided me that I have done little to prepare you for the social scene of university. I am sorry, there is only so much we can do in twenty-two months, but I can promise you two things: firstly, and most importantly, you

---

5   St Bede, *Bede's Ecclesiastical History of England*, ch. XIII.

will be fine – you are all excellent people and you will find friends at university at least as swiftly as you did here. Secondly, if you are ever in this part of London and in need of a friend, or at least a familiar face, then you will always be warmly welcomed at Steel House. You will have moved on, unstoppably, from student to alumna, but once part of Harris Westminster, always part of Harris Westminster.

Which leads us to the question of what it means to be part of Harris Westminster – and here I think that all three of our sages lead us astray, especially the Venerable Bede, whose sparrow flies briefly through the feasting hall taking advantage of a few moments of comfort but not interacting except for that. I do not feel that this is you – I hope that you do not feel like a sparrow who has flown into our hall of learning, has taken advantage of a few moments of scholarship, and now go about your business, somewhat warmer but otherwise unchanged. I hope you feel that you have been altered by your time here; at the very least that you can see two years of additional maturity in the eyes that look back from the morning's glass. In fact, I hope for rather more. I hope that you are more confident, that you know a little more about how amazing you are and how amazing you can be – I would be surprised if you thought yourself the finished article. I hope that you understand better your capacity for hard work and its capacity to enable achievement. I hope that you are more scholarly, more in love with your subjects and with learning in general. And I hope that you are more ambitious, that you see more clearly the good you can do in the world and are more determined to do it.

Isaac Newton, whose grave and memorial are behind me, said that every action has an equal and opposite reaction: when one body exerts a force on a second then the second inevitably applies an equivalent force on the first. We should therefore expect to see that you have shaped the school as it has shaped you – and indeed we do: classes, teachers, clubs, societies, routines and traditions are all formed by the daily interaction of students, and as you have been here over the last two years so, maybe slower than you would like, but inevitably, you have changed the institution. What is interesting to me, and very Newtonian, is that those of you who have worked the hardest to make your mark on the school have been affected most by your time here; maybe Bede was right after all, and some of you have passed right through, benefitting little, offering little. It is in the nature of things, as well as being a cliché, that the more you put into an experience, the more you get out. As you head out of the metaphorical door into the wintry world beyond, I hope you will remember that – and if you do then I think you will find the world far from wintry. The door you will leave from today opens on to the North Green, which I expect you will find basking in spring sunshine, leaving those of us behind in the dimly lit abbey – a metaphor for the opportunities that the world will offer you, a chance to do and see and be amazing things beside which Harris Westminster will seem small.

Seeming small is fine – it is Madonna's childhood playground that she remembers with fondness, not a theme park, and it is the homely spires, farms and hills of Shropshire that A. E. Housman recalls. As scholars we know that we are small, that our contribution is a drop in a much larger ocean, and that if we are able to see far it is not because of our intrinsic height but because we have stood on the shoulders of giants. That is Newton again – a giant of scholarship who understood his debt to those who had gone before. We follow behind him and the other greats of our subjects – and, indeed, others whose contribution is less but which is part of the pyramid up which we clamber. For Harris Westminster, Newton represents all of these past scholars, for his own work, the discoveries on which he built and for those who have followed after him, some of whom are remembered in the flagstones around his grave. As a symbol of this debt we owe to those who have gone before, and as a sign of how we mark and are marked by our experiences, Lee, the captain of this year's victorious house, will now lay flowers on Newton's memorial.

And now comes the moment of farewell – a moment of contradiction because we are sad that you are leaving but glad that you are going out into the world, blazing a trail for us to follow. Madonna asks, 'Why do they always say don't look back?' and the answer is that you should look forwards, look where you are going to, enjoy the moment and believe that the best is yet to come. If Harris Westminster has been a happy highway, then you can enjoy the memory without wishing you were still here; you can come back and tell us of your adventures without trying to preserve the experience. Thank you for your time in our feasting hall and now go, go out, not into the wintry night but into the glorious spring sunshine. Go!

There are echoes of 2016 in there, most particularly Bede's sparrow which has flown through the feasting hall every year despite the obvious flaws in the analogy. There is also the new tradition of placing flowers on Newton's memorial (which began in 2017 when the leavers' assembly moved into the nave to give the Year 13s more scope to process out through the quire). There is a lot to delight in that symbolism, starting with Newton's image of standing on the shoulders of giants (which feels particularly vibrant in the abbey where the memorials of his successors lie clustered at his feet). The placing of flowers, of making a mark on the fabric of the abbey is a sign that Harris Westminster students are expecting not just to see the beautiful, exciting and elite, but to change it, to shape it themselves; and it is right that we should choose as our representative the winning house captain – the prize for victory is service.

The last farewell is my own – in 2016, I spoke about my long-term ambition to retire to a veranda in order to shout theorems at passers-by (the follow-up being that anyone who shouts back the proof gets invited in to have a glass of lemonade). This is (at least partly) a joke, and a refusal to accept the inevitable truth that at some point I will have to hand over the office to a successor. It is a hard fact to face, and I can't imagine ever saying goodbye completely, turning my back on Harris Westminster (I hope that the adage about kings and queens in Narnia also applies to principals), but when one inevitably says goodbye to so many students (half the school) each year, it is one from which I can't get away.

This sad truth brings with it the responsibility that any leader has – to make sure that they have built something strong enough to continue without them. The time of testing has not come, for I am not ready to leave quite yet, but I hope that when I do hear the siren call of the veranda, that the school will have structures that support its ethos, and an ethos that is embedded in the community, and a community that is strong and wise enough to continue that which is worth keeping but bold enough to discard the fancies and affectations that will inevitably have accumulated. For a school built on ethos, that is the real test – an ethos that survives and thrives when the leadership moves on.

Final Thoughts

- The last moments of a student's time at a school are ones they will remember and so need to be planned and emphasised.

- Saying goodbye to good people is always hard but it doesn't need to be negative.

- Tradition is an ever changing and evolving thing; respecting it doesn't mean freezing it.

Coda: A Student's Reflection

I have learned a lot during my time as principal of Harris Westminster (which is a delight, given that learning is amazing) and much of it has come from talking to students, listening to them, seeing their ambitions, hearing about their background, sharing their creativity and insights. It is appropriate, therefore, to give the last words of this book to a student and appropriate to choose words spoken in Westminster Abbey.

Every year, at the Remembrance Service, one of the vice presidents speaks about their experience, their reflections, their hopes for the future, and every year I glow with pride seeing them bold and erudite, saying something profound and personal.

In 2018, the service was just a few days after a young man was killed in South London, someone who had been a classmate of students before they came to Harris Westminster. In 2018, therefore, there was something more immediate and weighty to talk about that went beyond our usual (and important) business of learning and persevering. That a Year 13 student would be able to handle such a topic sensitively and beautifully in front of an audience of their peers, teachers, parents and guests is remarkable and is the best example of the school's success that I could hope to offer. I leave you, then, with Yinka.

Malcolm – 13 November 2018

A reflection by Olayinka Aresa

Before I begin, I would like to put out a trigger warning: I will be using the words ambition, perseverance, legacy and scholarly a lot, so brace yourselves.

'At Harris Westminster we believe that learning is amazing and we believe that every student deserves a chance to excel, no matter their background, no matter how much their parents earn, no matter what part of London they come from, and crucial to achieving these goals are the three words: ambition, perseverance and legacy.' These words were my first introduction to this school in Year 11, when my friends and I started thinking about sixth forms. I remember them because of the reactions we had after watching the video. We thought, 'What episode of *Scandal* has this school been watching to get them so inspired?' and 'Wow, they are doing the most,' but we had no idea.

To us at that moment we didn't care about words like ambition, perseverance and legacy. Don't get me wrong, we had ambitions but 'not too much'. We were ambitiously desperate to get good GCSEs and get out into the world. We had perseverance – we had persevered for five years at a school that was constantly going through changes and budget cuts but at least we had teachers who cared. We didn't really think about legacy. I mean, what is legacy? The OED gives two main definitions: (1) an amount of money or property left to someone in a will, and (2) something left or handed down by a predecessor. We didn't think that either of these definitions applied to us.

At that moment in time these words seemed bigger than us; my friend Princess used to say, 'That's future Princess' problem.' We laughed about how officious the school was but we were still interested in the school disguised as an office building. So, on 26 September two years ago, about twenty of us jumped on the number 12 bus to go to the open evening. We were all excited because we were going into Westminster. I remember running across the bridge searching for the school, running across Parliament Square screaming (as you do) and when we finally found the school we became even more excited. We split up to see different sections of the school. I ran to the fifth floor while the majority of my friends ran to the second and third floors (scientists). I went into the English classroom where I saw Leanne and Beverly. Princess and I asked them about Harris Westminster. I kid you not, they spoke for thirty minutes straight about the school and about English and Austen. Again, Princess and I thought, 'Wow, the Kool-Aid they are drinking at this school is strong.' The passion they had about the school and their subjects was just inspiring. They were so scholarly and academically promiscuous. The way they spoke about the school made me excited to find out more. So, a week later I returned for the second open evening and then again, three weeks later, for the last open morning. At this point, our ambitions changed: we wanted to get the best GCSEs, we wanted to get into Harris Westminster and drink some of that Kool-Aid, we wanted to better ourselves because we were inspired by the scholars and their learning. We knew that the ability to achieve great things was in our hands. I can proudly say that we did it. We woke up on that cold January morning, went for the entrance exams, got our interviews and we got into the school.

By this point the school became something of a metaphor to me. It represented something bigger than just a sixth form. It represented the privilege of education. Harris Westminster was this school that was offering a private school education for free and I had the privilege to be offered this education. A lot of you in the abbey might be saying, 'Education is not a privilege, it is a right.' Well, maybe it should be, but if you come from a country like Nigeria where 10.5 million children don't have access to education, never mind free education, where 10.5 million children don't have the privilege to grumble about homework, where 4.5 million children are sold into modern day slavery in hopes for a better life – then education becomes a privilege.

I was asked to reflect on what it means to be a Harris Westminster student and so I asked some old Harris Westminsters. Leanne says being a Harris Westminster student is being able to grow in a diverse community. Vera says it means going beyond being just an academic student – it is a mini university with its societies, lab and sports. Lilian says Harris Westminster Sixth Form provides a step for its students to reach goals – you are pushed to the limit which, if you survive, makes you a better person. However, the school isn't all sunshine and rainbows. There are flaws and amazing students have left the school for one reason or another, but that is the thing about Harris Westminster Sixth Form – the school is willing to accept its flaws and begin to seek solutions.

School to me is more than just a place where you read books; it really is a community. I think of all the inspirational teachers who make it their mission to provide excellent education. Teachers like Mrs Pearson who makes every lesson an event and is always so enthusiastic, even when only Mariam gets it. School is a place where you meet the fantastic people who will make up your chosen family. A place where you meet people like my friend Malcolm who unfortunately lost his life to knife crime two Fridays ago. Malcolm was an amazing human who always had a smile on his face and sometimes, as Princess would say, makes the 'deadest jokes', and it is unbelievable to think that I will never bump into him on the streets again or see him on Joseph's Snapchat. But one thing I can say is that I am so glad that I got to know him and I am so proud to be able to say that he was my friend. Volunteering at the Armistice celebration on Sunday, laying down people's wreaths, I was able to read a lot of the personal messages written by families and see the legacies those soldiers and young people left to their mothers, fathers, brothers, friends and neighbours. Legacies of peace and safety of being decent human beings. For Malcolm Mide Madariola, his legacy was his positivity and the great words his friends and families are able to say about him. His name was Malcolm Mide Madariola and he will never be forgotten.

Harris Westminster asks you from the first day you see those words on those red walls, what will you do? What difference will you make? Who will you inspire?

References

Baldwin, J. (1955) 'Me and My House', *Harper's Magazine* (November).

Baldwin, J. (1962) 'A Letter to My Nephew', *The Progressive* (December). Available at: https://progressive.org/magazine/letter-nephew.

Beckett, S. (1983) *Worstward Ho* (London: John Calder).

Bunyan, J. (1678) *The Pilgrim's Progress from This World, to That Which Is to Come. Part 1: Delivered Under the Similitude of a Dream* (London: Printed for Nath. Ponder). Available at: http://www.gutenberg.org/ebooks/131.

Carroll, L. (1871) 'The Walrus and the Carpenter'. In *Through the Looking-Glass and What Alice Found There* (London: Macmillan and Co.).

Conrad, J. (1902) *Heart of Darkness*. In *Youth: A Narrative, and Two Other Stories* (Edinburgh and London: William Blackwood). Available at: http://www.gutenberg.org/ebooks/526.

Cooper, J. (1988) *Rivals* (London: Corgi).

Davies, C. (2009) 'PM's Apology to Codebreaker Alan Turing: We Were Inhumane', *The Guardian* (11 September). Available at: https://www.theguardian.com/world/2009/sep/11/pm-apology-to-alan-turing.

Davis, A. (2013) 'State Sixth Forms Aren't Inspiring Pupils, Says New Academy Head', *Evening Standard* (16 October). Available at: https://www.standard.co.uk/news/education/state-sixth-forms-aren-t-inspiring-pupils-says-new-academy-head-8883485.html.

Donne, J. (1959 [1623]) *Devotions Upon Emergent Occasions; Together with Death's Duel* (Ann Arbor, MI: University of Michigan Press). Available at: http://www.gutenberg.org/ebooks/23772.

Eliot, T. S. (1997 [1920]) 'Philip Massinger'. In *The Sacred Wood: Essays on Poetry and Criticism* (London: Faber & Faber), pp. 104–121.

Fitzgerald, F. S. (2000 [1926]) *The Great Gatsby* (London: Penguin).

Fullan, M. (2012) *Stratosphere: Integrating Technology, Pedagogy, and Change Knowledge* (Toronto: Pearson).

Garner, R. (2014) 'London Sixth-Form Heads Unite to Urge Michael Gove to Rethink New £45m Free School', *The Independent* (31 March). Available at: https://www.independent.co.uk/news/education/education-news/london-sixth-form-heads-unite-urge-michael-gove-rethink-new-ps45m-free-school-9226642.html.

Handscombe, R. D. and Patterson, E. A. (2004) *The Entropy Vector: Connecting Science and Business* (Singapore: World Scientific).

Housman, A. E. (1919) *A Shropshire Lad* (Boston, MA: Four Seas). Available at: http://www.gutenberg.org/ebooks/5720.

Lee, L. (2014 [1969]) *As I Walked Out One Midsummer Morning* (London: Penguin).

Levin, B. (1983) *Enthusiasms* (London: Sceptre).

Lewis, C. S. (2016 [1942]) *The Screwtape Letters* (Quebec: Samizdat University Press). Available at: http://www.samizdat.qc.ca/arts/lit/PDFs/ScrewtapeLetters_CSL.pdf.

Lewis, C. S. (2017 [1966]) 'Forms of Things Unknown', in *The Dark Tower and Other Stories* (New York: HarperCollins), pp. 165–178.

Macfarlane, A. J. and Dorkenoo, E. (2015) *Prevalence of Female Genital Mutilation in England and Wales: National and Local Estimates* (London: City University London in association with Equality Now). Available at: https://www.trustforlondon.org.uk/publications/prevalence-female-genital-mutilation-england-and-wales-national-and-local-estimates.

Marlowe, C. (1604) *The Tragical History of Doctor Faustus*. Available at: http://www.gutenberg.org/ebooks/779.

Mikes, G. (1973) *How to Be an Alien: A Handbook for Beginners and Advanced Pupils* (Harmondsworth: Penguin).

Mitchell, R. B. (n.d.) Underground Railroad: Information and Articles About Underground Railroad, One of the Causes of the Civil War, *HistoryNet*. Available at: https://www.historynet.com/underground-railroad.

Morris, W. (1919) 'The Beauty of Life' (lecture delivered at the Birmingham Society of Arts and School of Design, 19 February 1880). In *Hopes & Fears for Art: Five Lectures* (London: Longmans, Green, and Co.). Available at: http://www.gutenberg.org/ebooks/3773.

Motion, A. (2010) 'The Poem and the Path', *The Hudson Review* 63(1): 19–54. Available at: http://www.jstor.org/stable/25703712.

Murphy, J. (1986) *Five Minutes' Peace* (Harmondsworth: Penguin).

Nesbit, E. (1899) *The Story of the Treasure Seekers* (London: T. Fisher Unwin). Available at: http://www.gutenberg.org/ebooks/770.

Nicholl, C. (1993) *The Reckoning: The Murder of Christopher Marlowe* (London: Picador).

Nieto, L. D. (1979) 'Toward a Chicano Liberation Theology'. In G. H. Anderson and T. F. Stransky (eds), *Liberation Theologies in North America and Europe*. Mission Trends, no. 4 (New York: Paulist Press), pp. 277–282.

Phelps-Rogers, M. (2017) 'I Grew Up in the Westboro Baptist Church. Here's Why I Left', *TED.com* (February). Available at: https://www.ted.com/talks/megan_phelps_roper_i_grew_up_in_the_westboro_baptist_church_here_s_why_i_left?language=en.

Plato (1921) *Theaetetus*. In *Plato in Twelve Volumes*, Vol. XII, tr. H. N. Fowler (Cambridge, MA: Harvard University Press; London: William Heinemann).

Rowling, J. K. (1997) *Harry Potter and the Philosopher's Stone* (London: Bloomsbury Children's Books).

Rowling, J. K. (2007) *Harry Potter and the Deathly Hallo*ws (London: Bloomsbury Children's Books).

Rowling, J. K. (2008) 'The Fringe Benefits of Failure and the Importance of Imagination', Harvard University commencement address, 5 June. Available at: https://news.harvard.edu/gazette/story/2008/06/text-of-j-k-rowling-speech.

Rowling, J. T. (1999) The death of Christopher Marlowe, *Journal of the Royal Society of Medicine* 92: 44–46.

Roy, A. (2017 [1997]) *The God of Small Things* (London: HarperCollins).

Rumbelow, H. (2015) 'Could Harris Westminster Be the Most Elitist School in the Country?' *The Times* (16 April).

Save the Children (2018) *100 Years of Fighting for Children: Annual Report 2018*. Available at: https://www.savethechildren.org.uk/content/dam/gb/reports/annual-report-2018-save-the-children.pdf.

Schmidt, E. and Cohen, J. (2014) *The New Digital Age: Transforming Nations, Businesses, and Our Lives* (New York: Vintage).

Schott, B. (2002) *Schott's Original Miscellany* (London: Bloomsbury).

Shapiro, J. (2011) *Contested Will: Who Wrote Shakespeare?* (London: Faber and Faber).

Shelley, M. (1823) *Frankenstein; or, The Modern Prometheus* (London: G. and W. B. Whittaker). Available at: http://www.gutenberg.org/ebooks/84.

Smith, J. (2002) *The Learning Game: A Teacher's Inspirational Story* (London: Abacus).

St Bede (1907) *Bede's Ecclesiastical History of England*, tr. A. M. Sellar (London: George Bell and Sons).

Steinberg, J. (2015) *Why Switzerland?*, 3rd edn (Cambridge: Cambridge University Press).

Tagore, R. (2012) *My Reminiscences* (Zhingoora Books).

Ternisien, X. (2012) 'A "Charlie Hebdo", on n'a "pas l'impression d'égorger quelqu'un avec un feutre"', *Le Monde* (20 September). Available at: https://www.lemonde.fr/actualite-medias/article/2012/09/20/je-n-ai-pas-l-impression-d-egorger-quelqu-un-avec-un-feutre_1762748_3236.html.

This American Life (2012) *Red State Blue State* [podcast] (2 November). Available at: https://www.thisamericanlife.org/478/red-state-blue-state.

Turner, J. (2016) 'Girls Can't Escape From This Relentless Bullying', *The Times* (2 April).

UNHCR (2018) 'Four Million Refugee Children Go Without Schooling: UNHCR Report' (29 August). Available at: https://www.unhcr.org/uk/news/latest/2018/8/5b86342b4/four-million-refugee-children-schooling-unhcr-report.html.

Vonnegut, K. (1992 [1965]) *God Bless You, Mr Rosewater* (London: Vintage).

Wasserman, D. (2017) 'Purple America Has All But Disappeared', *FiveThirtyEight* (8 March). Available at: https://fivethirtyeight.com/features/purple-america-has-all-but-disappeared.

Weinersmith, Z. (2015) *Augie and the Green Knight* (Brooklyn: Breadpig).

Whyte, W. H. (1950) 'Is Anybody Listening?', *Fortune* (September).

Wilde, O. (1915) *The Importance of Being Earnest: A Trivial Comedy for Serious People* (London: Methuen). Available at: http://www.gutenberg.org/ebooks/844.

Index of Assemblies

About the Author

James Handscombe is the principal of Harris Westminster Sixth Form. Having grown up mostly in the north of England, with a comprehensive schooling in Sheffield, he gained a BA in mathematics from Oxford in 1995 and went on to specialise in algebraic geometry at Harvard. He has been in teaching since the last millennium and includes moving from teaching in south Wales to a school in New South Wales, Australia, (in order to properly compare the two versions) as one of his accomplishments.

Other achievements include having circumperambulated the island of Jersey and helping to deliver both a calf and a human baby (on separate occasions). Since 2003 he has lived in south-east London, which he claims has treasures and delights beyond the comprehension of those addicted to the underground – he is unwilling to be specific on what exactly these amazing features might be, but invites exploration of the region. He is firmly convinced of the maxim that 'learning is amazing' and current projects involve gaining a greater familiarity with the music of Shostakovich, committing a Dylan Thomas poem to memory and learning to play the bass recorder.

What If Everything You Knew About Education Was Wrong?
ISBN: 978-178583157-7
David Didau

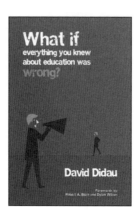

If you feel a bit cross at the presumption of some oik daring to suggest everything you know about education might be wrong, please take it with a pinch of salt. It's just a title. Of course, you probably think a great many things that aren't wrong.

The aim of this book is to help you 'murder your darlings'. David will question your most deeply held assumptions about teaching and learning, expose them to the fiery eye of reason and see if they can still walk in a straight line after the experience. It seems reasonable to suggest that only if a theory or approach can withstand the fiercest scrutiny should it be encouraged in classrooms. David makes no apologies for this; why wouldn't you be sceptical of what you're told and what you think you know? As educated professionals, we ought to strive to assemble a more accurate, informed or at least considered understanding of the world around us.

Making Kids Cleverer
A Manifesto for Closing the Advantage Gap
ISBN: 978-178583366-3
David Didau

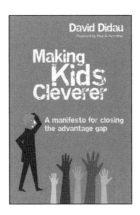

In this wide-ranging enquiry into psychology, sociology, philosophy and cognitive science, David argues that with greater access to culturally accumulated information – taught explicitly within a knowledge-rich curriculum – children are more likely to become cleverer, to think more critically and, subsequently, to live happier, healthier and more secure lives.

Furthermore, by sharing valuable insights into what children truly need to learn during their formative school years, he sets out the numerous practical ways in which policy makers and school leaders can make better choices about organising schools, and how teachers can communicate the knowledge that will make the most difference to young people as effectively and efficiently as possible.

Teach Like Nobody's Watching
The Essential Guide to Effective and Efficient Teaching
ISBN: 978-178583399-1
Mark Enser

In *Teach Like Nobody's Watching*, Mark Enser sets out a time-efficient approach to teaching that will reduce teachers' workload and enhance their pupils' levels of engagement and attainment.

At a time when schools are crying out for more autonomy and trust, teacher and bestselling author Mark Enser asks educators the critical question 'How would you teach if nobody were watching?' and empowers them with the tools and confidence to do just that.

Mark argues that a quality education is rooted in simplicity. In this book he convincingly strips away the layers of contradictory pedagogical advice that teachers have received over the years and lends weight to the three key pillars that underpin effective, efficient teaching: the lesson, the curriculum and the school's support structure.

Trivium 21c

Preparing Young People for the Future with Lessons from the Past

ISBN: 978-178135054-6

Martin Robinson

From Ancient Greece to the present day, *Trivium 21c* explores whether a contemporary trivium (Grammar, Dialectic, and Rhetoric) can unite progressive and traditionalist institutions, teachers, politicians and parents in the common pursuit of providing a great education for our children in the 21st century.

Education policy and practice is a battleground. Traditionalists argue for the teaching of a privileged type of hard knowledge and deride soft skills. Progressives deride learning about great works of the past preferring '21c skills' (21st century skills) such as creativity and critical thinking.

Whilst looking for a school for his daughter, the author became frustrated by schools' inability to value knowledge, as well as creativity, foster discipline alongside free-thinking, and value citizenship alongside independent learning. Drawing from his work as a creative teacher, Robinson finds inspiration in the arts and the need to nurture learners with the ability to deal with the uncertainties of our age.

Curriculum

Athena Versus the Machine
ISBN: 978-178583302-1
Martin Robinson

Rather than being seen as a data-driven machine, a school should be viewed as a place that enables children to develop thoughtful perspectives on the world, through which they can pursue wisdom and be free to join in with the ancient and continuing conversation: 'What is it to be human?'

Teachers need to be liberated from policy-led prescription in order to design curricula which bring the subjects being studied, rather than the blind pursuit of measurable outcomes, to the foreground of the school's teaching and learning agenda.

In *Curriculum*, Martin Robinson explores how this can be achieved.

The Machine demands data, order and regulation; Athena is the goddess of philosophy, courage and inspiration. An Athena curriculum celebrates wisdom and skills, and considers why it seeks to transmit the knowledge that it does. In this book, Martin examines how we can construct a curriculum that will allow liberal education to flourish.